Web-Based Instructional Learning

Mehdi Khosrow-Pour, D.B.A.
Executive Director
Information Resources Management Association

IRM Press
Publisher of innovative scholarly and professional
information technology titles in the cyberage

Hershey • London • Melbourne • Singapore • Beijing

Senior Editor:	Mehdi Khosrow-Pour
Managing Editor:	Jan Travers
Assistant Managing Editor:	Amanda Appicello
Copy Editor:	Jennifer Swenson
Cover Design:	Tedi Wingard
Printed at:	Integrated Book Technology

Published in the United States of America by
  IRM Press
  1331 E. Chocolate Avenue
  Hershey PA 17033-1117, USA
  Tel: 717-533-8845
  Fax: 717-533-8661
  E-mail: cust@idea-group.com
  Web site: http://www.irm-press.com

and in the United Kingdom by
  IRM Press
  3 Henrietta Street
  Covent Garden
  London WC2E 8LU
  Tel: 44 20 7240 0856
  Fax: 44 20 7379 3313
  Web site: http://www.eurospan.co.uk

Library of Congress Cataloguing-in-Publication Data

Web-based instructional learning / [edited by] Mehdi Khosrow-Pour.
     p. cm.
  Includes bibliographical references and index.
   ISBN 1-931777-04-7 (paper)
   1. Internet in education. 2. World Wide Web. 3. Distance education. I. Khosrowpour, Mehdi, 1951-

LB1044.87 .W433 2002
371.33'44678--dc21   2001059401

eISBN: 1-931777-22-5

British Cataloguing-in-Publication Data
A Cataloguing-in-Publication record for this book is available from the British Library.

Other New Releases from IRM Press

- **Effective Healthcare Information Systems,** Adi Armoni (Ed.)
  ISBN: 1-931777-01-2 / eISBN: 1-931777-20-9 / approx. 340 pages / US$59.95 / © 2002
- **Human Computer Interaction Developments and Management,** Tonya Barrier (Ed.)
  ISBN: 1-931777-13-6 / eISBN: 1-931777-35-7 / approx. 336 pages / US$59.95 / © 2002
- **Data Warehousing and Web Engineering,** Shirley Becker (Ed.)
  ISBN: 1-931777-02-0 / eISBN: 1-931777-21-7 / approx. 334 pages / US$59.95 / © 2002
- **Information Technology Education in the New Millennium,** Mohammad Dadashzadeh, Al Saber and Sherry Saber (Eds.) /
  ISBN: 1-931777-05-5 / eISBN: 1-931777-24-1 / approx. 308 pages / US$59.95 / © 2002
- **Information Technology Management in Developing Countries,** Mohammad Dadashzadeh (Ed.) / ISBN: 1-931-777-03-9 / eISBN: 1-931777-23-3 / approx. 348 pages / US$59.95 / © 2002
- **Strategies for eCommerce Success,** Bijan Fazlollahi (Ed.)
  ISBN: 1-931777-08-7 / eISBN: 1-931777-29-2 / approx. 352 pages / US$59.95 / © 2002
- **Collaborative Information Technologies,** Mehdi Khosrow-Pour (Ed.)
  ISBN: 1-931777-14-4 / eISBN: 1-931777-25-X / approx. 308 pages / US$59.95 / © 2002
- **Modern Organizations in Virtual Communities,** Jerzy Kisielnicki (Ed.)
  ISBN: 1-931777-16-0 / eISBN: 1-931777-36-5 / approx. 316 pages / US$59.95 / © 2002
- **Enterprise Resource Planning Solutions and Management,** Fiona Fui-Hoon Nah (Ed.)
  ISBN: 1-931777-06-3 / eISBN: 1-931777-26-8 / approx. 308 pages / US$59.95 / © 2002
- **Interactive Multimedia Systems,** Syed M. Rahman (Ed.)
  ISBN: 1-931777-07-1 / eISBN: 1-931777-28-4 / approx. 314 pages / US$59.95 / © 2002
- **Ethical Issues of Information Systems,** Ali Salehnia (Ed.)
  ISBN: 1-931777-15-2 / eISBN: 1-931777-27-6 / approx. 314 pages / US$59.95 / © 2002
- **Intelligent Support Systems: Knowledge Management,** Vijay Sugumaran (Ed.)
  ISBN: 1-931777-00-4 / eISBN: 1-931777-19-5 / approx. 318 pages / US$59.95 / © 2002
- **Human Factors in Information Systems,** Edward Szewczak and Coral Snodgrass (Eds.)
  ISBN: 1-931777-10-1 / eISBN: 1-931777-31-4 / approx. 342 pages / US$59.95 / © 2002
- **Global Perspective of Information Technology Management,** Felix B. Tan (Ed.)
  ISBN: 1-931777-11-4 / eISBN: 1-931777-32-2 / approx. 334 pages / US$59.95 / © 2002
- **Successful Software Reengineering,** Sal Valenti (Ed.)
  ISBN: 1-931777-12-8 / eISBN: 1-931777-33-0 / approx. 330 pages / US$59.95 / © 2002
- **Information Systems Evaluation Management,** Wim van Grembergen (Ed.)
  ISBN: 1-931777-18-7 / eISBN: 1-931777-37-3 / approx. 336 pages / US$59.95 / © 2002
- **Optimal Information Modeling Techniques,** Kees van Slooten (Ed.)
  ISBN: 1-931777-09-8 / eISBN: 1-931777-30-6 / approx. 306 pages / US$59.95 / © 2002
- **Knowledge Mapping and Management,** Don White (Ed.)
  ISBN: 1-931777-17-9 / eISBN: 1-931777-34-9 / approx. 340 pages / US$59.95 / © 2002

Excellent additions to your institution's library!
Recommend these titles to your Librarian!

To receive a copy of the IRM Press catalog, please contact
(toll free) 1/800-345-4332, fax 1/717-533-8661,
or visit the IRM Press Online Bookstore at: [http://www.irm-press.com]!

Note: All IRM Press books are also available as ebooks on netlibrary.com as well as
other ebook sources. Contact Ms. Carrie Stull at [cstull@idea-group.com] to receive
a complete list of sources where you can obtain ebook information or
IRM Press titles.

Web-Based Instructional Learning

Table of Contents

Foreword

During the past two decades, advances in computer technologies combined with telecommunication technologies have had tremendous impact on every facet of life. These technologies have offered many new opportunities to organizations of all types and sizes. No longer is computing considered the main use of computer technologies, instead today the primary use is in the area of communications and information retrieval and sharing. In recent years, through the use of Web-enabled technologies, businesses have managed to identify new ways of doing business and reaching customers and suppliers through the use of E-commerce; educational institutions have developed new ways of delivering education programs through distance learning programs; government entities have learned how to conduct their business and information sharing through E-government concepts; and libraries have begun disseminating vast library information resources electronically to all remote sites.

In the area of educational technologies, many colleges and universities worldwide now can offer academic programs and courses regardless of distance and location. Through the use of information technologies the communication gap between providers and receivers of education has been closing and narrowing. Many of the traditional students who could not previously attend campus-based educational programs now can attend educational programs that are either offered through various Web-based programs or offered through different distance learning technologies. In addition, these technologies have allowed students to be able to collaborate with each other more effectively and easily. Today, Web-enabled technologies allow everyone regardless of age, gender, and location around the world to have access to a vast number of Web-based sources of information knowledge. No longer is information or knowledge the domain of only a few entities with limited access due to their location limitation and restrictions. The idea of virtual libraries which until a few years ago was not even imagined now is a reality. Information technology now is the most effective facilitator of information and knowledge dissemination around the world, and as a result, the accumulation of knowledge related to all topics is multiplying by the second rather than the traditional pace of every year or two.

These technologies have been beneficial not only to academic programs but also to organizations and their training and knowledge management efforts. Through the use of collaborative learning technologies, organizations of all types and sizes now can collaborate in different organizational learning and developments. In reality, all organizations are knowledge–based entities that require constant processing, utilization and updating of their knowledge regarding different products, services, functions, and procedures. Information technologies of the modern years have allowed organizations to develop much more effective techniques and methodologies in managing organizational knowledge and information. Obviously, the collaborative technologies of recent years have been very instrumental toward organizational knowledge management and learning processes. Furthermore, these technologies have been utilized effectively in support of learning new and innovative ways of dealing with modern organizational reengineering and downsizing, paving the way toward more leaner and efficient organizations.

Like many other new technologies, these technologies are not free of controversies and challenges. Many of the technology related challenges are not technically oriented but instead they are related to the non-technical components—most in the area of human aspects. Perhaps we can argue that most challenges impacting the overall utilization and management of information technologies are "people-related challenges." These challenges range from training-related issues to overall innovation and adoption of emerging modern technologies in organizations. Modern organizational theorists should understand the true organization and management of these technologies and devise ways for contemporary organizations to cope more effectively with the issues of information technology management. No longer can effective organizations afford to place the majority of their focus on hardware and software technologies and ignore the "people" side of these technologies. It is time to place the major focus on the human side of technology and to recognize the true man-machine relationships.

The influence and impact of information technologies on organizations during the past two decades have far exceeded the majority of organizational scholars' and managers' imagination and foresight. No longer should information technology be viewed as technologies in support of organizational functions and day-to-day functions and operations, but, instead, successful organizations have been utilizing information technologies of modern years as major strategic tools. Information technology can reshape the overall focus and mission of the organizations in ways that were never imagined and envisioned. The biggest challenge facing organization leaders today is to understand the strategic values of information technology and to view the ways that technology can bring their organization cost savings methods, facilitate customer service, and identify new markets and growth areas. Information technology can be a very powerful strategic tool if it is correctly positioned and utilized within the overall organization structure.

Mehdi Khosrow-Pour, D.B.A.
Executive Director, Information Resources Management Association
November 6, 2001

Preface

Since the World Wide Web's conceptualization in 1991 as a method of making research findings and scientific materials available to researchers and teachers across the globe, it has become an indispensable tool for educators. Not only has the Web achieved making scientific findings more accessible, but also it is now being used as a mechanism of course delivery. Web-based education is fast becoming the new method of teaching. Some teachers use the web to post syllabi and give tests; other courses are offered exclusively on the Web. As this new technology grows in acceptance and use, it is essential for academics and practitioners to increase their knowledge about the uses and abuses of the Web in education and to stay up-to-date on the latest findings in Web-based education research. The chapters in this book address many aspects of Web education. From how to incorporate the Web into classroom-based classes to studies on which mechanism of instruction is more effective and how students feel about instruction from the Web, the authors of the following chapters, all experts in the fields they discuss, share their knowledge.

Chapter 1 entitled, "Web-Based Learning and Instruction: A Constructivist Approach" by Valerie Morphew of West Virginia Wesleyan College (USA) defines and explains constructivist thought and then applies it to learning and instruction. The author then offers recommendations for selecting curriculum and instruction based upon constructivist thought. The chapter contains concrete direction on planning instruction, monitoring students' responses and evaluating students and programs.

Chapter 2 entitled, "Implementing Corporate Distance Training Using Change Management, Strategic Planning and Project Management" by Zane Berge of University of Maryland Baltimore County and Donna Smith of T. Rowe Price Associates, Inc. (USA) offers a perspective for implementing distance education that integrates strategic planning, change management and project management as critical to successful overall implementation. Rather than prescribe specific models, the approach described in the chapter identifies the essence of what each discipline contributes to the process of implementing distance education.

Chapter 3 entitled, "Three Strategies of the Use of Distance Learning Technology in Higher Education" by William E. Rayburn of Austin Peay State University and Arkalgud Ramaprasad of Southern Illinois University (USA) identifies and describes strategies for using distance learning technologies at higher education institutions. The chapter describes three specific strategies: guest lecturer strategy, the automated correspondence course strategy and the large lecture hall strategy.

All of the three described strategies have antecedents in the recent history of higher education and each has its own implications for the future. The chapter discusses these implications.

Chapter 4 entitled, "Developing a Learning Environment: Applying Technology and TQM to Distance Learning" by C. Mitchell Adrian of Longwood College (USA) describes how to apply the concepts of total quality management (TQM) to the new and readily available electronic communication technologies. The chapter presents specific techniques that are designed for a distance education environment that allows for some degree of student-faculty interaction.

Chapter 5 entitled, "Web-Based Education" by A.K. Aggarwal and Regina Bento of University of Baltimore (USA) examines Web-based education and argues that it can successfully simulate face-to-face teaching models, while adding some unique features made possible by the technology. The chapter looks at several critical aspects of Web-based education, including technological, administrative, quality and control issues that need to be addressed in order to create an environment favorable to Web-based education.

Chapter 6 entitled, "Web-Based Teaching: Infrastructure Issues in the Third World" by Dushyanthi Hoole of Open University of Sri Lanka and S. Ratnajeevan H. Hoole of University of Peradeniya (Sri Lanka) discusses the problems faced by educators in the Third World who seek to incorporate the Web into their teaching. Specifically, the chapter describes the attempts by the authors in producing new ways or teaching with the Web and the development of an infrastructure for Web-based teaching at the Open University of Sri Lanka.

Chapter 7 entitled, "Cognitive Effects of Web Page Design" by Louis Berry of University of Pittsburgh (USA) addresses the cognitive implications of Web page design. The chapter does not focus on specific graphic layout and design criteria nor on visual display specifications, but rather it reviews and discusses the major theoretical and design issues impacting contemporary instructional Web page design.

Chapter 8 entitled, "Distance Education in the online World: Implications for Higher Education" by Stewart Marshall of Central Queensland University and Shirley Gregor of Australian National University (Australia) identifies the forces that lead to change in industries in the online world, including increasing global competition, increasingly powerful consumers and rapid changes in technology. The authors outline a "glocal" networked education paradigm that separates out global and local resource development learning facilitation

Chapter 9 entitled, "The Consequences of e-Learning" by Henry Emurian of University of Maryland Baltimore County (USA) offers a philosophical discussion about the future of e-learnng. The author discusses the role of the individual in the learning process, and concludes that the e-learning phenomena will produce a more informed learner and learning environments more conducive to different types of learners.

Chapter 10 entitled, "Student Perceptions of Virtual Education: An Exploratory Study" by Anil Kumar and Poonam Kumar of the University of Wisconsin-Whitewater and Suvojit Choton Basu of Northern Michigan University (USA)

explores the perceptions of students in a mid-western rural university regarding virtual education. The chapter also addresses the implications for the participants in the educational system. The chapter concludes by discussing the factors that encourage and discourage students from utilizing virtual education courses and provides insights for universities seeking to develop these programs.

Chapter 11 entitled, "Online Student Practice Quizzes and a Database Application to Generate Them" by Gary Randolph, Dewey Swanson, Dennis Owen and Jeffrey Griffin of Purdue University (USA) discusses a quiz database application that stores potential test questions and exports selected subsets of questions to a Web-based JavaScript program. The chapter explains how the database application works and how educators can obtain and use the application and provides guidance for constructing quiz questions that make the quiz a positive experience.

Chapter 12 entitled, "Classroom Component of an Online Learning Community: Case Study of an MBA Program at the University of St. Gallen" by Julia Gerhard, Peter Mayr and Sabine Seufert of the University of St. Gallen (Switzerland) discusses a way of designing an online learning environment and explains how to design a possible classroom component of a specific online learning community. The chapter first introduces the concept of online learning communities and then briefly describes the reference model for learning communities. The reference model is applied as a concrete MBA program, and the design of the classroom component of the MBA learning community is introduced.

Chapter 13 entitled, "Using Lotus Learning Space to Enhance Student Learning of Data Communications" by Michael Dixon and Tanya McGill of Murdoch University (Australia) and Johan Karlsson of Lund Institute of Technology (Sweden) describes how the authors deliver and manage part of a postgraduate degree in telecommunications. The aim of the degree is to foster learner-centered education while providing sufficient teacher centered activities to counter some of the known concerns with entirely learner-centered education. The Internet is used as the communication infrastructure to deliver teaching material globally and Lotus LearningSpace to provide the learning environment.

Chapter 14 entitled, "Development of a Distance Education Internet Based Foundation course for the MBA Program" by James LaBarre and E. Vance Wilson of University of Wisconsin-Eau Claire (USA) details the procedures to develop a distance education foundation course for an MBA program. All the MBA courses using this methodology are delivered to students enrolled in several universities within the Wisconsin systems.

Chapter 15 entitled, "Web-Based Learning: Is It Working? A Comparison of Student Performance and Achievement in Web-Based Courses and Their In-Classroom Counterparts" by Kathryn Marold, Gwynne Larsen and Abel Moreno of Metropolitan State College of Denver (USA) discusses the results of an in-depth study of Internet and classroom students' test grades and assignment grades spanning three semesters. In the comparison, students from the Internet set did better on the tests while classroom students performed better on the hands-on homework. The authors conclude that the findings support the theory that Internet delivered distance education courses require different designs and believe that their findings indicate that Web-based education is working.

Chapter 16 entitled, "Audio and Visual Streaming in Online Learning" by P.G. Muraleedharan of XStream Software (India) discusses two major players in media streaming technology, namely Microsoft and Real Networks. The chapter also addresses the two different types of media, on demand and broadcast, and the two types of connections for delivering these contents to the clients, unicast and multicast.

Chapter 17 entitled, "Relevant Aspects for Test Delivery Systems Evaluation" by Salvatore Valenti, Alessandro Cucchiareli and Maurizio Panti of the University of Ancona (Italy) presents a proposal for a framework that helps to identify guidelines for the selection of Test Delivery System. The chapter presents the metrics for the evaluation of the TDS at the elementary and system levels. The chapter then discusses how to avoid cheating and what countermeasures to adopt.

Chapter 18 entitled, "An Overview of Agent Technology and Its Application to Subject Management" by Paul Darbyshire and Glenn Lowry of Victoria University of Technology (Australia) provides an overview of agent software generally and autonomous agents specifically. The chapter then discusses the application of autonomous agents to educational courseware, and describes a project using autonomous agents to aid in Web-based subject management tasks.

Chapter 19 entitled, "A Comprehensive Approach to Teaching Visual Basic Programming" by Yun Wang of Mercy College (USA) introduces the background of the visual basic course taught at Mercy College and briefly outlines previous teaching approaches. The chapter describes the current teaching methodology in detail and examines existing course questions and proposes future revisions by studying the results of this new teaching approach.

Chapter 20 entitled, "What Do Good Designers Know That We Don't?" by Morgan Jennings of Metropolitan State College of Denver (USA) reports on an investigation of the immersive properties of game and learning environments. From the findings, the author develops prescriptive aesthetic framework based on data and aesthetic experience literature. The author chose aesthetics because popular multimedia environments appear to arouse the same experiences as aesthetic experience. The results reported indicate that this is the case.

Chapter 21 entitled, "Learning with Multimedia Cases in the Information Systems Area" by Rikke Orngreen of Copenhagen Business School (Denmark) and Paola Bielli of SDA Bocconi (Italy) presents research investigating possible learning scenarios for three Italian and three Danish cases through the collection of qualitative and quantitative empirical data. The objective of the research is to gain knowledge about how the chosen learning objectives from a multimedia case are best transferred to the users. The methodology and current experiences are described and preliminary results reported.

Chapter 22 entitled, "Who Benefits from WWW Presentations in the Basics of Informatics?" by Pekka Makkonen of the University of Jyväskylä describes the use of Web-based guided tours as a complementary addition to conventional lectures in the basics of informatics. The authors analyze the benefit of an optional coursework, including the use of guided tours, search engines, and directories on the World Wide Web. The chapter presents who benefits and who does not from the optional course work. The authors hypothesize that the students who are not familiar with computers and the Internet benefit more from the Web-based learning.

Chapter 23 entitled, "Towards an Automatic Massive Course Generation System" by Ahmed H. Kandil, Ahmed El-Bialy, and Khaled Wahba of Cairo University (Egypt) considers a system for massive course generation. The courses that are generated are built on top of open Internet standards and broadcast on the Web. The system described is equipped with an automatics system for final exam generation. The chapter discusses the implementation of the described systems in six courses in the biomedical engineering department at Cairo University.

Chapter 24 entitled, "A Case Study of One-to-One Video Conferencing Education over the Internet" by Hock C. Chan, Bernard C.Y. Tan and Wei-Ping Tan of National University of Singapore (Singapore) investigates the use of Internet video conferencing for one-to-one distance education. Through in-depth observations and interviews with two instructors and three students in Singapore, the chapter examines the impact of four critical factors, namely, system characteristics, mode characteristics, social presence and media richness, on the effectiveness of teaching and learning in such a context. This classroom focuses on the impact of virtual learning in small environments.

The Internet has changed the lives of individual students and educators in innumerable ways—it has also changed the face of education. Universities across the globe are offering Web-based courses and alternatives to classroom-based instruction, and teachers are incorporating Web-based activities and tests into their curriculum. The chapters in this book represent the best research currently available on Web-based education. They address the critical issues of how to select software for use, how to use the Web and associated technologies to generate tests and quizzes, how to measure the effectiveness of Web-based instruction and what the future of Web-based education is. Leading experts in the fields of education share their expertise and outline the road to successful implementation of the Internet in education as well as sharing practical tips on how to avoid some of the pitfalls that may lie ahead. This book provides practical guidelines for researchers and practitioners alike. It will be useful to teachers as they strive to improve and broaden their teaching, and the research of this book will prove to be an excellent resource for academicians and students alike as they explore this expanding field.

IRM Press
October 2001

Chapter 1

Web-Based Learning and Instruction: A Constructivist Approach

Valerie N. Morphew
West Virginia Wesleyan College

INTRODUCTION

The precipitous rise in Web-based education and employee training speaks volumes of technology's far-reaching potential. While most agree that Web-based instruction can be cost-effective and convenient, few academicians and practitioners have examined the efficacy of Web-based learning in terms of constructivism, the most widely accepted model of learning in education today.

The constructivist approach to learning acknowledges that both teacher and student bring prior knowledge to the learning experience. Over time and through interaction with others in the learning environment, the student co-constructs new meaning as a knowledge-building process—piece by piece, new knowledge is built onto former knowledge. This differs from the former notion of learning that considered children as empty vessels waiting to be filled (*tabula rasa*). While constructivism is widely accepted by educators in theory, it is not always evident in teaching practices, including Web-based instruction.

To help academicians and practitioners provide effective constructivist learning experiences for students and employees, the following issues will be addressed:

Previously Published in *Distance Learning Technologies: Issues, Trends and Opportunities* edited by Linda Lau, Copyright © 2000, Idea Group Publishing.

CONTEMPORARY CONSTRUCTIVIST THOUGHT

The constructivist perspective dominates learning theory today. Constructivists view knowledge as something that a learner actively constructs in his/her environment. Through meaningful learning experiences, a learner co-constructs new knowledge in tandem with those who share his/her learning environment. Knowledge is built piece by piece, and connections arise to join related pieces. In this view, knowledge is subjective—a learner's cumulative construction is uniquely erected.

Constructivism has its roots in various disciplines such as education, psychology, philosophy and the history of science. John Dewey, Jean Piaget, Edmund Husser and Thomas Kuhn are only a handful of theorists whose work impacts constructivist thought.

Dewey's emphasis on the role of experience in learning is significant to the constructivist perspective:

> When we experience something we act upon it, we do something with it; then we suffer or undergo the consequences. We do something to the thing and then it does something to us in return: such is the peculiar combination. The connection of these two phases of experience measures the fruitfulness or value of the experience. . . . Experience as trying involves change, but change is meaningless transition unless it is consciously connected with the return wave of consequences which flow from it. When an activity is continued *into* the undergoing of consequences, when the change made by action is reflected back into a change made in us, the mere flux is loaded with significance. We learn something (Dewey, 1944, p. 139).

Similarly, the mechanisms of knowledge development suggested by Piaget are significant to constructivist understanding. Piaget believed that thought developed by growing from one state of equilibrium to another. He believed that when a thinker encounters an experience consistent with prior beliefs, he simply needs to add it to his store of information. If an inconsistency arises, however, the thinker either ignores the new experience, modifies the experience in his mind to fit, or modifies his thinking to fit the experience. Progress in conceptual thinking occurs when the latter process is engaged (Baker & Piburn, 1997).

In the philosophical realm, Husserl's phenomenology similarly relates the construction of knowledge. In phenomenology, the subject's perceptions involve the transaction between the subject and the subject's field where things outside the subject are transformed into meaningful entities (in Morphew, 1994, from Tiryakian, 1973). When a subject experiences phenomena and perceives, meaning is possible (Morphew, 1994).

Husserl distinguished between types of meaning: meaning-intention and meaning-fulfillment. Meaning-intention corresponds to the ability of an expression to be meaningful and meaning-fulfillment to the possibility or impossibility of that meaning being carried to fulfillment (Husserl, 1970a, 1970b). Mohanty (1969) provides examples that illustrate meaning-intention and meaning-fulfillment: "Abcaderaf," "The present King of France," and "This white wall before me." "Abcaderaf" is meaningless and is not animated by meaning-intention. "The present King of France" is animated with meaning-intention as is "This white wall before me." They differ, however, in the possibility and nature of meaning-fulfillment since France no longer has a monarchy (p. 36, and Morphew, 1994).

According to Mohanty (1969), "Husserl would say that whereas thinking consists in the meaning-intending act, knowing consists in the appropriate fulfillment of the meaning-intention. So long as the meaning-intention is not fulfilled, we do not have knowledge" (p. 37). This exchange between the subject and the subject's field makes possible the learning experience.

In a collective process of learning, Kuhn (1962) described the process of acquiring new scientific understanding through his discussion of paradigm shifts. Kuhn uses "paradigm" to mean a world view involving models of explanations and models for the behavior of scientists. Most of the science done on a routine basis is normal science, a type of scientific puzzle solving. Normal science is carried out by scientists who perceive the world to operate in a particular fashion. If anomalies ("persistent failure of the puzzles of normal science") or counter-instances (new observations) arise and persist, the prevailing paradigm may be called into question and reexamined. Paradigm breakdown and blurred rules may open the door for the emergence of an alternate paradigm and for extraordinary research. As a result, a scientific revolution may emerge. This collective process of maintaining and modifying scientific thought is analogous to constructivist learning for individuals.

For the sake of this chapter, constructivism will follow the thinking of Husserl's phenomenology where meaning is defined as the co-created sense one makes of phenomena through the interaction of the subject and the subject's field (Morphew, 1994). In other words, constructivism is defined as the co-construction of meaning in the learning environment.

CONSTRUCTIVIST LEARNING AND INSTRUCTION IN THE TRADITIONAL CLASSROOM

Instruction includes planning, implementing, and evaluating the curriculum or the material covered in scope and sequence. The scope of the curriculum includes the breadth and depth of what is taught, and the sequence is the order in which it will be taught. Together the scope and sequence of the curriculum steer the act of instruction, though practically speaking, curriculum and instruction are inseparable (see Figure 1).

Theoretically, the curriculum that is taught should equal the curriculum learned (Passe, 1999). Unfortunately, in reality this seldom occurs. Instead, the difference in what is taught and learned shows itself in poor test scores and gross misconceptions. To bring the taught and learned curriculum closer together, the experiences made available to the learner must be amenable to what Dewey called "the flux" in learning. This attention to the experiences offered to learners helps ensure the act of co-construction of meaning.

In order for the learner to co-construct meaning, he/she must be open to the process of co-creation. To some degree instructors may influence the willingness of learners to learn, though much of this is intrinsically motivated. To a greater extent, instructors may impact the learning experience. Thus, the question arises, "What experiences should an instructor provide to help facilitate the act of co-construction?"

In traditional classrooms, instructors have adopted various teaching practices that maximize the potential for this flow by creating dynamic

Figure 1: Scope and Sequence Steering the Act of Instruction

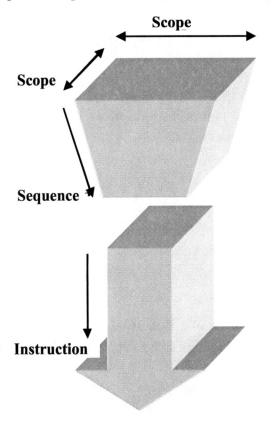

learning experiences. A number of experiences will be described that have proven effective.

Concept Maps and Semantic Webs

Concept maps are a visual representation diagramming concepts and relationships among concepts. Concepts are arranged hierarchically so that the most general concepts are located at the top of the diagram, and the most specific are located toward the bottom (Baker & Piburn, 1997). Connections between related concepts are shown in Figure 2. Semantic webs are also visual representations of concepts, yet they are not hierarchical in nature. Rather all concepts emanate from one overriding concept, showing relationships between the subordinate concepts and the main concept (Baker & Piburn, 1997). Figure 3 illustrates a semantic web for the skull. Concept maps and semantic Webs may be created by either the instructor, learner or both and may be introduced any time relationships among existing knowledge are made, or whenever new knowledge is constructed.

Venn Diagrams and Other Graphic Organizers

Venn diagrams, like concept maps and semantic webs, help show the connection between related concepts. They can be simple or complex and may be created by the instructor, learner, or both to accentuate connections between concepts or attributes of concepts (see Figure 4). Venn diagrams are a type of graphic organizer: any visual representation used to help make the abstract concrete. Figure 5 illustrates a graphic organizer that shows the patterns of inductive and deductive reasoning.

Models

Creation and utilization of models is another experience that provides learners with concrete examples of connections and relationships. For instance, relief maps help learners understand connections between flat topographic maps and changes in land elevation. A model of the solar system showing relative location and distance of the planets to the sun may be used to make the abstract concrete.

Analogies and Metaphors

Analogies and metaphors are helpful in making connections between prior knowledge and new knowledge. For example, a learner may benefit from understanding that the transmission of messages in a computer system is like the transmission of nerve impulses in the human body. Similarly,

Figure 2: Concept Map of Dogs

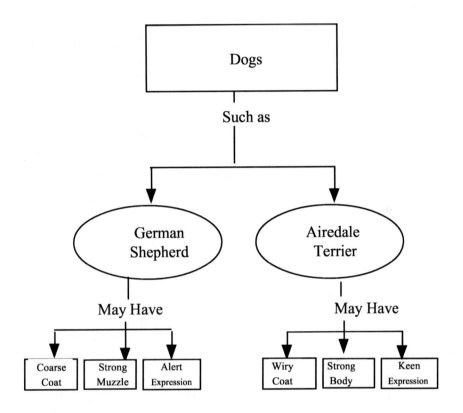

conceiving the human life span as a journey may help a learner more easily grasp the meaning of this experience.

Hypothesis Making and Testing

Hypothesis making and testing are experiences that help facilitate co-construction of meaning by requiring the learner to draw from a vast store of previously learned concepts to make inferences about new ones. Hypotheses are statements that show a cause and effect relationship between two or more factors. They are often written in the if-then format. "If temperature is increased, then pressure will increase." "If blue is added to red, then purple will result." These statements are meaning-building in their creation but also in their testing. In testing hypotheses, the learner must experiment to co-create new concept formation. This new knowledge will later be a part of future hypotheses making.

Figure 3: Semantic Web of the Skull

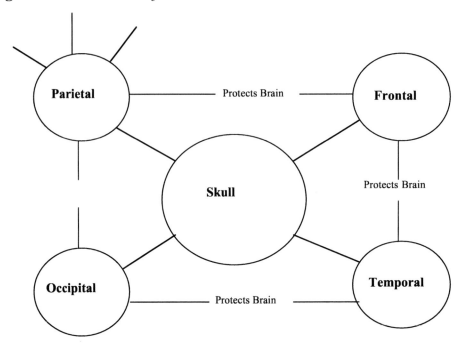

Figure 4: Venn Diagram Showing That All Dogs Grow Hair

Figure 5: Graphic Organizer Showing Inductive and Deductive Reasoning Patterns

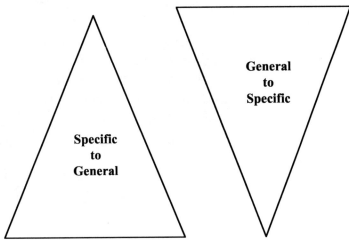

Integrated Themes

The relevancy of connections becomes apparent to learners when themes and concepts are integrated holistically. For example, the learner who constructs meaning about the life style of colonists during the American Revolution at the same time she learns about the science of that time and place has a better chance of building connections than if she were taught these concepts in isolation. Elementary instructors more often teach integrated thematic units than secondary instructors. Unfortunately, the traditional isolation of secondary teaching faculty doesn't allow for integrated planning and thus, presentation to learners.

Journaling

Journaling is the process of reflecting on a given statement or question to make sense of it in terms of the learner's past and current experiences. For example, learners may begin a journal at the beginning of a unit on space travel. Early in the journal learners may be asked to reflect and write on what it would be like to leave their familiar planet to journey for a new life wrought with uncertainties. As the learners progress through the unit, preferably thematically, they are asked to reflect on their travels as they journey farther and farther away from planet Earth. How are their survival needs being met? What kinds of hardships are they encountering? What improvements to their quality of life are they discovering? Like hypothesis testing, analogies, and metaphors, this type of experience forces the learner to reach back into her prior learning to co-construct meaning of the new.

Portfolios

Portfolios are a system of organizing various documents so that connections among the documents and their conceptual meaning may be made. Portfolios may contain paradigm statements or declarations of what students understand about a concept at that place and time in their life. For example, beginning teachers are often asked to document their educational philosophy early on in their careers and to revisit those statements as they grow up in the profession. By reflecting on where they have been, where they are, and where they might be going, connections can be made between prior, present, and future knowledge and experiences.

Another example may be at the beginning of a unit on particle physics; learners might be asked to explain their current understanding of the atom. As new concepts are introduced in their learning experience, the students would record how these concepts measure up to new ones in the process of co-construction of meaning.

Other instruments may be used to analyze current conceptions. Questionnaires, surveys and checklists may be periodically completed and updated as students move through the study of a concept. These documents may be added to the portfolio to help the learner understand how he/she constructs knowledge most fully. This act of self-observation and interpretation is called metacognition and is consistent with constructivist thought.

Dialogue and Cooperative Learning

Dialogue with others and cooperative learning provide students with experiences where the act of co-creation of meaning can occur simultaneously with other learners. When learners are asked to engage in dialogue, their prior knowledge is called up and constantly challenged as new concepts are introduced. In the cooperative learning experience, where groups of learners work together to construct meaning toward the solution of a given problem, similar connections are made.

For example, a cooperative group of learners, given the task of building a better mousetrap, will exchange prior knowledge about the construction of typical mousetraps. Different learners will likely be familiar with different types of traps. Together, the exchange of dialogue helps learners share and build new meaning. Cooperatively, the learners will test possible prototypes of new mousetraps and modify their existing understanding of what a mousetrap means.

Learning Cycle Lesson

The learning cycle lesson is a process of presenting material so that the learner capitalizes on the constructive nature of learning. The learning cycle lesson has several phases to its delivery. The first phase is the exploration phase, where students are given an opportunity to explore components of the curriculum. In a science lesson, students may be given different shells to observe. The students will be asked to record their observations and begin to make inferences about their observations.

The next phase is the explanation phase, where the instructor helps the student co-construct meaning of the observations and inferences. This phase, also known as the Term Invention phase, is where sense is made of the phenomenon. Here terminology, explanation and connections will make up the learning experience. In our example, perhaps the shells might be described in terms of their biological attributes. Connections to remains of other sea life would likely be addressed to connect former knowledge with new knowledge, and to help students discard any preconceived ideas that they now realize are incorrect.

The expansion phase, also known as the Concept Application phase, is where students are given an opportunity to apply what they just learned. Here students might develop a family tree of the shells and compare to the actual taxonomic relationship delineated by scientists. Learners would then have the opportunity to compare previous understanding with new and see how they measure up to one another.

In some versions of the learning cycle, an additional phase is listed. This phase, the evaluation phase, is actually an ongoing act of assessing for the co-construction of meaning. Student responses, questions, records and actions are all considered when assessing learning.

RECOMMENDATIONS FOR WEB-BASED CONSTRUCTIVIST LEARNING AND INSTRUCTION

The foregoing discussion on experiences used by constructivist instructors in the traditional classroom has numerous implications for distance learning education. With some creativity, much of the same experiences that stimulate thinking and facilitate the co-construction of meaning in traditional settings can be made available to the distance learner.

For example, as a distance learning educator plans for instruction, he/she must keep in mind that the experience is paramount in the constructivist learning process. But before the experiences can be selected, the scope and sequence of the curriculum must be decided. Questions such as, "What knowledge of this topic is worth knowing and significant to understanding other concepts?" and "What depth of understanding is essential for learners to make important connections?" will be helpful in narrowing down the plethora of material on a given topic.

Next, the distance learning educator must decide what planning will be necessary to deliver the curriculum. Choices must be made regarding related Web sites, CD-ROMs and other technology that will be used to help make the curriculum deliverable.

Once the technology is selected, careful attention must be paid to the experiences that will be provided to learners to make meaning possible. The appropriateness of every experience described previously should be evaluated to determine the degree to which it would bring the taught curriculum closer to the learned curriculum.

Following this planning, the distance learning educator must orchestrate all the technologies and experiences for the implementation phase of instruction. During this phase, educators should closely monitor the growth in the learners and efficacy of the program by keeping abreast of journal responses, paradigm statements, or whatever other experiences are being used as part of the distance learning education program. Instructional plans should be modified based on this feedback to most fully ensure co-construction of meaning by the learners. This process of monitoring and modifying should be ongoing throughout the distance learning education program.

During the evaluation phase of instruction, the distance learning educator should review growth of the learners in terms of meaning construction and should assess how closely the curriculum taught and the curriculum learned match. In this way, evaluation of the learner and program can be accomplished simultaneously. Figure 6 illustrates a conceptual model of constructivist learning and instruction via Web-based instruction.

FUTURE RESEARCH OPPORTUNITIES

Jonassen, Peck, and Wilson (1999) propose a conceptual model of learning environments for technology. According to their model, Constructivist Learning Environments (CLEs) should engage students in investigation of the problem, critique of related cases, review of information resources, develop-

Figure 6

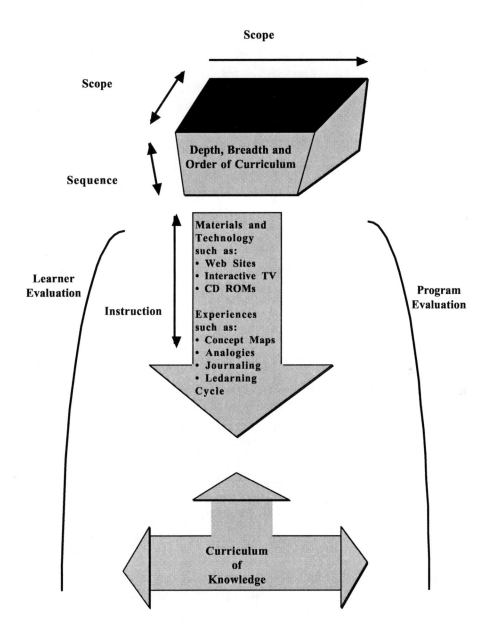

ment of necessary skills, collaboration with others and use of social support in implementation of the learning experience. Perhaps merging of the conceptual model of constructivist distance learning education described in this chapter and that presented by Jonassen, et al. will better serve distance learning educators and learners alike. Learner and program evaluation will testify to the efficacy of Web-based constructivist learning and instruction.

The degree to which this process will bring about the desired learning is a question for future study. Most Web-based instruction today is based on behaviorism, viewing the learner as an empty vessel waiting to be filled. Distance learning educators should acknowledge constructivism as the new paradigm for learning and must also be willing to shift their teaching practices for consistency and constructivist learning.

REFERENCES

Baker, D. R., & Piburn, M. D. (1997). *Constructing science in middle and secondary school classrooms*. Boston: Allyn and Bacon.

Dewey, J. (1944). *Democracy and education*. New York: The Free Press.

Husserl, E. (1970a). *Logical investigations, Volume I* (J. N. Findlay, Trans.). New York: Humanities Press. (Original work published 1921-22).

Husserl E. (1970b). *Logical investigations, Volume II* (J. N. Findlay, Trans.). New York: Humanities Press. (Original work published 1921-22).

Jonassen, D. H., Peck, K. L., Wilson, B. G. (1999). *Learning with technology: A constructivist perspective*. Upper Saddle River, NJ: Prentice Hall, Inc.

Kuhn, T. S. (1962). *The structure of scientific revolutions*. Chicago: The University of Chicago Press.

Mohanty, J. N. (1969). *Edmund Husserl's theory of meaning*. (2nd ed.). The Hague: Martinus Nijhoff.

Morphew, V. N. (1994). *Change in meaning, change in action: A phenomenological study*. Unpublished doctoral dissertation. West Virginia University, Morgantown.

Passe, J. (1999). *Elementary school curriculum* (2nd ed.). Boston: McGraw.

Tiryakian, E. A. (1973). Sociology and existential phenomenology. In M. Natanson (Ed.), *Phenomenology and the Social Sciences, Volume I* Evanston: Northwestern University Press, 187-222 .

Chapter 2

Implementing Corporate Distance Training Using Change Management, StrategicPlanning and Project Management

Zane L. Berge
University of Maryland, Baltimore County

Donna L. Smith
T. Rowe Price Associates, Inc.

As businesses expand to become more globally competitive, their needs grow to train geographically dispersed employees in a cost-effective manner. What must businesses do to implement distance education? An important role of the training and performance specialists in business is to help management solve complex problems within an organization. Still, distance education is usually not accomplished by a single group within an organization, nor through a single process. To change the way training is done, performance managers must use what is known about change management, strategic planning and project management in order to successfully implement technology-enhanced learning globally. One of the methods being used increasingly in the workplace is distance training.

Early in the company's implementation of distance training, it is useful to think about two approaches: a change approach and a project approach. As

Previously Published in *Distance Learning Technologies: Issues, Trends and Opportunities* edited by Linda Lau, Copyright © 2000, Idea Group Publishing.

the level of the organization's maturity with distance training grows, (i.e., as distance training becomes institutionalized), the amount of change by definition decreases, and reliance shifts from change management to strategic planning. Similarly, as distance training permeates the organization, the shift is away from "individual events" and toward distance training as simply "how the organization does business."

Offered here is a perspective for implementing distance education which integrates strategic planning, change management and project management as critical to successful overall implementation. Rather than prescribe specific models, this approach identifies the essence of what each discipline contributes to the process of implementing distance education.

WHAT IS CORPORATE DISTANCE TRAINING

Distance training and distance education are used synonymously throughout this article unless otherwise noted. Essentially, we mean that the training or teaching function is implemented remotely using some type of technology and two-way communication system. This is especially in contrast to in-person training. Our focus is on how to introduce and sustain technologically-mediated learning in the workplace. Included are applications such as internet/intranet, computer-mediated communication, video-conference, satellite broadcast, audiographics and e-mail. Corporate distance training is defined differently by different authors, but here it means bringing together resources and learners to address the business problems in which training is at least part of the solution. This needs to be done in a cost-effective, timely manner. An emphasis is on the business challenge of training geographically disperse employees and managing resource and productivity across the system.

In addition, we view corporate distance training as an "innovation" (Schreiber and Berge, 1998). We propose an approach where training at a distance represents a significant departure from how the business currently conducts training activities—a change which will meet some level of resistance. This results not only in applying new technology but also "creating a different kind of structure for learning and teaching" (Kearsley, 1998, p.49). The decision to implement distance education must be made during strategic planning, where it is determined whether distance education programs fit into the mission of the institution and how best to integrate it into the mainstream (Berge and Schrum, 1998).

THE NATURE OF DISTANCE EDUCATION IMPLEMENTATION

What does distance education "implementation" mean? Fowler and Levine (1993) define implementation as the process of putting an innovation or technology into use in an organization's or individual's work environment. Schreiber (1998) distinguishes between a technologically mature company's making distance education part of the *profile of the organization* compared with a less technologically mature organizations implementation of distance learning *events*. Many change models see implementation as synonymous with "adoption" (DLRN Technology Resources Guide, Chapter 8). Early technologically based models show implementation as the last (or nearly last) step in a linear process—framing it as a discrete step or event. Dormant (1992) notes that "the problem with the implementation-comes-last approach is that. . . it separates those involved in implementation from those making decisions about development" (p. 168). Implementation is closely tied to adoption by end users. It is gradual, sporadic, and accomplished over time. Projects are one major means of accomplishing implementation, although the complexity of distance education's impact on an organization requires careful attention to how implementation is carried out.

LESSONS LEARNED

Much of the research for implementing distance education is being conducted by higher education institutions. In borrowing what is learned from higher education for application in business, care must be taken to respect the similarities and differences of each environment, so that the integrity of the generalizations is maintained. As a preface to "mixing" experience from education and business, the fundamental missions of the two should be considered (Chute, Thompson, and Hancock, 1999). Traditional education is focused on individuals, with a secondary mission to achieve productive results. Business is focused on productivity, with a secondary mission of educating individuals, as a means to the corporate end of profitability. However, in both cases, leaders concern themselves with creating an atmosphere, relationships and processes that will achieve the organization's goal—whether it is learning as a direct or indirect goal. Business and higher education can each pull from principles of strategy, change management and project planning to implement distance education.

CRITICAL COMPONENTS OF IMPLEMENTING DISTANCE EDUCATION

The framework here (see Figure 1), recognizes the unique contributions of the three disciplines of change management, strategic planning and project management.

Context: Change management provides the *context* for making strategic decisions and setting up projects. By context, we mean the necessary circumstances and linkages to theory which predict patterns of behavior. One significant theory underlying change management models is "diffusion of innovation." By this is meant the process by which an innovation is communicated through certain channels over time among the members of a social system (Rogers, 1995). The process used to communicate innovation provides the backdrop for making decisions about time lines, resources and human factors. Managing change can thereby guide strategy decisions, thus connecting strategic planning to the end users implementing distance training projects. Change management and diffusion theory are critical models that place in context that which strategy makers interested in sustaining changes in the organization must work.

Conditions: Strategic planning provides conditions under which distance education is implemented. Conditions are any constraints or limitations imposed upon the organization because of their mission, goals, values, priorities, etc., including time, budget, and culture. Strategic plans give rise to funding allocations, assignment of resources and the elevation of distance education by the company's leaders to a critical goal. It also facilitates the

Figure 1. Critical Components of Implementing Distance Training

Strategic Planning
(Conditions)

Project Management
(Conduits)

Distance Ed.
Implementation

Change Management
(Context)

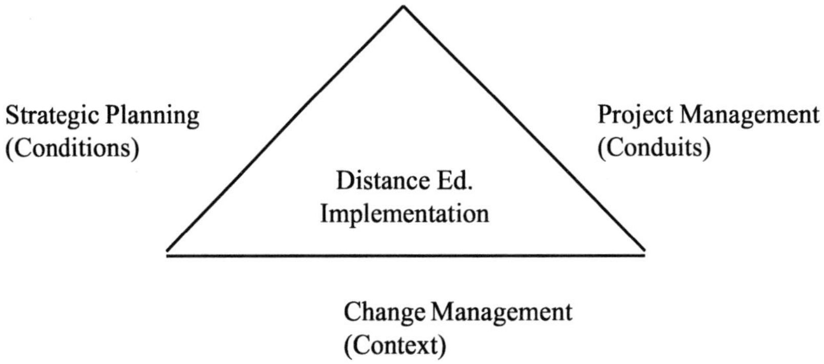

identification of issues and constraints around funding, resources, infrastructure and organizational readiness. Many strategic planning models also have processes for connecting users and implementers to the plans early in the development process. Involving the implementers, as change theory tells us, will facilitate adoption. This linkage of strategy makers and users provides a reality check for distance education implementation.

Conduits: Early in an organization's use of distance training, projects function as conduits for implementation. Projects function as vehicles for realizing tangible results and measurement which are needed for justification and reinforcement in the context of corporate culture. For any large scale innovation, such as distance education, projects are also critical because of the cross-functional nature of project management. Project participants develop learning that serves as feedback for strategic planing. Change models and strategic plan models both incorporate projects as a way to implement change. Projects that run concurrent to strategic planning provide methods to track status, monitor progress, manage resources of time, money, people, and measure results. Thus, the success of distance education depends on project implementation.

CHANGE MANAGEMENT AS CONTEXT FOR DISTANCE EDUCATION IMPLEMENTATION

Change management provides a context in which to implement distance education activities. Rogers' (1995) work provided a foundation for diffusion of innovation theory, which underlies the discipline of change management. His work provides guiding principles for types and rates of adoption of an innovation (early adopter/innovators, middle adopters/opinion leaders, late adopters/laggards). The work also provides predictable patterns of adoption (s-curve) with implications for time lines, resources and other logistical considerations. These can help managers avoid "rash" actions and decisions in the name of getting results quickly. Change management for distance education capitalizes on involving early adopters in strategic projects such as first attempts and pilots of new technology. It also includes consideration of adoption rates in planning for large capital expenditures or resources and planning for sequence and locations of early projects, as well as planning for overcoming barriers in throughout.

Change management helps in focusing on human nature as a business consideration and also provides guidelines for managing the human side of implementing distance education. Surry (1997) cites problems with diffusion of instructional technologies due to ignoring the many factors that influence adoption of innovations. In distance training, these factors include lack of comfort with the nature of teaching and learning in distance environments; lack of trust among different functions with different expertise; lack of skill with technologies; lack of resources; or poor learning design. These and other factors which influence adoption must be identified and included in planning so persons charged with implementation can explain, predict and account for those issues that facilitate or impede an organization's acceptance of the innovation.

Related to this impact on people and why this affects long term acceptance is the notion of cultural change. Implementing distance training and new technologies is often considered a "cultural change" or organization development (OD) initiative. For example, Finney (1997) notes that the intranet's many-to-many communication model forces companies out of a hierarchical structure and towards individual empowerment. Strangelove (1994) addresses this cultural impact by stating that any new form of communication creates a new cultural paradigm, such as the internet's creation of "mass participation in bidirectional, uncensored mass communication" where "audience and content provider act as one" (p.7). There are many other examples, but the view of distance education implementation as requiring change management is implied in Wagner's (1992) listing of technological integration and organizational readiness as areas which influence successful diffusion of distance education technologies. He cautions that organizations not ready to show how these solutions improve the current state will find "diffusion of the innovation slow and disruptive" (p. 521). Competency in change management and understanding of diffusion theory improves the context in which distance education can be implemented, providing guidelines, predictive patterns of behavior and focus on human issues. It creates the context for implementing distance education.

STRATEGIC PLANNING FOR DISTANCE TRAINING

With regard to implementing distance training, strategic planning provides the conditions, or constraints, of the organization as they are derived from the mission, goals, values, priorities, etc. Powers (1992) defines strategic alignment as the "systematic arrangement of crucial business systems behind a common purpose" and lists the following strategic alignment model components: mission, values, aims and goals, objectives, job roles, selection, expectations, tools, training, feedback, rewards, financial and other management systems, for quality performance (p.258). Organizations must take time to establish a "big picture" on how implementing distance education will change the organization, and also how it will fit the organization, asking many questions up front to address issues like need, cost savings, audiences, technical requirements, infrastructure, resources, communication, incentives, support, etc. (Wagner, 1992).

Pearson (as cited in DLRN Chapter 7) identified 20 critical factors for implementing distance training. In rank order, the top ten were based on human and fiscal resources such as time, people, and funding. But the top critical factor for implementing distance education is to identify the need for it. Assuming that exploration of distance education is triggered by an implied or expressed need for distance education, managers should plan for and commit resources; contract with executive "sponsors;" and investigate any existing internal drives to apply distance education technology in a similar fashion to other business functions of the company (e.g. intranet, internet, e-mail communication, etc.). While some exploration and demonstration of concept is needed, it may be dangerous in the long run to view distance education technologies as a quick fix solution until the impact upon the organization is considered using the strategic planning process. Otherwise, among other things, organizations risk unnecessary resistance to the changes implied by the adoption of distance education.

The strategic planning team must assess organizational readiness by looking at factors such as numbers and locations of potential users; projected demand for distance education delivery; and technology's perceived value to the organization, to managers and to trainers themselves (Wagner,1992). Other factors to consider might be prerequisite skill sets of learners and trainers; barriers relating to accessibility of distance education; whether other major changes are distracting employees and resources; etc. Wagner cautions that it is "not sufficient to provide people with solutions without also showing them how these solutions can be applied to improve on the ways in which things have always been done" (p. 521). Jellison (1998) goes even further advocating "progressive transformation," a way to break down emotional barriers by changing people's actions in small ways instead of trying to make them believe they should change all at once. An example here may be using technology in meaningful ways in conjunction with in-person training as a stepping stone for training at a distance.

Once it is determined that the organization has a true need for distance education as a business solution, the strategic planning process must connect to the end users and/or implementers (Berge and Schrum, 1998). We characterize implementation as something that is local, must be accomplished by end users usually using a gradual, iterative process rather than a discrete event in a linear chain. If distance education is directly connected to the mission and goals of the organization, then implementers can make strong argument for management support, and users will support it to the extent they support strategic plan (Dormant, p. 174).

Noblitt (1997) notes that "top-down folks" are charged with administrative or institutional duties concerned with infrastructure while "bottom-up people" are charged with instructional or research duties and demands for time and resources to get their projects done. Their deep mutual dependency carves out different roles for each. The top-down program advocate relies on success stories to justify large investments in technology and the bottom-up project advocate needs a well-conceived and reliable working environment for successful implementation for innovative concepts (pp. 38-39). Noblitt also calls for a context-sensitive implementation plan, and this means that top-down and bottom-up people must work together on setting priorities (p. 43). For distance education, this applies as end users (trainers and learners) and strategic planners (executive management) working together with sensitivity to how changes caused by distance education can be smoothly integrated with involvement of all stakeholders (Pollack and Masters, 1997; Vazquez and Abad, 1992).

PROJECTS AS CONDUITS FOR DISTANCE EDUCATION

Change management and strategic planning both value projects as a way to manage change. Projects connect adopters, users, or implementers to the distance education initiative. In this way, projects function as the conduits for implementing distance education. Early in an organization's attempts to implement distance education, project management tools and techniques help structure distance training (Formby and Ostrander, 1997) within good business practice focusing on schedule, cost and scope issues.

The Project Management Institute (Duncan, 1996) defines a project as a "temporary endeavor undertaken to create a unique product or service" (p. 4). A project has a beginning and end; is performed by people; constrained by limited resources; and planned, executed, and controlled. Wideman's (1991) typical project life cycle includes the four stages of Concept, Development, Implementation and Termination. Within each phase are activities, methods, tools and formats reflecting classical project management techniques. Examples include feasibility study, risk analysis, scope, work breakdown structure, resource allocation, schedule, etc. Since implementation of learning technologies results in a business product with cost, schedule and scope elements to be managed and economics as an influence on successful diffusion (Wagner, 1992), it can benefit in many ways from having individuals who are competent in project management. Projects function as the conduit not only for tactical implementation of strategy but also for the change management process. Jackson and Addison (1992) note that:

> any project activity will represent some degree of change for virtually everyone affected... A critical responsibility of the project manager is to help ensure that the changes introduced by project activities are as easy and rewarding as it is feasible to make them. More than one technologically sound project has been seriously damaged simply because people in the organization saw the process as unnecessarily difficult, unpleasant, or time-consuming" (p. 71).

Projects also function as the conduits for the organizational learning that informs strategy. Nadler (1994) contends that structure leads to strategy which emerges over time from a pattern of decisions. In the process, project groups help develop new relationships and new learning within the organization (Systemic Reform, 1994, p. 3). So projects carry learning between the "top" and the "bottom" of the organization. When informed by skills in change management, project managers play a key role in successful distance education implementation. Additionally, projects are good for distance education because of their interdisciplinary nature. Schreiber and Berge (1998) cite overcoming barriers to interdisciplinary efforts as critical to successful implementation and institutionalization of distance education since it requires managers, educators, and technologists to evolve the organization into a sophisticated user of technology.

Project management as a practice provides a rigorous discipline for getting results. Schaffer and Thomson (1992) distinguish between activity-centered and results-centered programs and recommend introducing innovations in increments to support specific performance goals. With tangible results, managers and employees can enjoy success and build confidence and skill for continued improvements. They recommend using each project to test new ways of managing, measuring, and organizing for results. Marrying long-term goals with short-term projects helps turn strategy into reality. Eventually, implementation and integration of distance education into the business and training culture will result to the extent distance training aligns with strategic planning in the organization. Each design project has its own project manager, project schedule, scope, budget and objectives which "dovetail" with the concepts laid out in strategic planning. Targeted distance education projects aligned with business strategies, learner needs, and corporate objectives will move the organization toward acceptance.

CONCLUSIONS

Our approach views the implementation of distance education as a long term strategic change in the organization. Especially at the beginning stages, projects provide a structured way to synthesize what is learned and connect users to persons charged with strategic planning. Practice of the three disciplines is simultaneous and nonlinear, with overlapping aspects. Diffusion of innovation and change theory provide a background (context) for making strategic and tactical decisions, increasing likelihood of positive results. The strategic planning results (conditions/constraints) are continuously informed by what is being "learned" and evaluated in the projects (conduits).

In short, distance education must not be explored or conceived as a solution waiting for a problem. Consideration of conditions and constraints of the organization, as raised by the strategic planning process, are critical to successful implementation. The primary consideration is that distance education arises out of true need. Once this is established, the planning process is informed by connection to users. To implement distance education requires overcoming barriers and dealing with complex issues. Training and performance stakeholders can benefit from leveraging existing skills of project management, change management, and strategic planning and applying these disciplines to distance training.

REFERENCES

Berge, Z.L. & Schrum, L. (1998). Strategic planning linked with program implementation for distance education. *CAUSE/EFFECT*. 21(3), 31-38. [Online.] http://www.educause.edu/ir/library/html/cem9836.html.

Chute, A.G., Thompson, M.M., and Hancock, B.W. (Eds.) (1999). *The McGraw-Hill Handbook of Distance Learning*. New York: McGraw-Hill.

DLRN Technology Resource Guide. Steps of change: basics of innovation diffusion. Chapters 7 & 8. [Online.] http://www.wested.org/tre/dlrn/plan.html.

Dormant, D. (1992). Implementing human performance technology in organizations. In H. Stolovitch and E. Keeps (Eds.) *Handbook of Human Performance Technology*. San Francisco: Jossey-Bass, 167-187.

Duncan, W.R. (1996). *Guide to the project management body of knowledge*. Project Management Institute Standards Committee, 130 South State Road, Upper Darby PA19082 USA.

Finney, M. (1997, February). Harness the power within. *HR Magazine.*, 66-74.

Formby, S. and Ostrander, G. (August, 1997). Managing change the project management way. *PM Network.*

Fowler, P. and Levine, L. (December, 1993). *A conceptual framework for software technology transition*. Carnegie-Melon University. Software Engineering Institute.

Jackson, S. and Addison, R. (1992). Planning and managing projects. In H. Stolovitch and E. Keeps (Eds.) *Handbook of Human Performance Technology*. San Francisco: Jossey-Bass, 66-76.

Jellison, J. (1998). PIA human relations conference preview: Change is emotional. [Online.] http://www.printing.org/prhrpre.htm.

Kearsley, G. (1998, April) Educational technology: A critique. *Educational Technology*, 47-51.

Nadler, D. (1994, Set.-Oct.) Collaborative strategic thinking. *Planning Review*. p.31

Noblitt, J. (May-June 1997.) Top-down meets bottom-up." *Education Review*. 32(3), 38-43.

Pollock, C., and Masters, R. (1997). Using internet technologies to enhance training. *Performance Improvement*. *36*(2), 28-31.

Powers, B. (1992). Strategic alignment.. In H. Stolovitch and E. Keeps (Eds.) *Handbook of Human Performance Technology*. San Francisco: Jossey-Bass, 247-258.

Rogers, R. (1995). *Diffusion of innovations*. (4th. ed.). New York, N.Y.: Macmillan.

Schaffer, R. and Thomson, H. (January-February 1992). Successful change programs begin with results. *Harvard Business Review.*

Schreiber, D. (1998) Best practices of distance training. In D. Schreiber and Z. Berge (Eds.) *Distance Training: How Innovative Organizations are Using Technology to Maximize Learning and Meet Business Objectives*. San Francisco, CA: Jossey-Bass Inc., Publisher. pp. 393-409.

Schreiber, D.A. & Berge, Z.L. (Eds.) (1998). *Distance Training: How Innovative Organizations are Using Technology to Maximize Learning and Meet Business Objectives*. San Francisco, CA: Jossey-Bass Inc., Publishers.

Strangelove, M. (1994, December) The internet as a catalyst for a paradigm shift. *Distance Education Magazine,* 8, 7.

Surry, D.W. (1997, February 20,). Diffusion theory and instructional technology. [Online.] http://intro.base.org/docs/diffusion/, 1-11.

Systemic Reform (1994, September). Perspectives on Personalizing Education http//www.ed.gov/pubs/EdReformStudies/SysReforms/stiegel7.html

Vazquez-Abad, J., and Winer, L. (1992) Emerging trends in human performance interventions In H. Stolovitch and E. Keeps (Eds.) *Handbook of Human Performance Technology*. San Francisco: Jossey-Bass, 672-687.

Wagner, E. (1992). Distance education systems. In H. Stolovitch and E. Keeps (Eds.) *Handbook of Human Performance Technology*. San Francisco: Jossey-Bass, 513-525.

Wideman, R. (1991). A framework for project and program management integration, preliminary edition. The *PMBOK Handbook Series. 1.*

Chapter 3

Three Strategies for the Use of Distance Learning Technology in Higher Education

William E. Rayburn
Austin Peay State University

Arkalgud Ramaprasad
Southern Illinois University

INTRODUCTION

"University A" is a small, private liberal arts school with a religious affiliation. Located in a large city, it draws locally and from its particular religious group. With an enrollment under 3,000, it carries a Carnegie Classification of Baccalaureate II and has its own board of trustees. The school has pushed the use of new technology in instruction. For instance, it was one of the first schools in its area to install a fiber optic network across campus. Programs such as business feature the active use of technology to enhance learning. For example, in an international business course, students develop links with fellow students in other countries. However, University A differs from other schools that have embraced new information and communication technology; it has rejected some uses as not appropriate to the mission of the school. For instance, University A will not use videoconferencing to send instruction to remote sites. Why? School leaders feel that a significant part of a student's experience at University A comes from faculty providing role models, and that role modeling cannot be done through a television monitor.

Previously Published in *Distance Learning Technologies: Issues, Trends and Opportunities* edited by Linda Lau, Copyright © 2000, Idea Group Publishing.

"University B" is a regional public university located in a small town in a heavily rural portion of its state. The nearest small city is an hour's drive away, and it draws students regionally, mostly from nearby counties. With an enrollment under 10,000, the school carries a Carnegie Classification of Master's I. For years, University B has used its Continuing Education program in aggressively serving the region, beginning with such means as "circuit rider" faculty who traveled to remote sites to teach classes and broadcast television instruction through local public television. The school has continued its aggressive outreach with new technology. In the 1990s, University B quickly moved into videoconferencing (compressed video) to phase out at least some of the circuit rider faculty. At the same time, the school has expanded the off-campus sites to which it sends instruction. Lastly, University B has augmented its MBA program by bringing in a health care administration concentration from another university via videoconferencing, and it has been considering the future servicing of majors in declining programs such as geography by outsourcing instruction.

Officers at the two universities described above were among those at several schools who participated in a series of case studies (Rayburn, 1997). The two schools use distance learning technology (DLT) in very different ways, but they do share at least one common trait: they have clear pictures of how to use available technology. Put another way, they have identifiable strategies for using technology that conform to the missions of the schools.

The point of this chapter is to identify and describe strategies for using distance learning technology (DLT) at higher education institutions. Research suggests three major strategies, the "Guest Lecturer" strategy, the "Automated Correspondence Course" strategy, and the "Large Lecture Hall" strategy. All three strategies have antecedents in the recent history of higher education, and each has its own implications for the future. The next section looks at literature and field research on the strategic use of DLT.

BACKGROUND

The literature provides many examples of how institutions have used distance learning technology (DLT). The case study research that included University A and University B, while adding to the body of knowledge on distance learning from an *organizational* perspective, also suggested a useful working taxonomy of DLT strategies. Both history and current literature support this taxonomy.

Schools employ DLT to achieve different goals. Those goals also have antecedents elsewhere in academe. Broadly speaking, the goals fall into three major categories: making instruction more effective, reaching new students and making programs more efficient. These goals translate into the three strategies mentioned in the introduction. An historic antecedent lends its name to each strategy.

Guest Lecturer Strategy

Institutions with the first goal, making instruction more effective, pursue the Guest Lecturer strategy. Just as with business, schools seek to improve the quality of their product (Baldwin, 1991), although some see DLT as a threat to a quality product (Jacobson, 1994b). The choice of the Guest Lecturer title does not suggest that its exclusive use is only to bring in a guest who could not otherwise attend class; rather, it is just an archetype. Examples of the Guest Lecturer strategy include digital libraries and archives (Basinger, 1999; Blumenstyk, 1998b; Guernsey, 1998), virtual communities (Glassman, 1997), on-line conferences for students and faculty (Kiernan, 1998; Morrison, 1997), Web-based simulations (Robbin, 1996), electronic field trips (Carey, 1991; Hawkins, 1991), the telecommuting of personnel (Berge, Collins, and Day, 1995), "cultural context" in language instruction (Lambert, 1991) and of course guest lecturers and outside experts (Carey, 1991; Berge and Collins, 1995). The case study research added the viewing of satellite programs to the list as well. DLT used this way serves as a catalyst to improve the learning experience itself. Here the antecedent is the guest lecturer whose input enhances the value of the class to the student. In its most extreme use, DLT can transform the process (how the instruction takes place) (Dede, 1991). In this regard, the potential impact of DLT on instruction conforms to the concepts of Zuboff and Scott Morton. Zuboff stated that information technology impacts beyond mere automation; she proposed that the technology had the power to *informate* processes (Zuboff, 1988). Scott Morton took Zuboff's idea further, saying that information technology has the power to *transform* process and organization entirely (Scott Morton, 1991).

Automated Correspondence Course Strategy

The second goal, reaching new students, manifests itself in business terms as seeking new markets (newly available student groups) and/or gaining existing market share (students who would otherwise attend another school) (Albrecht and Bardsley, 1994). Schools that pursue this goal use the Automated Correspondence Course strategy. With this strategy, institutions seek to expand availability and provide flexibility to previously unserved or underserved groups (Johnstone and Jones, 1997; Keller, 1997; Vines, Thorpe, and Threlkeld, 1997). Examples of the Automated Correspondence Course strategy include reaching students physically remote from on-campus programs (Schmidt, 1999), serving students constrained not only by place but also by time (Blumenstyk, 1998a) and providing students with greater choice in programs, perhaps appealing to them with niche programs (Lively and Blumenstyk, 1999; Mangan, 1999). The case study research confirmed efforts at outreach. An antecedent for this goal is the traditional correspondence course offered to students who could not come to a central campus. DLT provides the opportunity for schools to deliver classes to remote sites and at different times from the campus schedule (Godbey, 1993).

Large Lecture Hall Strategy
The third goal, making programs more efficient, mirrors productivity concerns in business. Schools seek to reduce costs or increase revenues—they act to leverage instructional resources. With this goal, institutions follow the Large Lecture Hall strategy. The Large Lecture Hall strategy reveals itself in concerns to deliver instruction more productively *at less cost* (Gubernick and Ebeling, 1997; Schmidt, 1999) or to more students for greater revenue (Biemiller and Young, 1997; Green, 1997). An antecedent for this goal is the movement to house lower-level or survey classes in large lecture halls so fewer instructors can teach more students. DLT provides schools with the means to leverage instruction—increasing the number of students who take any one instructor's class (Ohler, 1991). However, DLT also incurs its own unique costs such as equipment and new staffing which a school must consider when using DLT (Threlkeld and Brzoska, 1994).

Links to Porter's Strategies
Evidence from the case study research also links the three strategies for using DLT to Michael Porter's three competitive strategies - the introduction of new products and services, the enhancement of existing products and services, and the altering of industry structure (Porter, 1980; Stair and Reynolds, 1998). First, the Automated Correspondence Course strategy resembles Porter's new products and services strategy. Here the strategy affects the scope of instruction: the breadth of what the school offers students.

When DLT provides the means for one school's MBA program to import a Health Care Concentration from a second school, that illustrates Porter's new products and services strategy. In fact, schools using this strategy can be both providers as well as receivers. For instance, the same institution that imports a special MBA concentration can in turn provide special instruction to area high schools via DLT. Finally, schools can both send and receive instruction in the same program, whether it is just a simple exchange of two accounting courses one semester or a collaboration of two schools' unique strengths to plan a joint graduate nursing program.

Second, the Guest Lecturer strategy mirrors Porter's strategy of improving existing products. When schools use DLT to change the process of instruction or how they go about the actual instruction, they are enhancing an existing product or service. Moving from traditional lecture to automation to transformation under the Zuboff and Scott Morton framework illustrates the enhancement of the product. When a school uses DLT to link its students to resources outside the boundary of the classroom, or when it uses DLT to connect students and instructors in content-rich exchanges outside the classroom setting, it follows the Porter strategy of improving an existing product. Some schools eschew all other applications of DLT and consciously focus only on using technology to improve the product they now have.

Third, the Large Lecture Hall strategy corresponds to Porter's strategy of altering industry structure. When schools use DLT to change scale (how many students receive instruction), they often follow the Porter strategy of altering industry structure. When schools seek to leverage on-campus instruction by sending it to one or more remote sites, they follow this strategy. Using remote sites to gain a cost advantage conforms to altering the industry structure. The case study research found multiple instances where a school takes existing classes and sends them to other classrooms. For example, one school uses compressed video to send its instruction not just to other area schools but also to businesses, and extensive networks promote this change in where learning takes place. Even more dramatic are Internet-based courses to provide instruction anytime, anywhere. With these methods, the boundaries of space and time and the constraints of the old classroom disappear.

The three option framework provides a means for exploring the strategic use of DLT and its implications for higher education. It is supported by the literature and confirmed by case study. The next section considers strategic issues in detail.

MAIN THRUST OF THE CHAPTER

Technological innovation of any sort affects its environment. Distance learning technology (DLT) does not differ in its potential to affect higher education. This section looks at issues surrounding the use of distance learning technology. Some of these issues are general and some pertain to only one or two of the three defined strategies. Broadly, these issues fall into the categories of personnel, funding, markets, competition, fraud and alliances. An overarching concern is the relationship between the school's mission and available technology. Each issue is examined in turn, beginning with personnel.

Personnel

The personnel category breaks down into four issues: faculty skills required, new personnel needed, "faculty recompense," and resistance to technology. First, using DLT in any strategy requires certain training for effective use. When considering teaching skills in both the routine and the creative use of technology, schools must address two challenges: they must adequately train current faculty to use DLT effectively and they must weigh what technology-based skills they look for in future faculty. The Guest Lecturer strategy stresses the creative use of DLT to enhance the student's experience, such as with the current spotlight on multimedia. On the other hand, both the Automated Correspondence Course and the Large Lecture Hall strategies demand skill in translating "old-style" teaching into a wider, perhaps non-interactive realm. Examples of this need found in the case study research include learning to instruct through compressed video. The need exists for Web-based courses as well. Schools must commit funding to train, support, and perhaps recruit faculty to use DLT in a manner compatible with their goals.

Second, higher education institutions must adapt personnel beyond just the faculty. These include support personnel: technicians to maintain equipment (Parisot and Waring, 1994), proctors to manage remote sites and classes (Moses, Edgerton, Shaw, and Grubb, 1991; Jordahl, 1995; Parisot and Waring, 1994) and staff to train faculty and prepare materials (Rayburn, 1997). Interview comments during the case study research suggested that new personnel may also include a management team to establish and promote DLT use. Again, schools must commit funding for staff. Technology, be it mainframe computers in the 1970s, microcomputer labs in the 1980s, or DLT in the 1990s, requires enough trained personnel to make the investment worthwhile. As one school officer in the case study research pointed out, institutions have often embraced innovation and bought into technology yet failed to support equipment with needed staff. Concerns about support personnel focus on the Automated Correspondence Course strategy because of its reliance on DLT such as compressed video. However, staff support also impacts the Large Lecture Hall strategy and to a lesser extent the Guest Lecturer strategy.

A great unresolved issue about personnel called "faculty recompense" begins with the question, "What does an instructor get in return for teaching in a DLT environment?". This issue transcends just monetary compensation; it includes a variety of concerns such as tenure, release time and course load. Together, these concerns come under the umbrella term "faculty recompense." First of course comes money: schools vary in how much if any premium instructors get paid for teaching via DLT. Some would hold that teaching with DLT is but one of many forms of teaching and nothing to merit higher pay, while others advocate extra compensation due either to the larger volume of students or to special teaching demands beyond that of the traditional classroom. Inconsistency about release time and course load mirror that of money. They all vary from one school to another, and the philosophy behind school policy varies as well. For instance, one view holds that teaching twenty students on campus and another twenty off campus at a remote site via compressed video equates to two courses not one. As such, that course with DLT counts as two in figuring course loads. As for release time, some schools acknowledge the need to adapt instruction to the DLT classroom and set aside schedule time at least for those new to teaching via DLT. Finally, some raise the idea of separate tenure tracks from the traditional one. There might be a special tenure track for teaching in a technology-rich environment, focusing efforts on the development of new tools and techniques. While an important issue in using any of the three DLT strategies, faculty recompense applies especially to the Automated Correspondence Course strategy when an instructor may be teaching in a mixture of the traditional classroom and the DLT realm. DLT instruction calls into question old views of course load, pay scales and job expectations.

Finally, higher education in the late 1990s has seen an increase in faculty resistance to technology. Any prior technology mixed into instruction has caused resistance, and DLT is no different. The rise of microcomputing in the 1980s saw resistance as well. Opposition to using DLT in the late 1990s has three levels. First, some faculty express discomfort with using DLT itself (Young, 1997). The history of DLT such as compressed video, with frequent downtime and faulty equipment, has bolstered such resistance. This type of resistance is possible with any of the three DLT strategies used. Second, some contend that a vital part of the educational experience is lost or distorted using DLT (Biemiller, 1998; Blumenstyk, 1998a; Neal, 1998). They worry that the interaction between instructor and student, which they consider part of the learning experience, diminishes or vanishes. This type of concern would occur when a school uses the Automated Correspondence Course strategy or the Large Lecture Hall strategy. With the Automated Correspondence Course, some would worry about the sacrifice made in instruction to reach new markets. Third, and even more profound, some see DLT instruction as a threat to them specifically and also to their accustomed way of academic life (Monaghan, 1998; Selingo, 1999; Young, 1998). An increasing use of the Large Lecture Hall strategy, minimizing costs and maximizing revenues, provokes these fears. While institutions and governing boards do not directly speak of such, some faculty have perceived that technology could and perhaps would indeed threaten not just individual faculty but also institutions themselves (Ives and Jarvenpaa, 1996). In a nutshell, they fear replacement by software.

Current policies regarding personnel, especially faculty recompense, appear ad-hoc at best. Schools must clearly assess the demands of teaching through DLT compared to traditional teaching and resolve questions on pay, tenure and course load. If schools enter into DLT-enabled courses and programs full-scale, they must reconcile these new labor concerns. Also, schools must recognize, define, and adequately staff new personnel categories such as remote-site facilitators, technicians and producers and course development specialists. Merely acquiring DLT without matching it with labor resources creates new problems. A final challenge is to integrate new or modified personnel types into the overall organization.

Funding

Funding concerns the commitment and allocation of financial resources. As with other information and communication technology, DLT is not cheap. Further, as with computers, the equipment becomes dated quickly. Success in using DLT comes with commitment. One academic officer interviewed in the case study research described a philosophical change of view: more and more, schools should view information technology as an *operating expense*, not a capital expense. Apart from specific accounting rules, this idea points schools toward an ongoing duty to maintain and replace hardware as needed. Threlkeld and Brzoska (1994) support the idea that DLT has higher fixed costs versus lower variable costs in comparison to traditional instruction.

Markets

Market issues involve changes in the quantity, location and nature of students. In particular, the Automated Correspondence Course strategy affects enrollments. DLT usage to reach new students means that those students will be greater in number, remote from campus (Schmidt, 1999), nontraditional (Green, 1997) or some blend of those traits. To reach those students, schools have to adapt not just to DLT but to student schedules, locations, and finances. Market issues have a less direct link to the Guest Lecturer and the Large Lecture Hall strategies; rather, competition is more important with them.

Competition

Technology changes competition: it resets boundaries, strengthens or weaknesses current rivals and opens the door to new parties. All three DLT strategies affect competition. The Guest Lecturer strategy impacts competition based on quality. As one officer at a large private school in the case study research pointed out, students who choose among that school and similar rivals look at how those schools use DLT to enhance the basic instruction. Those students regard creative or cutting-edge use of DLT as a plus when they compare schools. With the Automated Correspondence Course strategy, schools are trying to reach those students they could not before. Those new students could be either ones no school could reach before due to constraints such as time or distance, or ones who would have taken courses from some other school. In either case, the school would be building market share in business terms. Using the Large Lecture Hall strategy, a school or other entity alters the long-standing structure on which competition is based.

Institutions face varying degrees of competition, and DLT affects that degree of competition. Schools compete for the same students based on certain criteria such as intellect, geography, career interests and finances. Even if unacknowledged, each institution has an understood set of competitors. However, DLT has the potential to alter "groupings" of competition. The removal of geography as a competitive criteria is the most obvious example.

Literature frequently cites how DLT can change competition. New levels of competition may come from three sources. First, the competition with existing competitors may intensify (Dede, 1991). DLT can make one institution's programs more attractive due to factors such as program enhancement, time flexibility or location expansion. Second, other established institutions may enter markets previously unavailable to them (Albrecht and

Bardsley, 1994; Godbey, 1993). The MBA degree market is a leading example, with "brand-name" schools offering courses and programs on-line (Mangan, 1999). Schools can now enter attractive new markets that they could not reach before (Jacobson, 1994a; Deloughry, 1996). State public schools may fight over and redefine "territories" within their states based on using DLT. Across state borders, the competition is less regulated and more intense. For example, in part using DLT, one school can locate a satellite program just across the state line from another school and tap into an attractive market (Gold, 1998). Third, new entrants such as for-profit programs can come into the market. One leading example as of this writing is the University of Phoenix (Fischetti, Anderson, Watrous, Tanz, and Gynne, 1998).

Fraud

Related to the changing competitive environment is academic fraud. Fraud relates in particular to the Automated Correspondence Course strategy, and it of course is not new. Getting a degree through the mail a generation ago would raise suspicion, getting it on-line from certain sources does the same today. DLT can facilitate a scam degree operation and also obscure it (Guernsey, 1997; Lord, 1998). With a rush into on-line programs by established institutions, the large volume of choices can mask a bogus operation in the eyes of the public (Lord, 1998).

Alliances

Finally, DLT promotes alliances. These alliances take many forms, the most transforming of which is the virtual university (Johnstone and Jones 1997). An option when schools pursue the Large Lecture Hall strategy is to enter an alliance with other schools. Alliances provide the means to bring courses and programs to students without having to add teaching resources. For example, two schools can enter an alliance using DLT that draws on both their resources to jointly offer a program, as were the plans of one school in the case study to join with a second school in starting a graduate nursing degree. Otherwise, the schools in the alliance would duplicate instructional resources.

FUTURE TRENDS

Two trends that apply to all three strategies are (1) distance learning technology (DLT) will continue to both evolve and then standardize and (2) DLT will continue to require a learning curve. Technology of all sorts goes through periods of growth and a certain degree of chaos, but over time certain standards form. Both personal computers, moving from over thirty different systems to now only two (IBM-compatible and Apple Macintosh) and VCRs, moving to the VHS format and away from the Beta format, provide recent examples. DLT will likely follow the same path, perhaps later rather than sooner. Regardless of what DLT equipment wins out, schools and staff will continue to endure a learning curve in using DLT.

Changes in tenure may occur, prompted by the DLT teaching environment. Though some have championed change over the years, tenure has remained mostly unaltered. However, technology serves as a catalyst of change and one might be in tenure. Diverse tenure tracks could address special situations such as teaching (and developing curriculum) in a DLT environment. Certainly if a school moves to the Automated Correspondence Course or Large Lecture Hall strategy, the school might use a special tenure track to push (rapid) development of "marketable products."

The market will continue to change. In particular with the Automated Correspondence Course strategy, schools will be looking to increase enrollment. The enlarged needs of the marketplace, for example, may come from geographically remote students (Gransden, 1994; Watkins, 1994) or from new demand for higher degree programs (Baldwin, 1991). It is interesting but perhaps logical that greater availability of courses and programs might itself stimulate bigger market for higher degrees.

The most radical change in the higher education landscape may come from use of the Large Lecture Hall strategy. One outgrowth of trying to reduce instruction cost or to spread that cost over more students might be outsourcing. Colleges and universities, while lagging behind industries such as manufacturing, have increasingly used outsourcing to hand over operations such as food services (King, 1997a; King 1997b), information systems and services (Wallace, 1997), bookstores (Freeman, 1997) security, and custodial services (Nicklin, 1997). A typical reason given is that cost pressures force administrators to look elsewhere, and that outsourcing allows the institution to focus on its core function: instruction. What if, as part of a Large Lecture Hall strategy, a school defined its core function more precisely? For instance, a state engineering school might define its mission strictly in terms of schooling engineers. If that was the case, school leaders might decide to focus resources on the engineering curriculum. To do that, they might consider outsourcing the history department, getting those courses from some other school via DLT. Schools might focus on what they do best and outsource the rest, becoming both the provider and receiver of instruction through DLT. If such a scenario came true, it would lead to greater specialization among institutions.

Three research opportunities in the strategic use of DLT are (1) the strategies themselves, (2) the confusion over faculty recompense, and (3) the transformation of the process of instruction. First, each strategy bears watching, and interesting future case research would compare the success of schools that chose the same strategy. Second, the case research revealed policy on faculty recompense all over the board. It even varied from one college to another at the same school. Will a standard policy emerge? Finally, technology affects process in other organizations, and higher education institutions will be no different. Future research could explore the change in process in terms of the Zuboff and Scott Morton framework.

CONCLUSION

The central issues regarding DLT revolve not around the technology itself, but how it is used (or not used). Those schools that employ DLT must make effective choices in how they use it and address how the organization relates to it. Perhaps the best gauge of how schools may use DLT comes from what they do now. Do they focus on quality or creative instruction? Maybe they will follow the Guest Lecturer strategy. Do they have a history of outreach? They may pursue the Automated Correspondence Course strategy. Do they serve large numbers of students? Then they may consider the Large Lecture Hall strategy.

Schools may pursue any of the three strategies or some combination of them. What matters most is not the technology but the plan for using it. DLT use must conform to the larger mission of the school, and the school must also be aware of how others are using the same technology. To do less in either case is to put a school at a distinct competitive disadvantage.

REFERENCES

Albrecht, R. & Bardsley, G. (1994). Strategic planning and academic planning for distance education. Willis, Barry (Ed.), *Distance Education Strategy and Tools* (pp.67-86). Englewood Cliffs, NJ: Educational Technology Publications, Inc.

Baldwin, L. V. (1991, March). Higher-education partnerships in engineering and science. V. M. Horner & L. G. Roberts (Eds.), *Annals of the American*

Academy of Political and Social Science: Electronic Links For Learning (514) (pp. 76-91). Newbury Park, CA: Sage Publications.

Basinger, J. (1999, January 22). Former Michigan president seeks to turn higher education into a 'knowledge industry.' *The Chronicle of Higher Education*, A30.

Berge, Z. L., Collins, M. P., & Day, M. (1995). Introduction. In Zane L. Berge & Mauri P. Collins (Eds.), *Volume one: Computer-mediated communication and the online classroom: Overview and perspectives*). Cresskill, NJ: Hampton Press, 1-10.

Biemiller, L. (1998, October 9). U. of Utah president issues a pointed warning about virtual universities. *The Chronicle of Higher Education*, A32.

Biemiller, L. & Young, J. R. (1997, November 7). EDUCOM notebook: Merger plans, high-tech colleges, and the death of the book. *The Chronicle of Higher Education*, A29.

Blumenstyk, G. (1998a, February 6). Western Governors U. takes shape as a new model for higher education. *The Chronicle of Higher Education*, A21.

Blumenstyk, G. (1998b, July 17). Museums collaborate to put images of thousands of their art treasures on line. *The Chronicle of Higher Education*, A29.

Carey, J. (1991, March). Plato at the keyboard: telecommunications technology and education policy. *Annals of the American Academy of Political and Social Science: Electronic Links For Learning (514)*, Vivian M. Horner & Linda G. Roberts (eds.), Sage Publications, Newbury Park, CA, 11-21.

Dede, C. J. (1991, March). Emerging technologies: Impacts on distance learning. *Annals of the American Academy of Political and Social Science: Electronic Links For Learning (514)*. V. M. Horner & L. G. Roberts (eds.), Sage Publications, Newbury Park, CA. 146-158.

Deloughry, T. J. (1996, September 20). New school for social research bolsters flagging enrollment with 90 on-line courses. *The Chronicle of Higher Education*, A27-A28.

Fischetti, M., Anderson, J., Watrous, M., Tanz, J., & Gynne, P. (1998). The march of Phoenix," *University Business*, 46-51.

Freeman, L. (1997, January). Bookstore contract boosts revenues. *School Planning and Management*, 20F(3).

Glassman, B. (1997, July/August). Oh pioneer! *On the Horizon*, 15-16.

Godbey, G. (1993, Spring). Beyond TQM: Competition and cooperation create the agile institution. *Educational Record (74:2)*, 37-42.

Gold, E. L. (1998, November 18). MSU center won't be on HCC campus. *Kentucky New Era*, pp. 1-2.

Gransden, G. (1994, July 13). Bringing education to the remote expanses of Siberia. *The Chronicle of Higher Education*, A36.

Green, K. C. (1997, November/December). Money, technology, and distance education. *On The Horizon*. 1-7.

Gubernick, L. & Ebeling, A. (1997, June 16). I got my degree through e-mail," *Forbes*, 84.

Guernsey, L. (1997, December 19). Is the Internet becoming a bonanza for diploma mills? *The Chronicle of Higher Education*, 22.

Guernsey, L. (1998, May 8). Historians form new organization on technology in teaching and research. *The Chronicle of Higher Education*, A30.

Hawkins, J. (1991, March). Technology-mediated communities for learning: Designs and consequences. In Vivian M. Horner & Linda G. Roberts (Eds.), *Annals of the American Academy of Political and Social Science: Electronic Links For Learning (514), 159-74*). Newbury Park, CA: Sage Publications.

Ives, B. & Jarvenpaa, S. L. (1996 Spring). Will the Internet revolutionize business education and research? *Sloan Management Review*, 33-41.

Jacobson, R. L. (1994a, July 6). Extending the reach of 'virtual' classrooms. *The Chronicle of Higher Education*, A19-A23.

Jacobson, R. L. (1994b, July 6). 2-Way video praised by many educators; others question its benefits and costs. *The Chronicle of Higher Education*, A20.

Johnstone, S. M. & Jones, D. (1997, November/December). New higher education trends reflected in the design of Western Governors University. *On the Horizon*, 8-11.

Jordahl, G. (1995, January). Bringing schools closer with 'distance' learning. *Technology & Learning (15:4)*, 16-19.

Keller, G. (1997, May/June). Beyond bytes and bandwidth. *On the Horizon*, 14-15.

Kiernan, V. (1998, December 4). Escaping the chilly ballroom: Researchers to attend a biomedical conference on line. *The Chronicle of Higher Education*, A22.

King, P. (1997a, July 7, 1997). Contractors give 'the old college try' in battle for university food dollars. *Nation's Restaurant News*, 57(4).

King, P. (1997b, August 25). NACUFS [National Association of College and University Food Services] needs to settle contractor debate. *Nation's Restaurant News*, 34(1).

Lambert, R. D. (1991, March). Distance education and foreign languages. *Annals of the American Academy of Political and Social Science: Elec-*

tronic Links For Learning (514), Vivian M. Horner & Linda G. Roberts (eds.), Sage Publications, Newbury Park, CA, 35-48.

Lively, K. & Blumenstyk, G. (1999, January 29). Sylvan Learning Systems to start a network of for-profit universities overseas. *The Chronicle of Higher Education*, A43.

Lord, M. (1998, September 28). Sheepskin fleecers. *U.S. News & World Report*, 72-73.

Mangan, K. S. (1999, January 15). Top business schools seek to ride a bull market in on-line M.B.A.'s. *The Chronicle of Higher Education*, A27.

Monaghan, P. (1998, June 19). U. of Washington professors decry governor's visions for technology. *The Chronicle of Higher Education*, A23.

Morrison, J. L. (1997, March/April). Academic cybermalls. *On the Horizon*, 2-3.

Moses, K. D., Edgerton, D., Shaw, W. E., & Grubb, R. (1991, March). International case studies of distance learning. *Annals of the American Academy of Political and Social Science: Electronic Links For Learning (514)*, V. M. Horner & L. G. Roberts (eds.), Sage Publications, Newbury Park, CA, 58-75.

Neal, E. (1998, June 19). Using technology in teaching: We need to exercise healthy skepticism. *The Chronicle of Higher Education*, B4.

Nicklin, J. L. (1997, November 21). Universities seek to cut costs by 'outsourcing' more operations. *The Chronicle of Higher Education*, A35(2).

Ohler, J. (1991, March). Why distance education? *Annals of the American Academy of Political and Social Science: Electronic Links For Learning (514)*, Vivian M. Horner & Linda G. Roberts (eds.), Sage Publication, Newbury Park, CA, 22-34.

Parisot, A. & Waring, S. (1994, March / April). At a distance. *Adult Learning (5:4)*, 10-11.

Porter, M. E. (1980). *Competitive Strategy*, Free Press.

Rayburn, W. (1997). Not what but how: The role of institutional and environmental factors in the use of distance learning technology for higher education. Southern Illinois University.

Robbin, L. K. (1996, November 11). Modern technology: A quantum leap forward on today's Christian college campuses. *Christianity Today*, 60.

Schmidt, P. (1999, January 29). Concept of university centers has appeal in several states. *The Chronicle of Higher Education*, A41.

Scott-Morton, M. S. (1991). Introduction. *The Corporation of the 1990s*, Michael S. Scott Morton (ed.), Oxford University Press, 3-23.

Selingo, J. (1999, February 5), Plan to reshape California State U. disturbs many faculty members. *The Chronicle of Higher Education*, A32.

Stair, R. M. & Reynolds, G. W. (1998). *Principles of Information Systems: A Managerial Approach*, Course Technology.

Threlkeld, R. & Brzoska, K. (1994). Research in distance education. *Distance Education Strategy and Tools*, Barry Willis (ed.), Educational Technology Publications, Inc., Englewood Cliffs, NJ, 41-66.

Vines, D., Thorpe, B., & Threlkeld, R. (1997, November/December). California higher education extends its reach. *On the Horizon*, 11-14.

Wallace, B. (1997, June 30). More firms outsource remote support; IS hopes to cut big access bills. *Computerworld*, 49.

Watkins, B. T. (1994, August 10). Uniting North Dakota. *The Chronicle of Higher Education*, A17-A19.

Young, J. (1997, October 3). Canadian university promises it won't require professors to use technology, *The Chronicle of Higher Education*, A28.

Young, J. R. (1998, May 8). Skeptical academics see perils in information technology. *The Chronicle of Higher Education*, A29.

Zuboff, S. (1988). *In the Age of the Smart Machine*, Basic Books.

Chapter 4

Developing a Learning Environment: Applying Technology and TQM to Distance Learning

C. Mitchell Adrian
Longwood College

INTRODUCTION

It is known that good classroom management techniques help promote a suitable learning environment, an environment in which students are interested and participate as a community of learners (Brophy & Alleman, 1998). In this type of environment, learning occurs when faculty develop and encourage discussion through the use of social interaction (Brophy & Alleman, 1998). The problem in applying these concepts to a distance education program is "how to develop or maintain an environment of social interaction?"

To contribute to the learning environment in a distance education program, a combination of new and readily available electronic communication technologies can be combined with concepts taken from Total Quality Management (TQM). The term "distance education" covers a wide range of educational practices, ranging from the traditional correspondence course to synchronous teleconferencing via multiple classrooms. The techniques discussed here are designed primarily for a distance environment that allows for some degree of student-faculty interaction.

Regardless of the learning methods used, a distance education program is dependent upon student commitment and the TQM approach gives students a high degree of ownership of the learning process. Likewise, electronic communication technology allows faculty to assess student progress and provide feedback in a timely fashion – regardless of the geographic distance between the student and the faculty member.

Changes in Academia

Academia in America has felt profound change while progressing from the 20th to the 21st centuries. Society no longer accepts the "ivory tower" premise and is beginning to value teaching efforts as much as research. In summary, social pressures are demanding university accountability for student learning (Hill, 1997). These pressures reach state-funded campuses in the form of financial incentives (or disincentives) from state legislators, who seek quantifiable results of educational contributions to society. Reacting to these pressures, institutions of higher education have pushed faculty to focus efforts on enhancing the student's learning process (Hill, 1997).

The Growth of Distance Education

As an outgrowth of the increased focus on quantifiable contributions to society, higher education has attempted to "reach out" to an increasingly larger population of potential students. Many schools are attempting to reach these students through what is hoped to be a cost-effective method of distance education (Noon, 1996). As a result, a 1999 study indicated that 58% of two-year and 62% of four-year public colleges offer courses through the Internet (Hodgson, 1999).

The concept of distance education and distance learning has gone through many changes over the past few decades inspired mostly by advancements in technology. Once relegated to the level of a "correspondence course," electronic communications technology now allows a distance learning course to function much more like a traditional course, including "real-time" lectures and discussions.

The downside to advances in electronic technology is that developments have progressed faster than faculty can learn to apply the new technologies. This growth of electronic and communications technology has forced many faculty to question how to apply this technology to student education (Black, 1997). Faculty are now expected to be masters of technology and delivery management as well as experts in their subject (Laird, 1999). In order to make distance education an effective learning tool, the role of the teacher will be essential in using technology to its best advantage (Bayram, 1999). Therefore, to develop an effective learning environment in distance education we must first understand a few basic concepts of learning theory.

Learning Theory

Efforts focused on understanding how we learn have lead to a broad range of learning theories. If we focus on learning in higher education and theories regarding adult learners then a few basic foundations for learning can be found. Primarily, adults learn best through high levels of immersion (or hands-on practice) and teacher-student dialog. For instance, in the "holistic" learning theory it is believed that all facets of a student's life are part of their total learning (immersion). The role of the faculty member is to assist students at interpreting and comprehending various inputs from the world around them (Argyris, 1997). In addition, collaborative activities by students help participants learn from each other, suggesting that active participation is more important than passive listening (Pike & Mansfield, 1996). In a concept called productive constructivism, the teacher's job is to fuse students' knowledge with what experts know, typically accomplished through teacher-student dialogue (Zahorik, 1997). Discussion allows students to refute traditional concepts while at the same time incorporating new ideas.

What these theories have in common is that learning centers on student immersion and faculty-student dialog. While we may take the existence of dialog for granted in a traditional classroom environment, specific efforts must be made to effectively utilize faculty-student dialog in the application of a distance learning course. In addition, distance learning on the Web has the potential to offer a greater level of student immersion than traditional courses (Mirabito, 1996).

APPLICATIONS OF DISTANCE LEARNING AND ELECTRONIC TECHNOLOGY: A THREE STEP APPROACH

The first question that most faculty face when considering a distance learning program and the use of new technologies for their educational efforts is "how to do it." Some faculty fear potential problems of having to learn to apply new electronic technologies, while others embrace the idea and make great efforts to incorporate electronic technologies to the classroom environment. In either instance, however, we must constantly remind ourselves that distance does not necessitate reduced communication and that new technologies are tools rather than ends in themselves. Educators, like professionals in many other fields, become swept up by the "bells and whistles" that are offered with various technological packages and often lose sight of their original objectives.

What are arguably the most important educational criteria for all faculty to remember are that of *organization* and *clarity*. Whether a traditional course or a distance learning course, organization and clarity may be the two most important factors in student understanding and comprehension of the tasks and materials. This is compounded in courses that are heavily dependent on electronic communications (as are most distance learning courses). If organization and clarity are not present, the electronic communication tools tend to make these deficiencies even more prominent. For that reason, a three-step course development and implementation process has been established.

Step 1: Design Course Objectives

Just as with traditional courses, a faculty member's first step is to determine the primary course objectives. This is an even greater priority in a distance learning course and courses using electronic and communications technology. Not only should the contextual learning objectives be defined, but also the more general and overriding objectives regarding course design. For instance, it is assumed here that the primary objective will always be student learning and that faculty will want to create a sense of "enjoyment" regarding learning to encourage students to become lifelong learners.

The course design must contribute to the development of a learning environment, even in a distance learning program. Again, one essential ingredient for developing this learning environment is teacher-student dialogue (Pike & Mansfield, 1996; Zahorik, 1997).

Step 2: Design the Course Structure

Even more than a traditional class, success in a distance learning environment is more dependent upon a beneficial melding of synchronous and asynchronous teaching. Typically we think of most traditional courses as focusing on synchronous techniques and most distance courses as focusing on asynchronous techniques. However, electronic technologies allow us to deviate from this traditional model. Each technique has advantages and disadvantages, but building a strong distance learning program may depend upon the degree of synchronous learning that can be effectively incorporated into the program.

In order to design a distance learning course that provides an adequate mix of synchronous and asynchronous learning, philosophies from Total Quality Management can be mated to electronic technology to work in tandem. Following a quality initiative may be an effective way to motivate students to learn (Chen & Rogers, 1995; Bonser, 1992; Del Valle, 1994; Hequet, 1995; Harvard Business Review, 1991; Peak,1995) and may thus be a logical foundation for a distance learning environment.

Transferring the Quality Philosophy to the Distance Classroom

To establish a foundation for applying concepts of quality management to education, insights from leading writers in the field can be combined into the key elements of quality (Brocka & Brocka, 1992). Most notable of these elements are: (1) knowing and satisfying the customer, (2) empowering employees, and (3) having managers function as leaders. (Beaver, 1994; Brocka & Brocka, 1992).

Several of the basic tenets from TQM can be applied to the classroom to establish a system of Total Quality Education (TQE) and, thus, enhance the learning environment. However, one dilemma is that not all of the principles of TQM seem applicable to the classroom setting (Arnold, 1994). For that reason, a specific set of assumptions and procedures should be developed for educational purposes.

ASSUMPTIONS

Students should be viewed as the employee/product.

While some may argue that students are the customer (e.g., Beaver, 1994; Froiland, 1993; Knappenberger, 1995), it is more appropriate to consider other instructors as internal customers and businesses that hire new graduates as external customers (Arnold, 1994). Thus, the student is viewed as both product and employee. To improve the product (the student), we must examine and adjust the learning process. Inputs are the body of knowledge pertinent to the course. The instructor serves as the manager, students serve as employees (or processors), and the resulting knowledge and skills possessed by students is the output (Arnold, 1994).

Colleges and Universities are Suppliers

Internally, students completing a basic course are supplied to later courses which base their content on previously learned information. Externally, colleges are suppliers to employers. The products offered are graduates who possess the knowledge and skills required by industry (Arnold, 1994).

The Majority of Students are Capable of
Performing at a Quality Level

If students do not perform at acceptable quality levels, instructors must analyze the entire learning process to determine what barriers are hindering performance. Deming (1986) states that most assignable variation is caused by problems in the process. Thus, it is dangerous for faculty to begin with the assumption that students do not perform at acceptable quality levels because they are defective inputs (Arnold, 1994). This assumption erroneously focuses attention on a defective input and away from problems in the learning system which may be preventing quality performance.

Instruction Does Not Necessarily Equal Learning

As managers, instructors must create an environment that allows employees (students), to produce a quality product (themselves). The more traditional thought in higher education is that it is the instructor's job to "profess" and the students' job to learn (Arnold, 1994). However, this allows the manager to avoid all responsibility for unacceptable quality. We must create a classroom situation that facilitates the learning process. Students, as employees who build the product, are responsible for their learning with faculty serving as the mangers who are responsible for providing students the tools they need to accomplish the task of learning. (Arnold, 1994).

Applying a Quality Philosophy

When applying quality concepts in the classroom, the initial difficulty is in translating concepts designed for the production process to an educational environment. In the original experiments attempted by Arnold (1994) and later by the author, it was found that a specific set of guidelines can be used for implementing Total Quality Education.

Quality Output is Required

To achieve quality performance, the employee (students) must understand how quality is defined and determined within their environment. The manager/instructor must emphasize the expectation of high performance. The instructor must also emphasize how he/she will provide the tools necessary for students to achieve this level of performance (Arnold, 1994).

Emphasize the Entire Learning Process

The learning process, the sum of all educational experiences, results in some level of quality. Consequently, improving quality depends on adding,

Table 1: Parameters for Course Design

a.	Limit lecture.
b.	Apply a variety of learning experiences.
c.	Use written learning experiences.
d.	Use oral learning experiences.
e.	At least one performance must be a team activity.
f.	Participation is part of the quality imperative.
g.	Tests are mandatory; use subjective tests when possible.

modifying, improving, or replacing segments of the learning processes (Arnold, 1994). To better design the learning process in distance education, a non-inclusive set of parameters for course design has been established (Table 1). It must be remembered that the learning process includes the student's "out of class" study activities. To better facilitate learning, a non-inclusive list of suggested learning experience ideas are provided in Table 2.

Customer Satisfaction

Customer satisfaction is the most relevant measure of the quality of our product. Employers and future instructors receiving our students are viewed as the relevant customers. A survey of employers provides the best indication of external market satisfaction with product quality (graduates). In lieu of a survey, general market indexes can be used by examining the knowledge, skills and abilities reported as desirable by most firms.

Empowerment

Empowerment involves delegating power or authority to employees. Since students are viewed as employees in the classroom situation, the students must be empowered (Arnold, 1994). A key method of empowering students is to give them ownership of as many tasks as possible. While it is the instructor's role to determine primary goals and objectives of the course, students should be empowered to develop intermediate goals and the processes by which they will achieve those goals. Note that empowerment does not imply a democracy or complete freedom. Instead, empowerment must occur within specific parameters established by management (Arnold, 1994). Empowerment may be the key to applying TQE in distance learning. Geographic separation forces students in distant locals to take increased responsibility for their learning. By formalizing the process and empowering these students their motivation level is increased.

Table 2: Distance Learning Experience Alternatives

Lecture by Instructor (limited)	Group discussions
Presentation of Chapter Material	Studying for Written Exams
Writing an Original Case	Case Analysis (individual or team)
Problem/Case Solutions	Video Tapes
Term Papers	Internet Exercises
Business Simulation	Chapter Summary
Computer Games	Viewing and Analyzing Existing Business
Role Playing	Term Paper
Preparing Test Questions	Library
Presentations	Analysis of Business
Written Assignments	

As stated, empowerment, or allowing employees the authority to develop production goals and procedures is a foundation of the quality initiative. Traditionally, academic expectation is defined as the level of achievement that students must reach in order to satisfy a standard established by the teacher. Unlike academic expectations, goal setting is a target to aim for rather than a standard that must be reached (Madden, 1997). Schunk (1984) states that goal setting for the learner involves the establishment of an objective to serve as the aim of one's actions. Punnett (1986) says that the perceived ability of the learner to achieve the goal is necessary for successful goal setting. Consequently, individual goals are more effective than one goal for all students. Motivation is the desire to achieve a goal that has value for the individual (Linskie, 1977). Motivation is a process that leads students into experiences in which they can learn, that keeps them focused on a specific task, and which helps fulfill their needs for immediate achievement and a sense of moving toward larger goals (Madden, 1997). As a result, students are interested in the things which they plan themselves. They work much harder on self-made goals than they ever would on the expectations of someone else.

Leadership
With the instructor in the role of manager, he/she is responsible for providing leadership. This is especially important in a distance learning environment. The instructor must design and articulate the quality approach while implementing and sustaining it throughout the semester (Arnold, 1994). The instructor must demonstrate a commitment to quality and continuous improvement in every aspect of the course (Arnold, 1994).

Cross Functional Management

This concept is normally implemented in business by eliminating barriers between various functional areas. In a distance learning program, this is interpreted to mean that students should be involved in some type of team assignments (Arnold, 1994). One very useful team is to group volunteer students together in Quality Control Circles (or QC groups) that will meet regularly to help each prepare assignments, review performance of group members, receive feedback from the instructor and provide feedback to the instructor.

The use of a modified QC group can be particularly useful in a distance learning program. QC members can meet either in person or electronically as required by their geographic dispersion. Their task is to learn from other class members what processes students feel are working correctly and what processes need improvement. By communicating these ideas to the faculty member and other QC members, they can develop plans for improvement. In this role, QC members function as a communication link between students and faculty and focus on developing ideas for improving the learning process.

Continuous Improvement

Continuous improvement applies to processes, products/services, and people. An important difference between a quality approach and a traditional teaching approach is the commitment to change as a means of achieving improvement. If a process is not working as envisioned or a better method arises, the instructor must be committed to making the necessary change immediately, not at the end of the semester (Arnold, 1994). To facilitate continuous improvement, work with QC member to discuss class processes and relay information from instructor to students (Arnold, 1994).

Continuous Information

Continuous improvement requires continuous information. This means frequent feedback. For the manager/instructor, frequent information can be provided by the Quality Team. For the students/workers, frequent information requires frequent feedback on their performances (Arnold, 1994). Defective work (inadequate learning) should be detected and corrected quickly. Therefore, tests should be given frequently and cover relatively small amounts of material (Arnold, 1994).

Drive Out Fear

Students' fears seem to be associated with low grades and test taking. In a distance learning program, there are additional fears associated with application of new technologies and a somewhat unorthodox learning environment (Bayram, 1999). Fear can be eliminated through several steps. The instructor should be able to tell students exactly what he/she wants them to know about the course material and what constitutes quality performance (Arnold, 1994). In addition, technology can be used to eliminate some fears normally felt by students.

Applying Electronic Technology

Given the objective of student learning through the use of a total learning environment, Quality Management concepts serve as a template for the application of electronic technologies and distance learning. Rather than having technology determine the direction and function of the class, technology serves as the tool to support the desired structure for student learning. In general, the electronic components assumed here are the Internet (including course material and on-line testing), e-mail, bulletin boards, chat, audio/video conferencing and in-class presentation material.

To develop the Internet portion of the course, a storyboard method should be used to map out the desired content and determine levels of access and linkage (Figure 1). In this example of a storyboard, this portion of the course provides continuous information to the students and revolves around the professor's homepage. A multilayered approach links class homepages and various other materials to the professor's homepage. From the class homepage, chapter notes, discussion areas and online testing can be reached.

In addition to the Internet components, communication is increased using e-mail and discussion groups. What must be remembered is that electronic communications have yet to fully replace the intricacies involved in face-to-face communication (Bayram, 1999; Jones, et. al. 1998) and were never intended as a replacement for classroom interaction. However, electronic communications are a beneficial supplement to face-to-face verbal communication. E-mail allows students and instructors to communicate one-on-one in a timely and efficient manner. In addition, a threaded discussion list should be designed into the Internet component of the course allowing ongoing discussions of topics, with the original idea and it's subsequent responses accessible to all viewers.

The use of e-mail and discussion groups allows instructors to remain in relative contact with students on a 24 hour a day, 7-day per week basis. It is

Figure 1

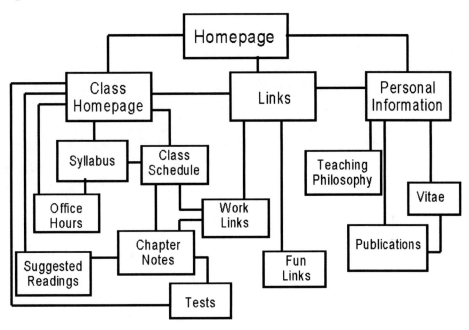

no longer necessary to wait until the next scheduled class period to share or discuss a new idea. It can be immediately broadcast to the class and read by students.

Step 3: Implementation and Follow-Up

It has been found that the use of electronic and communication technologies have been particularly supportive of a distance learning environment. In addition, electronic and communication technology are very supportive of the quality philosophies used for course design. For instance, students can expand their concepts of learning to include more activities outside of the classroom. The ability of students to easily communicate at their leisure greatly increases the level and intensity of spontaneous academic interaction and provides an emphasis on the entire learning process.

Student empowerment is supported by the increased availability of contextual resources. Increased resources and increased communication facilitate the decision-making process of an empowered student body. This results largely from the continuous information provided by numerous "online" tests and quizzes, each with instant feedback of student performance. Increased feedback allows for continuous improvement efforts. Students can discover the errors in their performance while the subject is still fresh in their minds. However, to make such efforts work, true leadership is required on the part of the instructor. Some specific ideas for linking technology and TQM can include:

Emphasize the Entire Learning Process

This is undoubtedly the most taxing and most enjoyable portion of implementing a quality distance learning environment. Internet-based activities (class web pages, etc.), management simulations, group activities, etc. can be used. The number and type of these activities is limited only by the imagination.

Empowerment

Empowering students has often proven to be a challenge. Deming (1986) states that workers know how to do their job and should be allowed to do it unhindered. Unfortunately, most students do not yet have enough experience in information delivery formats to know what will help them learn. For this reason, instructors should suggest new instructional methods such as group discussion, group chat, student presentation of chapter material via PowerPoint™ saved in HTML format, etc., and encourage students to experiment with these techniques. As students gain experience in various learning techniques they will be better equipped to design their own learning program.

Continuous Information

It is generally supported by most learning theories that testing has distinct advantages for learning. When using multiple choice type tests combined with commercial Internet-based testing software, grading and performance feedback can be done instantly. However, there are also problems associated with testing in a distance learning environment. One recommended use of today's technology is to develop substantial practice tests. Most online testing programs contain a feature in which the student must pass test X before being allowed access to test Y. In addition, most will create tests from a bank of questions established by the instructor. Thus, a student can take a practice test that must be passed before attempting the graded test. If the student fails the practice test, they can retake a test on the same material with a new list of questions. This utilizes technology to reduce test-taking fears while immersing students in the material until they have demonstrated the ability to perform at a quality level.

Maintaining Dialog

Ironically, what has developed as the single most significant result of the adoption of electronic and communication technologies to a TQM approach to distance learning is the improvement of dialog with students. The addition of student dialog through electronic communications serves as a primer for class discussions utilizing teleconferencing and group chat sessions. Based on previous electronic discussions, students often enter real-time discussions with a topic they wish to explore. The net result can be an undergraduate level class that performs at a near-graduate level, particularly in regards to topic discussions.

The Next Step: Continuous Improvement

Constructing knowledge is a constant, naturally occurring process as students view new information in terms of their prior knowledge (Zahorik, 1997). It is the responsibility of instructors to nurture this process. While it is not claimed that the instructional methods described above are the final answer, the guiding philosophy may be a step forward in creating a better process for management/business education, especially in a distance learning environment. Student responses to the processes mentioned have to be overwhelmingly good. While many students are apprehensive of a new process at first, they tend to quickly adapt.

SUMMARY - BENEFITS OF THIS APPROACH

To recap and summarize the process, the implementation of a distance learning program differs little from traditional courses in that there are three basic steps to course design. *Step1: Design Course Objectives. Step 2: Design Course Structure, and Step 3: Implement the Process and Follow-Up on Performance.* When applying the quality philosophy to distance learning, remember that 1) *Quality output is required,* 2) *The entire learning process should be emphasized,* 3) *Customer satisfaction must guide goal formation,* 4) *Students must be empowered to influence the learning process,* 5) *Faculty must serve in the leadership role,* and 6) *There must be efforts for continuous improvement through continuous information, feedback and teamwork.* To make technology work, faculty must A) *Design the course, then apply the technology,* B) *Use technology in its fullest regarding faculty/student and student/student dialog,* and C) *Be creative in finding ways for technology to help accomplish various learning experiences.*

The application of Quality Philosophies to the distance education process typically results in students' feeling a greater amount of freedom in regards to the learning process. Student development of the learning process and goals increases the level of students' perception of course organization and clarity.

The use of Internet and e-mail technology has opened new doors for communication links between faculty and students. The procedures outlined above have resulted in students becoming more involved in discussion of course material in both synchronous and asynchronous environments. As the level of discussion increases, students become interested not only in the topic but also in learning in general.

The technologies used in this process are readily available to most institutions of higher education. As stated earlier, the primary tools are the Internet and e-mail, and this technology is now quite common. The TQM techniques used are not new although their application in education is not yet widespread. Overall, the methods discussed here focus on the learning process and how applied Quality Philosophies combined with technology can assist learning. Once applied, students become interested and active learners while faculty gain more freedom to explore and discuss issues in their field of interest.

REFERENCES

Adrian, C. M., McWee, W., and Palmer, D. (1997a). Moving from total quality management to total quality education. *SAM International Management Proceedings*, (March), 283-289.

Adrian, C. M., McWee, W., and Palmer, D. (1997b). Total quality education: Expanding the educational experience. *American Society of Business and Behavioral Sciences*, (Feb.), 6-12.

Argyris, C. (1997). Initiating change that perseveres. *American Behavioral Scientist*, 40, 3, 299-310.

Arnold, D. R. (1994). *TQM in the Classroom*. Unpublished Manuscript.

Bayram, S. (1999). Internet learning initiatives: How well do Turkish virtual classrooms work? *T H E Journal (Technological Horizons In Education)*, 26, 10, (May), 65.

Bayram, S. and Uzuncarsill, U. (1998). Virtual classrooms on the web: Problems and solution in Turkey. presented at the *Conference of the European Educational Research Association, Scottish Council for Research in Education (SCRE) and European Conference on Educational Research*, (September 17-28), Ljubjana, Slovenia.

Beaver, W. (1994). Is TQM appropriate for the classroom? *College Teaching*, 42, 3, 111-114.

Black, J. (1997). Technical difficulties. *CNET News.com*, [Online] February 28, 5:30 p.m. PT, Available WWW: http://www.news.com/SpecialFeatures/0,5,8354,00.html.

Bonser, C. F. (1992). Total quality education? *Public Administration Review*, 52, 504-512.

Brocka, B. and Brocka, M. S. (1992). *Quality Management: Implementing the Best Ideas of the Masters*, Homewood, Ill; Richard D. Irwin Inc.

Brophy, J. and Alleman, J. (1998). Classroom management in a social studies learning community. *Social Education*, 62, 1, (Jan.), 56-58.

Chen, A. Y. S. and Rodgers, J. L. (1995). Teaching the teachers TQM. *Management Accounting*, (May), 42-46.

Del Valle, C. (1994). Total quality management: Now, it's a class act. *Business Week*, (October 31), 72.

Deming, E. W. (1986). *Out of Crisis*, Cambridge, Mass.: Center for Advanced Engineering study, MIT Press.

Duis, M. (1996). Using schema theory to teach American History. *Social Education*, 60, 3, 144-146.

Froiland, P. (1993). TQM invades business schools. *Training*, (July), 52-56.

Harvard Business Review. (1991). An open letter: TQM on the campus. (Nov.-Dec.), 94-95.

Hequet, M. (1995). Quality goes to school. *Training*, 32, (September), 47-52.

Hill, R. P. (1997). The future of business education's functional areas. *Marketing Educator*, 16, (Winter), 1, 7.

Hodgson, P. (1999). How to teach in cyberspace. *Techniques*, 74, 5 (May), 34.

Jones, G.R, George, J. M., and Hill, C. W. (1998). *Contemporary Management*. Boston Mass.: Irwin McGraw-Hill.

Knappenberger, J. A. (1995). Total quality management. *Business Education Forum*, (Feb.), 5-8.

Laird, Ellen (1999). Distance-learning instructors: watch out for the cutting edge. *The Chronicle of Higher Education*, 45, 38, (May 28), B6.

Leinhardt, G. (1992). What research on learning tells us about teaching. *Educational Leadership* 49, 20-25.

Linskie, R. (1977). *The Learning Process: Theory and Practice*. New York: D. Van Nostrand Company.

Loughlin, K. (1994). GED teaching and adult learning theory: Practical approaches. *Adult Learning*, 6, 2, (Nov-Dec), 13-14.

Madden, L. E. (1997). Motivating students to learn better through own goal-setting. *Education*, 117, 3, (Spring), 411-414.

Mirabito, M. (1996). Establishing an online educational program. *T.H.E. Journal*, 24, I, 57-60.

Noon, J. (1996). Publisher 's corner. *Syllabus*, 9, 9, 4.

Peak, M. H. (1995). TQM transforms the classroom. *Management Review*, 84, (September), 13-14.

Pike, B., & Mansfield, J. (1996). Adult learning theory increases the success of teaching interns. *Adult Learning*, 7, 5 (May-June), 13-14.

Punnett, B. (1986). Goal setting and performance among elementary school students. *Journal of Educational Research* 80, 40-42.

Tobin, K., and Tippins, D. (1993). Constructivism as a referent for teaching and learning. In *The Practice of Constructivism In Science Education*, edited by K. Tobin. Hillsdale, N.J.: Lawrence Erlbaum, 3-21.

Von Glaserfeld, E. (1995). A constructivist approach to teaching. In *Constructivism in Education*, edited by L. Steffe and J. Gale. Hillsdale, N. J.

Zahorik, J. A. (1997). Encouraging - and challenging - Students' Understandings. *Educational Leadership*, 54, 6 (March), 30-33.

Chapter 5

Web-Based Education

A.K. Aggarwal and Regina Bento
University of Baltimore, USA

The Internet is changing the very nature of society in ways unparalleled since the industrial revolution. It is affecting local, national and global economies and their infrastructures. Information is available at any time from any place to any Internet user. This is creating tremendous opportunities for universities to provide a learning environment that is accessible to all. The "same time, same place, only some people" traditional educational environment is giving way to "anytime, anyplace and anybody" instructional models. For universities, the question becomes how to preserve and expand the desirable aspects of face-to-face teaching models when translating them into the new environment of Web-based education (WBE). This challenge is made even more complex when seen in the context of other trends in education: the transition from passive classroom lectures to hands-on, student-centered, interactive learning; the perception of students as "customers," with increased control over the learning process; a higher education market where traditional universities have to compete with for-profit enterprises.

This chapter examines Web-based education and argues that it can successfully simulate face-to-face teaching models, while adding some unique features made possible by the technology. To be successful, however, this simulation requires adjustments in many areas, including student assessment, faculty training and expectations, and student expectations and motivation. In addition, the chapter examines several critical aspects of Web-

Previously Published in *Web-Based Learning and Teaching Technologies: Opportunities and Challenges* edited by Anil Aggarwal, Copyright © 2000, Idea Group Publishing.

based education, including technological, administrative, quality and control issues that need to be addressed in order to create favorable environments for Web-based education.

Information technology, especially the Internet, is creating tremendous opportunities in many areas and education is no exception. Electronic commerce is increasing by leaps and bounds, having already surpassed in 1999 the $300 billion mark that the Department of Commerce had estimated for the year 2003 (Church, 1999). The Web is becoming a virtual library where information about anyone and anything is available at practically little or no cost. People are planning trips, getting medical advice, meeting friends, playing games and chatting with like-minded strangers on the Internet.

Education is not far behind. Many virtual educational organizations are emerging and providing full-fledged curricula, sometimes with very little in-house staff, contracting out faculty to teach specific courses. The University of Phoenix is probably the most successful example of a university dedicated to Web-based teaching. With little or no physical presence in any given geographical area, the University of Phoenix has been able to attract many students and faculty worldwide. Several traditional universities, like Duke, MIT, NYU, and Georgia Tech, have successfully joined the Web movement (Schroede, 1998). There is a great variety of Web offerings in traditional universities, ranging from only a few select courses or topics in continuous studies to full curricula and formal degrees (www.uis.edu/~schroede/sources.htm). Some universities offer Web courses directly, while others create on-line "extensions" of their regular programs.

The Web-based education phenomenon is being felt throughout the world. Organizations such as the Commonwealth of Learning (COL) are emerging to help developing nations improve access to quality Web-based education and training. Web-based courses are being offered in universities in developing countries and regions as varied as India, Sri Lanka, Africa and South America. For example, in India, Web-based courses in engineering and business are being jointly offered by strategic alliances between "Education To Home" (http://education.eth.net) and several well-established universities.

WHY WEB-BASED EDUCATION?

Traditional universities face some basic questions when confronted with this new electronic environment. Can the Internet be used effectively for their educational purposes? Can Web-based teaching provide students with the same (or perhaps even better) quality of learning as the traditional face-to-face environment? Should traditional universities go into Web-based teaching and compete with virtual or for-profit universities?

Well-established universities are reexamining their missions and looking for different or supplemental ways of accomplishing them (Berge, 1999; Laurillard, 1993; Nasseh, 1998; Schlager et al, 1998). Such redefinition in non-profit universities often includes the goal of providing lifelong quality learning to as many students as possible without limitation of time, place, language and individual economic status. In order to achieve this goal, universities are moving from their traditional emphasis on classroom instruction to an environment where learning can be pursued through any media of instruction, be it the classroom, television or the Web.

Advances in information technology and telecommunications are allowing Web-based courses to replicate more seamlessly the features of face-to-face instruction through the use of audio, video, and high-speed Internet connections that facilitate synchronous and asynchronous communication in chat groups, Web discussion boards and virtual forums. Traditional instructional activities such as lecture preparation and delivery, student participation, discussion, feedback and evaluation can be easily translated to the Web environment. With the ever growing demand for technologies that will allow virtual classrooms to more fully replicate all the features of face-to-face environments, innovation is being driven by market-pull forces, rather than a technology-push model.

Some of the strongest pressures for changes in higher education are coming from students. A growing segment of working, self-motivated students want to acquire skills that they feel are useful and also want to be able to choose how they will learn those skills. Convenience is becoming increasingly important, and there is growing demand for a 21st century education that is:

- independent of time and space;
- oriented toward goals and outcomes;
- centered in the student/learner;
- geared to active, hands-on learning; and
- able to accommodate differences in skills and language.

There is growing research support for these educational trends. A renewed emphasis on student-centered, learning-oriented instruction is advocated by authors like Bonk and Cummings (1998) and Merill (www.coe.usu.edu/it/td2/ddc297.htm). They question the assumptions of conventional face-to-face learning and argue that traditional models may not fully satisfy the needs of the learner. In a constructivist learning environment, part of the ownership for learning is shifted from teacher to students. This traditional reliance on highly abstract exercises and problems is replaced by project-based learning, which rebuilds real-world complexity into assignments (Berge, 1999; Fishman and others, 1991). Goal-based scenarios provide a context that models real-world applications and a structure that facilitates adaptive learning environments (Henze and Nejdl, 1997; Schank, 1994).

The next section discusses the different ways in which traditional universities can use the Web to support or create different types of teaching environments, describes various models of using the Web for teaching and discusses opportunities and issues involved in Web-based education.

LEARNING ENVIRONMENTS AND THE WEB

Learning can take place in a variety of environments beyond the traditional classroom, and the Web may be used to replicate and expand the possibilities of each of those environments. Two critical dimensions, time and place, allow us to classify those teaching environments into four major types, as shown in Table 1.

Type I represents the traditional face-to-face classroom, where students congregate at the same time, in the same place, to be taught simultaneously the same material by the same person. The interaction between students and faculty is "many-to-one" during class time and one-to-one during office hours. Students work individually or in a group during class time and/or on

Table 1: Time and place dimensions of teaching environments

		TIME	
		SAME	ANY
PLACE	SAME	Type I Traditional classrooms	Type II Lab modules
	ANY	Type III Distance learning video, audio programs	Type IV Correspondence courses

their own time. Type II represents teaching environments where students come at different times to receive modularized instruction at the same place, such as a lab, information center, or library. Type III environments are distance learning programs where students from widely dispersed geographic areas can be taught simultaneously through one-way or interactive audio and video technology. Type IV environments have traditionally been represented by correspondence courses, where students can learn on their own anywhere, anytime, and take exams as needed.

The Web can be used to support or simulate all four types of teaching environments. When synchronous teaching environments (traditional Type I classrooms or distributed Type III sites) are enriched with live Internet connections and projection capabilities, the Web can be used to support or simulate lectures, case discussions and classroom interactions in multiple ways by:

- serving as a platform for simultaneously delivering presentations (text, audio and video) to students in a classroom (Type I) and/ or dispersed throughout the world (Type III);
- allowing synchronous virtual visits to sites dedicated to relevant topics or organizations;
- enabling real time or almost synchronous discussions and impromptu dialogue through text-based technologies such as chat-rooms and Web boards, or full video and audio interaction through software such as CU-SeeMe and NetMeeting.

The same Web capabilities can be used asynchronously to support and expand Types II and IV environments. When the Web is used in Type II environments, students gain access to an unprecedented wealth of multimedia information, tutorials, materials, and resources to perform lab assignments, do library research, or complete modules of instruction at their own pace. They also gain the capability to interact asynchronously, outside of class, with their classmates, teams, and instructors through chat, Web board or interactive Web-based video technology.

In Type IV environments, the Web allows students to benefit from the anytime / anyplace flexibility of earlier correspondence courses, without having to sacrifice the spontaneity and interactivity traditionally associated with synchronous modes of instruction. This is where Web-based teaching achieves its maximum contribution in eliminating time and space barriers, while still achieving interaction. When the Web is used to create a Type IV environment, education and human contact are available any time, from any place. Students can learn from home, office, or wherever they are, by accessing Web-based lectures, tutorials, materials, and books, completing and submitting Web-based assignments, exercises, and research, interacting in Web-based forums and taking Web-based quizzes and exams.

A few words of caution are needed at this point. Although the Web *can* support and even replicate all four types of teaching environments, this does not necessarily mean that it *should*. For example, if a traditional university strongly encourages or forces all instructors to use the Web to support a Type I environment teaching, the quality of instruction may suffer. Instructors who are technologically-inclined may become so enamored of the technology that they concentrate on form rather than content in their lectures, they may grow so dependent on the technology that they can no longer function in a classroom when the network goes down, and they may become so focused on their new gadgets that there is not enough time or energy left to stimulate class discussion and dialogue. These dangers are compounded when a traditional university starts using the Web as the exclusive medium for delivering instruction in a given course or program, as will be discussed later.

Though it is feasible to use the Web to simulate a face-to-face environment, this may require more than a linear translation. In the Web, instructional aspects such as mode of lecture delivery, student interaction and assessment and faculty roles may be very different. The emphasis should remain on "what" is being learned and "how" learning takes place, not on the medium itself. There is growing research to suggest that educational outcomes comparable to traditional classrooms can also be achieved on the Web through interactive asynchronous hands-on approaches (http://cuda.teleeducation.nb.ca/ nosignificantdifference). It is important, however, to keep the focus on learning, particularly in situations where instruction is exclusively Web-based.

WEB TEACHING MODELS

Traditional universities have been exploring different models of using the Web for teaching, ranging from simple forms of Web support for regular face-to-face classes, all the way to full-fledged Web-based teaching. We classify this range of Web usage into the following basic models:

A) Web Support for Information Storage, Dissemination and Retrieval

In this model, the Web supports synchronous or asynchronous teaching when faculty and students use it to store, disseminate and retrieve information that is relevant to the course. As can be seen in Table 2, this type of support

Table 2: Type of Web Support

Place of Web Usage

		Inside Classroom	Outside Classroom
Type of	Course-Specific	ACCESS I	ACCESS II
Information	Public	ACCESS III	ACCESS IV

may take place outside or within the classroom and may involve public or course-specific information.

When the classroom is equipped with live Web access and projection capabilities, faculty may support a regular face-to-face lecture or discussion by taking students into virtual field trips to public Web sites (ACCESS III). For example, faculty may show Web pages that deal with the topics or companies being studied, or demonstrate how to conduct electronic searches. If course-specific materials are posted on the Web (such as lecture notes or presentations, syllabi, tutorials, assignments or exercises), faculty may also use them during class to support a presentation, solve problems, and recall rules or deadlines. (ACCESS I).

When students have access to the Web outside of class, they can take advantage of the any time /any place flexibility of the Web to access public and course-specific information. From home, work, a public library or anywhere they have Web access, students can do readings, assignments and research by visiting the Web sites of news and academic organizations, libraries, professional associations, companies, etc. (ACCESS IV). The hypertext nature of Web-based materials allows students to pursue topics in non-linear ways, following their interests and curiosity.

If course-specific materials are online, students can take tutorials at their own pace, review lecture notes, and never lose the course syllabus! (ACCESS II). Moreover, if the textbook adopted in the course has a corresponding Web site, students may benefit from readings and resources specifically tailored to the chapters being covered, and even take online, interactive quizzes. A good example of these features can be found in the Web site for Robbins (1998) text book on Organizational Behavior at http://cw.prenhall.com/robbinsorgbeh/.

B) Web Support for Two-Way Interaction

The Web is far more than a vast repository of information. It also allows faculty and students to interact in powerful and dynamic ways to create vibrant learning communities (Schlager et al, 1998). Chat rooms (public or course-specific) provide real-time interaction, and are best suited for informal exchanges or quick questions and answers. Web discussion boards combine almost real-time capabilities with the flexibility and potential depth of asynchronous communication.

Threaded discussions on Web boards make it possible for dialogues on different topics to be pursued without confusion. Materials posted to a Web board can be accessed from anywhere, anytime, while privacy and confidentiality may be preserved through different levels of password protection (keeping the general public from posting and/or reading the postings). Many Web boards allow posted materials to be searched by thread, author, date, and category. Some allow creation of special areas for different teams to interact virtually. These features make Web boards an ideal forum for outside-of-class interaction, where faculty and students can conduct case discussions, explore topics and share resources.

C) Web-Based Teaching

The information and interaction capabilities of the Web have led to the development of "exclusively Web-based courses", where all (or almost all) teaching takes place on the Web, with no (or very little) face-to-face interaction. This model has several variations, depending on decisions made in the following areas:

c1) Course development: A Web course may be developed by (a) the faculty member who will teach it; by (b) another faculty member in the same university, who then supervises the teaching faculty; (c) cooperatively with faculty from the same or different universities, where each develops one or more course modules (see the Socrates initiative, http://www.esocrates.com); or (d) by a team of instructional and Web specialists, either in-house or by contract with an external company.

c2) Place of course delivery: The course can be entirely Web-based, with faculty and students never meeting face-to-face, and with students in places throughout the world; the course can be taught mostly on the Web, with a few face-to-face interactions required (usually at the beginning and end, sometimes the middle of the course); and the course can be taught in a mixed mode, with some students taking it in the classroom (supported with Web information and interaction), and others taking it entirely on the Web.

c3) Timing of course delivery: The course can be structured so that there are time limits for students to complete each unit or module, i.e., the course starts and ends at a certain date, and course units or topics are taken in lockstep by a cohort of students within certain time periods (e.g.,

Week 1 covers Topics A and B, and students can choose anytime during that week to do their work on those topics, but may not submit assignments after the week is over); or the course can be taken without time limits, i.e., the students are free to progress at their own pace through the materials.

c4) Level of interaction: The course can place varying degrees of emphasis on using the Web for transmission of information or for interaction between students and faculty. It is always possible to use the Web as a part of, rather than as a complete Web-supported course.

ISSUES IN WEB-BASED TEACHING

Many technical, administrative and pedagogical issues arise when traditional universities use the Web to move into a fully Web-based, any place/any time educational environment. Technical issues involve the constantly changing hardware and software used in Web-based teaching. Administrative issues include the logistics of providing remote students with the same support available to on-campus students (library, bookstore, advising, registration, career services etc.) and pedagogical considerations involve the twin challenges of quality and control.

Technical issues

A good way to appreciate the technical issues involved in Web-based education is to consider what one is trying to accomplish when translating to the Web the activities that normally take place in a Type I face-to-face learning environments (Table III).

The activities in Table III can be combined into a few basic categories:
- Content
  - Content preparation
  - HW preparation
- Delivery
  - Lecture delivery
  - Student presentations
- Access
  - Contents (lecture and HW)
  - Teacher
  - Peer/group
- Interaction
  - Between students
    - synchronous (class, lab, telephone)

Table 3: Typical activities in Type I Teaching

Place of support

Activities	Inside classroom	Outside classroom
Faculty	Deliver course syllabus & HW Deliver lecture Video/audio/software presentations Lab demonstrations Lab classes and practices	Prepare syllabus and HW Respond to student questions
Student	Get course Syllabus & HW Get reading assignment for next class Listen to lecture Get Home work assignments Take exam(s) Instructor Evaluation	Read assignment Do HW Review notes Seek additional information (library, Internet or other sources)
Student/faculty & student/student	In-class interaction with instructor Class/Case discussions with peers Student/group class presentations Get feedback from instructor	Interact with faculty out of class Phone/fax/e-mail classmates Meet, prepare group presentation Seek additional Information

- Asynchronous (voice mail, e-mail)
  - Between Faculty and Students
    - Synchronous (class, office, lab)
    - Asynchronous (voice mail, e-mail)
- Assessment/Feedback
  - Exams
  - Home work(s)
  - Individual and group presentations

Thanks to existing technology, these categories of activities normally found in face-to-face models of instruction can be translated into a Web-based environment:

- **Content**: Lectures and homework can be developed for the Web by using any word-processing package with html capabilities, or the html editor available with many browsers. Examples include Microsoft Word, WordPerfect, AOL Press, Homesite, Navigator Gold and Microsoft's FrontPage
- **Delivery:** Instead of being delivered in-class, lectures can be placed on a server (owned by the university or by the service provider contracted for Web-based teaching). For example, Eduprise (www.eduprice.com) allows instructors to post lectures on the Web, including plug-ins with video, animation and audio capabilities. Many universities are providing videotaped lectures which can be seen in real-time.

- **Access:** Web-based courses require Internet access through an Internet service provider (ISP) with FTP access. Multimedia data require high-speed modems (e.g., 56.6 K baud rates), or the faster ISDN connections available through local service providers. For students on the move, wireless connection is also becoming economically feasible. AOL, MSN, Prodigy, Erols, Comcast and others provide high-speed access to the Internet. In addition, students may need a Java capable browser with plug-ins capable of running streaming audio, video and animation. Netscape Navigator, Microsoft's Internet Explorer, *Excite@home*, Lycos and many other browsers are capable of viewing multimedia data.

- **Interaction:** One of the biggest advantages of the Type I learning environment is face-to-face interaction. Due to bandwidth restrictions, this is not yet easily translated into the Web-based environment, in spite of the many video-conferencing packages currently available, such as PictureTel, NetMeeting, and CUSeeMe. However, a highly interactive learning environment can be created using Web tools such as threaded discussion boards, forums, document sharing, message centers, bulletin boards, e-mail and others for asynchronous communication and online chatrooms for synchronous interaction. Many of these conferencing tools provide features to support group activities and presentations, including plug-ins on the electronic boards. Some of the popular conferencing packages are LOTUS Notes, FirstClass, WebBoard, Forums, WebCT, Web-in-a-Box and Microsoft Exchange.

- **Assessment/ Feedback:** Traditional forms of student assessment and feedback can be adapted to Web-based environments. For example, students can take on-line exams that may be automatically graded online, in real time (e.g., multiple choice, True/False tests) or may be electronically sent to the instructor for grading, which in many cases reduces feedback time.

In the last few years there have been rapid technological advances in Web-education. Several recent Web-education products like Learning Space from LOTUS, Centra's Symposium, Real Education, Blackboard, Web Course-in-a-Box and many other "integrated" packages that provide conferencing, lecture preparation examination and assessment capabilities are available in the market today. As bandwidth becomes less of a concern, it will be possible to economically simulate on the Web many of the audiovisual aspects of face-to-face environments. The ultimate goal in this area is to provide a seamless learning environment, independent of platforms and tools.

Administrative Issues

If education is offered electronically, all student-oriented administrative activities, from registration to graduation, should also be available online. On-line offerings should include:

General Information
University/College/Program/courses
    Hardware/software requirements
Net Etiquette
Registration
    Advising/Counseling
Application
    Fee payment
    Confirmation
Assistance
Hardware/software problems
Course demos
Tutors/tutorials
Mentor
Library resources
Social interactions
Graduation

Although these on-line activities replicate what happens in Type I learning environments, several policy issues require special attention. For example, fee structures, intellectual property rights and faculty contracts may have to be revised to reflect the nature of Web education. Flat fees may be challenged by the marketplace, since many students will never use physical facilities such as student centers or labs (if a campus even exists!), nor participate in student activities. Instead, there may be more demand for a fee structure based on credit hours or services used. Intellectual property rights is another hotly debated issue, which may end up being resolved in the courts. The legal system will have to address issues such as who owns Web courses, the university or the faculty who developed them.

Another main concern in Web-based education is class size (Boettcher, 1998). There are suggestions that on-line courses not go beyond 8 to 13 students in a class, and that the courses should be taught by fully qualified faculty in order to preserve the high level of interaction required for quality learning (Arvan et al., 1998). Trinkle (1999) argues strongly in favor of small class sizes and warns that technology may be most effective when integrated in face-to-face teaching environments.

The choice of courses and programs to be offered on the Web can be quite challenging. Should Web-based curricula be designed for cohorts pursuing a degree in lockstep or should they follow Type I model, where students can choose from a variety of courses being offered in a given term? These decisions may be affected by several factors, such as competition, number of students and faculty, server capacity and course duration.

In many cases, a parallel system for on-line administration may emerge which might not be economical. For this reason, many traditional universities are offering Web-based education as an extension of their current program or through collaboration with other universities. Irrespective of the strategy chosen, in order for Web-based education to succeed there must be a high-level champion in the organization who is willing to realign the current administrative structure to support the Web programs and enhance their visibility.

Quality Issues

Quality is one area where Web-based education often comes under heavy criticism. A recent conference on "Digital Diploma Mills" raised numerous questions about the "quality" of Web education (http://www.oreilly.com/people/staff/stevet/netfuture/1998/Jun0298_72.html#3). For every success report there is a cautionary study, and it seems that the jury is still out on the quality issue. Can Web-based education be effective? Can it provide the same or better quality as conventional face-to-face instruction? In order to answer these critical questions, traditional universities need to ask a variety of other questions, requiring a reexamination of the roles of students and faculty.

Student Factors In Quality

There is no denying that Web-based courses open new educational access to non-traditional and geographically dispersed students. The on-line setting provides a level of flexibility and convenience not provided by traditional classroom courses. However, effective Web-based teaching requires responsible, motivated students whose aims are to learn and not to simply get a passing grades. Many students seek on-line courses driven by personal situations such as time and distance constraints, and work and family responsibilities. Yet, to be successful in a Web learning environment students have to be highly motivated self-learners. Will students be able to learn on their own? Will they seek advice from instructors when needed? Will they be motivated to seek useful information, to go beyond the assigned instructional materials to explore the richness of the Web, without becoming stuck in the moving sands of information overload? Will students be able to manage their time so that the "any time" nature of instruction does not lead to procrastination? As Web-based education matures it will become clearer which students are more likely to master the challenges of this new environment

Although motivation is an essential element for students to succeed in Web-based education, ability is also a crucial factor, particularly in terms of computer literacy. In a recent study, Nasseh (1998) reported that 81 percent of students thought there should be a computer training and orientation program for all students before the start of classes. Many online courses require students to do electronic searches, exchange e-mail, download files, browse sites, use Web-boards, take on-line exams, discuss on-line cases, participate in on-line groups and play plug-ins. This requires students to go beyond simple computer training and become truly Internet-literate. Adequate preparation is an essential pre-condition for successful Web-based education. Students who attempt to learn simultaneously the technology and the course material are more likely to fail.

Faculty Factors In Quality

There are serious issues involved when a traditional university moves faculty from a Type I to a Type IV environment without providing them with adequate technological and pedagogical training and resources, as well as enough time and motivation for course development and delivery. In these circumstances, faculty might simply transfer their existing materials to the Web with minimal modifications and no consideration of the peculiar nature of the medium. When this happens, the course may suffer from the pedagogical costs associated with losing the richness, spontaneity and synergy of face-to-face interaction. Moreover, the problem may be compounded if the faculty member does not know how to help students reap the benefits of the highly interactive, continuously fresh and virtually inexhaustible nature of Web resources.

Web-based teaching raises new questions about the very role of faculty in course design and administration. Who should design Web courses and develop Web-based materials? Some universities try to compensate for the traditional faculty's lack of familiarity with the technical and pedagogical challenges of the Web by outsourcing the task of course development. As more and more for-profit businesses get in the education market, course content will at times be driven by technical issues of hardware and software convenience rather than pedagogical considerations. Occasionally, courses are developed jointly by traditional faculty and internal or external instructional specialists and technical experts, raising complex issues in terms of course ownership, intellectual property rights and so on.

In addition, what about the role of traditional faculty in delivering Web-courses, either developed by themselves or others? Some virtual universities have no full-time faculty, simply providing instructional materials on the Web and hiring part-time instructors for a few chat sessions. However, effective on-line instruction requires the same, if not more, faculty involvement as in face-to-face courses (Nasseh, 1998). Faculty need to be able to stimulate critical thinking in Web-board discussions, give individualized attention to students who need more help, provide timely and thorough feedback for assignments, and engage in ad-hoc problem solving. In fact, responsible on-line instructors are finding that their "cyber hours" may far exceed the time they normally spend in regular class and office hours.

In Web-based education, the instructor's roles are that of a facilitator, mentor and coach. As a facilitator, the instructor needs to know how to facilitate discussions in small groups, keep students task-oriented and move them toward some sort of consensus. In case of dominance by some group members, the instructor needs to intervene and encourage input from non-participating members. As a mentor and a coach, the instructor will have to advise students on their progress, provide one-on-one counseling and offer prompt and constructive feedback. In some cases, the instructor may need to fight the temptation to become a 24- hour help-desk where students seek help on any topic, personal or professional.

To accommodate these new roles, faculty involved in Web-based education need pedagogical and technical training. Pedagogical training is necessary for faculty to take full advantage of the new learning opportunities opened up by the Web. A linear transfer of in-class lectures to the Internet will ignore the strengths of the new technology. Technical training is also needed for faculty to effectively develop and deliver course content, communicate with students, answer technical questions and be able to offer "total" on-line assistance. In addition, faculty may require some training in content analysis, so that they can extract from the students' textual (or multi media) messages the same clues found in face-to-face education, such as body language, facial expression and other nonverbal communication.

Control Issues

How can traditional universities control Web-based education to assure its effectiveness? In addition to the addressing quality issues discussed above, universities must also pay special attention to how traditional methods of evaluating learning are translated into an exclusively Web-based environment. Face-to-face courses typically involve homework, presentations, papers, group assignments and exams that need to be submitted and graded. All of those can be replicated on the Web, with minor or major modifications.

A typical area of concern in traditional universities relates to the modifications needed to ensure the ethics of an exam when all contacts between faculty and students happen on the Web, i.e., student validation and authenticity of assignments. Of course, face-to-face interaction does not eliminate the possibility of cheating, but does make it more difficult, for example, for a student to hire someone else to take an exam or substitute for them during an entire semester. In Web-based teaching, some of the most obvious ethical problems may require changing the nature of the requirements (less reliance on Web-based exams and more on interactions and projects throughout the course) or modifying their administration (e.g., by requiring exams to be taken in places like public libraries or other cooperating institutions, where someone can verify the student's identity and proctor the administration of the exam).

Advances in video streaming and real-time data capture will eventually automate the validation process. In the same way that fingerprints, photographs, voice-recognition, and profiles are used to identify workers in a face-to-face environment, student images will be automatically captured and validated in real time in the Web environment. In addition, cookies could also be used to authenticate the student's machine environment. Computerized validation process will alleviate some of the problems of student validation and authenticity of submissions increasing reliability of Web-based exams and real time submissions.

FUTURE RESEARCH

Web-based education is in its infancy. Things are evolving and changing as we enter the 21st century. Nothing in society will remain immune from technological change. Selling, marketing, buying, advertising, banking, and even education are going through an unprecedented revolution, changing the boundaries of time, place and language, as well as gender, race, nationality, economy and religion. Academic institutions have traditionally been pioneers in innovation and this time is no exception. What is happening, however, is that many schools are simply joining the Web-education bandwagon, without much analysis or forethought, in fear of being left behind. Instead, they need to take advantage of whatever guidance already exists. Much new research is needed to answer many critically important questions.

- Who is interested in Web-based education and why? What motivates a student to take Web-based courses? Should some students be discouraged from taking them? What should be the admission requirements? Are the typical standardized tests, such as GRE, GMAT and SAT, appropriate predictors of success in Web-based education, or should new tests be devised to include personality and aptitude for self-learning and self-motivation?
- Is the quality of learning the same in Web-based education as it is in the classroom environment? Should universities differentiate between digital degrees and regular on-campus degrees? How will employers of on-line graduates perceive the quality of their education?
- What types of faculty are needed to teach on the Web? How can institutions retrain faculty to be effective online? Should on-line offerings include full degrees, isolated courses or continuing education initiatives? Should traditional universities develop on-line courses on their own or engage in strategic alliances with other schools and providers?

As in any emerging field, once these issues are resolved many new ones will emerge. This is a continuously iterative process, an ongoing search for consensus between educators, learners and administrators.

CONCLUSION

This chapter has raised more questions than answers in regard to Web-based education, which reflects the new and evolving nature of the medium. There are no clear-cut rules or simple solutions, and it is no wonder that an increasing number of journals, conferences and workshops are being dedicated to exploring the issues involved in Web-teaching.

Our belief is that each of the four types of learning environments discussed here has its advantages and drawbacks, and that the Web can be used to support or replicate any of them. When used effectively, the Web opens a door to inexhaustible and constantly replenishing resources, allowing us to reap the benefits of flexibility in time and/or place without compromising the interactivity, synergism, and spontaneity usually associated with being at the same time in the same place. However, the web's potential for good is matched, if not surpassed, by its potential for disaster. Depending on how we address the challenges involved in Web-based education, we may find out that it can sacrifice the benefits of other traditional environments while compounding, rather than reducing, their costs.

Technology may enrich, but should not dictate, education. The Web is a wonderful hammer, a tool with unprecedented, exciting possibilities for education that must be explored and expanded. But traditional universities should not indiscriminately transform all courses into nails that need hammering, or they may smash their fingers in the process.

REFERENCES

Arvan L., Ory J., Bullock C., Burnaska K, and Hanson M. (1998). The Scale efficiency Project, *JALN*, volume 2, issue 2. Also available at www.aln.org/alnweb/journal/vol2_issue2/arvan2.htm.

Berge, Z. L. (1999). Conceptual Frameworks in Distance Training and Education. In D.A. Schreiber and Z.L. Berge, (Eds). *Distance Training: How innovative organizations are using technology to maximize learning and meet business objectives*. San Francisco: Jossey-Bass, 19-36.

Boettcher, J. (1998). How Many students Are Just Right in a Web course?. CREN, http://www.cren.net/~jboettch/number.htm (retrieved May 1999).

Bonk, C.J. & Cummings, J.A. (1998). A dozen recommendations for placing the student at the center of Web-based learning. *Educational Media International*, 35 (2) 82-89.

Church, G. (1999). The Economy of the Future? TIME E-Commerce Special, October 4, 113-116.

Fishman, B.J., Honebein, P.C., Duffy T.M. (1991). Constructivism and the Design of Learning Environment:Context and Activities for Learning. NATO Advanced Workshop on the Design of Constructivist Learning Environments.

Henze, N., and Nejdl, W. (1997). A Web-Based Learning Environment:Applying Constructivist Teaching Concepts in Vitual Learning Environment. Available http://www.kbs.uni-hannover.de/paper/97/ifip97/paper15.html (retrieved may 1999).

Laurillard, Diana, (1993) Rethinking University Teaching: a framework for the effective use of educational technology, London: New York: Routledge.

Mendez, R. (1996). The World Lecture Hall. Available: http://www.utexas.edu/world/lecture/index.html.

Merrill, David, Learning-Oriented Instructional Development Tools. Available http://www.coe.usu.edu/it/id2/DDC297.htm.

Nasseh, B (1998). Training and Support programs, and Faculty's New Roles In Computer-Based Distance Education in Higher Education Institutions. Available at http://www.bsu.edu/classes/nasseh/study/res98.html

Robbins, S.P. (1998). *Organizational Behavior: Concepts, Controversies and Applications*. 8th Ed. Upper Saddle River, NJ: Prentice-Hall. Available http://cw.prenhall.com/robbinsorgbeh/.

Schank, R and Cleary, C. (1994). *Engines for Education*. Hillsdale, NJ :Lawrence Erlbaum Associates.

Schlager M., Fusco J, and Schank P.(1998). Cornerstones for an On-line Community of Educational Professionals. *IEEE Technology and Society*, 17(4), 15-21,40. Also available at http://www.tappedin.org/info/papers/ieee.html.

Schroede, R (1999). Online Higher Education Notebook. Available http://www.uis.edu/~schroede/sources.htm.

Talbolt, S. (1998). NETFUTURE: Technology and Human Responsibility. *Conference Report*, June 2, 1998. Available http://www.oreilly.com/people/staff/stevet/netfuture/1998/Jun0298_72.html#3.

Trinkle, D.(1999). Distance Education: A Means to an End, No More, No Less. *The Chronicle of Higher Education*.

Trinkle, D. (1999). History and the Computer Revolutions: A Survey of Current Practices, JAHC, 2(1), April. Also available at http://www.mcel.pacificu.edu/JAHC/JAHCII1/ArticlesII1/Trinkle/Trinkleindex.html.

Winner, L. (1998). Report from the Digital Diploma Mills Conference. Available http://www.oreilly.com/people/staff/stevet/netfuture/1998/Jun0298_72.html#3.

Chapter 6

Web-Based Teaching: Infrastructure Issues in the Third World

Dushyanthi Hoole
Open University of Sri Lanka

S. Ratnajeevan H. Hoole
University of Peradeniya, Sri Lanka

INTRODUCTION/BACKGROUND

The use of educational technologies is widely recognised as beneficial (IEEE, 1998; Hoole, 1988). However, cogent arguments have been made by those who have invested much time in the development of courseware for teaching (Hoberg, 1993; Vanderplaats, 1993) that the use of the technology dominates the class so much that the subject being taught tends to get lost.

In this milieu, the appearance of the Internet and the Web, and following that, Web-based teaching, offers new opportunities with caution as a caveat. Unlike courseware where an individual instructor sits down and writes programs for his class, the difference with the Web is that demands in terms of infrastructure are heavy. Not only that, while in the West, things such as a networked campus, Internet connections, etc. are taken for granted, in the Third World (defined for the purposes of this article as those countries that are not a part of North America, Europe, Australia and the newly industrialised countries of Asia such as Singapore, Japan, Korea, and Taiwan), these facilities are rare. Simply asking for all the relevant infrastructure one needs for teaching will often not produce the funds. As a result, Third World instructors wishing to embark on Web-based teaching must create a wide

Previously Published in *Web-Based Learning and Teaching Technologies: Opportunities and Challenges* edited by Anil Aggarwal, Copyright © 2000, Idea Group Publishing.

demand based on needs that go beyond simply teaching for these facilities and, thereby try to get what they want. They must also improvise and produce new ways of teaching with the Web.

This chapter spells out the attempts by the authors, still experimental, in producing new ways of teaching with the Web and the attempts by which an infrastructure for Web-based teaching was created at the Open University of Sri Lanka.

THE OPEN UNIVERSITY OF SRI LANKA

Distance teaching is increasingly found to be the way to go. It stresses the fact that education does not end after four years and one knows all that is there to know, but rather is a life-long process. It democratises education by giving late-comers, the marginalised such as women and minorities, villagers and others left out of conventional education, a new opportunity. The Open University of Sri Lanka is a state university founded by an Act of Parliament and caters to some 18,000 students while the Sri Lankan conventional universities together have a total student enrollment of approximately 32,000, showing the demand for distance education. Indeed, the fact that the vast majority of science students at OUSL are women, shows the service provided to women and underscores the success of the university in meeting its goals and thereby fulfilling its mission.

Demographic patterns also give pause to planners. The heavy success of the Sri Lankan state in its family planning overtures to society, say policy-planners (Rajapakse et al., 1997), means that the labour force will trail off in the year 2011 AD. This would put Sri Lanka in the place where countries like Singapore and Hong Kong now are, looking for and hiring labour from neighbours. But in 2011 AD, would there be countries for Sri Lanka to hire such labour from, competing with more advanced countries which also would be even more labour-short than they now are and competing for the same labour with better remuneration? It is now therefore increasingly agreed that while the Sri Lankan economy needs more graduates to shift to less labour-intensive work, the conventional universities cannot meet this demand because of lack of teaching staff and cash-limits on infrastructure expansion. The experience in Sri Lanka is that as new universities are opened in a country with a fixed number of qualified staff, poaching occurs – especially by attracting junior staff from the established universities to senior positions in the new universities. As a result, country-wide the staff quality goes down. However, since in open education, a teacher mainly prepares lessons and needs little else in terms of heavy infrastructure, it is now recognised that open education must be relied upon more and more to meet the anticipated shortage of graduates.

Presently, OUSL teaches through the printed medium where the material can be rather drab and the students do not have peer interaction to gauge for themselves how effectively they are studying. It was decided at the Senate of the OUSL therefore to try out two experimental courses on the Web as an alternative (or even a supplement) to the print medium. This chapter is a result of that effort.

BENEFITS OF THE WEB

Before proceeding, it is useful to describe the benefits of Web-based teaching based on a campus-wide network to keep in context the comments being made here. The described benefits are also based on the authors' experience in teaching in California. These are:

- Ideal to link/integrate a university community.
- In a linked community, the main disadvantage of open, distance education – learning in isolation and the attendant boredom and the inability to gauge the adequacy of ones level of work input that results in a high failure rate – is ameliorated.
- Lesson materials can use colour, sound and animation and can include the instructor's voice as in the lessons the authors have developed. It is noted that the incorporation of colour in print is relatively very expensive.
- E-Mail is offered to all students and enhances communication between teacher and student
- Bulletin boards/campus notices that are computer-based enhance the flow of information. Unlike in conventional distance education, the questions raised by students and the answers are available to the whole class through the bulletin board.
- Full-time list manager managing List Server allows easy communication to class with one E-mail address for each course.
- All assignments by e-mail use the list-server. Problems raised by students are also posted. Corrections, tips, etc., can be issued immediately without waiting for the next meeting.
- Questions to instructor by e-mail, which all students will see if the list-server is used.
- Quick announcements to class by e-Mail such as of mistakes in (or clarifications to) notes.

- Paper drafts by e-mail; these can be commented on quickly by the instructor on the same document and returned to the students. This results in quick turnaround and fewer problems with interpreting the teacher's handwriting.
- Extensive Writing Experience for Students by using e-mail since questions go from voice (in-class) to writing on the computer. Writing experience, it is now widely accepted, is very important to a well-trained graduate.

ALTERNATIVE USES OF THE WEB

The use of Web-based teaching, presupposes access to the Internet. In the Third World however, modern telecommunication lines do not exist. Although the technology exists, it is not offered because telecommunications agencies are usually government organisations with a monopoly. As a result of the poor network-links, accessing Web pages is very slow.

It was decided that although Web-based lessons would be placed on the network, alternative forms would also be used. These alternative forms included placing the lessons on CD and distributing them to all registered students. The material on a CD can be exactly that placed on the Web site. It is relevant to mention that a CD, when bought in bulk, costs about a US dollar and can contain as many as 20 regular textbooks (since writing the article, the retail price of a CD disk has come down to this level). That is, the cost is lower than that of a printed book. Further, when material from a CD is read directly from the CD drive of a computer, the access speed is several times faster than from the Internet. Naturally, there is a downside which is that updates will not be as easy as on a Web site since even with re-writable CDs, they need to be recalled and writing time can be as much as 15 minutes or more per CD. Another disadvantage is that unlike the book, the CD cannot be read from bed or the toilet.

The authors have made the case that teaching can be cheaper but as effective with only a campus-wide network and no Internet access (Hoole, 1998a). With such a system, one CD or material on the magnetic disc of a server would do for on-campus access – and this ameliorates the problem of updates and that of writing and issuing many copies of a CD. To address the problem of students not having access to computers and the need to offer geographically distributed access to the material, at least five computers have been placed at each of OUSL's 22 regional study centres spread across the country, the more important and extensively used centres such as those in the cities of Colombo, Matara and Kandy having more. Local area networks at the study centres are designed to have a server that may carry the lessons alternatively. The material is available on the newly inaugurated Campus-wide Network on the instructor's PC using Microsoft's Personal Web

Server™, with the machine being seen over the network. As such, any student can come to the campus and access the material from the student computers very rapidly and leave messages on the bulletin boards. In this mode of offering lessons too, the access speed is significantly faster than through the Internet. In this scheme, using dial-up services, the material can be updated quickly at the regional centres as lapses are found, particularly if the material is on a disc rather than on a CD.

THE COURSES

The courses selected for transformation to the Web (Hoole, 1998b; Hoole, 1999) were both from chemistry. One, Analytical Chemistry, was a long-standing course. It had been prepared for the printed medium. The text therefore existed in Word Perfect™. It was transformed to Microsoft Word™ by a simple process that merely involves opening the file with MS Word. In the latest version of MS Word, there is facility to "save as" a document for the Web. The process was easy, but lacked the incorporation of elegant styles that bear on pedagogy. Thereafter it was a matter of editing the document to incorporate design and stylistic issues with Netscape Composer™ and/or Frontpage 98™, perhaps the two most widely used Web-page editors. The graphics was scanned, but more often redone for better effect. The result by either program looked equally good to the authors. Frontpage 98 appeared to give a more colourful appearance, but the rigidity of the templates sometimes made the text difficult to read.

The second course is a new course developed from scratch, Food Chemistry. It can also be a stand-alone course for non-degree seeking students and is deliberately designed as such to investigate the differences that must be there between a course that is part of a programme of study and one that is taken for itself. Features incorporated include speech by the instructor, music as background if the student wants it, sound-ef-

Figure 1: Felix used in Asking Questions.

Q 1 What is meant by a gravimetric analysis?

A. Chemical Analysis by weight measurement
B. Chemical Analysis by volume measurement
C. Both
D. Neither

Hint

fects when going to a new page, and a bulletin board carrying all important questions to the instructor from individual students and the instructor's answers. One feature that the authors are particularly proud of involves addressing students not knowing if their answers to practice questions are right by interactive Web-pages. Here, "Felix the Cat" pensively walks back and forth as the question is asked (see Figure 1). The right answer brings up a computer-generated dancing infant in perfect rhythm with the accompanying music; a wrong answer elicits a word of encouragement by the instructor's voice and takes the student to that part of the text relevant to the question to help with further reading. It is noted that this cannot be done with the printed medium.

INFRASTRUCTURE

Offering access to the Web clearly presupposes the existence of a local area network. To place the costs in context, the cost of the network for the Colombo Regional Centre of OUSL was Rs. 12 million while the equipment budget for the whole university was 4.5 million. Comparatively, the authors found that the installation of a network with at least twice as many nodes as at the Open University for a college in California four years ago was about US $200,000, roughly Rs. 10 million. That is, the costs were significantly more in Sri Lanka while income in Sri Lanka is tens times lower. This underscores the difficulties in the Third World. To make a Third World university make such a monumental investment, other uses of the network must be demonstrated. It usually cannot be justified on grounds of greater teaching effectiveness alone.

In this particular instance, the justification indeed came partly from enhanced teaching effectiveness, faster communications through e-mail and better research facilities through Web-pages and associated search engines. But the main argument was successfully made on the use of a Management Information System (MIS) for the first time in Sri Lanka. Most university records in Sri Lanka are done by hand. In an open education system (where there are few prerequisites, many compulsory assignments, tests and examinations per course and a minimum attendance requirement at face-to-face sessions) record keeping is horrendous. The possibility of a wide range of course combinations unlike in a programme of study increases the complexity.

The support for the Web, therefore, came through the development of an MIS through funding by Great Britain's Department for International Development. This MIS development, now ongoing at the Information Technology Division of OUSL, is almost done. Modules such as student registration and report generation for research purposes are already available for use and accessible over the network. Other modules continue to be developed. These will allow comprehensive record keeping, automatic generation of transcripts and research on the demand for courses, failure rates etc. This MIS has a client-server architecture where grade/score entry is decentralised to faculty offices. Thus each instructor has to enter marks directly via the network on the server. It is a feature that is essential to any effective open education system. The authors suggest that Third World educators should muster every reason possible to get these facilities that are routinely assumed in the West. With the advantages of the MIS, OUSL quickly committed the funds. The campus-wide network, constructed under the supervision of one of the authors, is completed and presently services are being added one by one; Internet services were the first made available in March 1999.

The other infrastructural need for the Web, perhaps as costly when the system is mature, is having a desktop computer on every instructor's desk. In normal circumstances, a Third World university can develop this only gradually, not overnight and certainly not at the same time as the network. The desktops are necessary for communications with students, development of Web pages, updating of Web pages, etc.. Thankfully, the MIS under DfID funding also requires the same thing for each instructor to operate the database in a decentralised mode. Therefore, with DfID funding together with some university support, many instructors do now have access to computers and over time every instructor will have a desktop. Presently, computers have been made available to students in clusters at key regional centres. Instructors have access to clusters of computers dedicated for network and Web use by the Deans' offices with additional facilities such as scanning and photo-editing. The traditional videotape making Media Centre is also available for graphics editing.

In addition to these facilities, the vice-chancellor of the university has promised to support a request for a desktop computer connected to the network from every instructor who would convert from traditional methods of teaching to Web-based. This by itself has proved a great incentive to many instructors.

Software is another issue. Unlike in the West, most basic word-processing software is unlicensed in the Third World. For instance, when buying a computer in Sri Lanka, vendors would place pirated copies of anything one asks for. However, this illegal mode of operation cannot be sustained when one displays products on the Web – for example when Microsoft recognises a Web-page as having been created by their Frontpage, a lawsuit would surely follow. One of the first acts the authors undertook was to legalise the situation. Thankfully,

Microsoft has a university licence programme for US $2220 per year for all their software. This legalised us at a fraction of the cost we would have paid if we had tried to buy each program at market value.

TRAINING

For OUSL to go into Web-based teaching, a part of the required infrastructure is a trained teaching staff. Workshops have been offered by the authors and many university teachers from the entire system of national universities have participated. (Ceylon Daily News, 1998) We are perhaps at the same stage as when some years ago many shifted from typewriters to computers while others refused to learn. While many teachers at OUSL have been trained, others resist and prefer to continue with the printed material. Training programmes for instructors who wish to create their own Web-based courses continue to be offered by the IT Division under one of the authors on a periodic basis. Unfortunately, because of needed computer skills, few from the Faculty of Humanities and Social Sciences have participated. Special efforts clearly need to be made to involve that faculty with the largest proportion of students as at most universities. Clearly, a new generation of staff skilled in the use of computers is required. This process of cultivating such teachers has just begun. Keeping in mind:

a) that World Bank funding is now focused on teacher education,
b) that it will soon be necessary for even school teachers to teach computers to their students at least in the national schools which are geographically distributed all over the island and get the best of the students and resources and
c) that ultimately it is those who do their M.A.s who join the faculty after their Ph.D.s,

one of these authors, together with the Faculty of Education, developed a proposal for a soft loan from the World Bank for developing an M.A. programme in Teacher Education with a significant IT content. The proposal was funded in the middle of this year and the programme begins in January 2000. We expect that even existing members of the faculty will be involved and with those newly trained, some of these issues in the Faculty of Humanities and Social Sciences will be satisfactorily addressed.

To have more courses transformed to the Web, it will have to be a slow and gradual process of inculturation. Many argue that to speak of sophisticated networks when we, in the Third World, are struggling for simple things like photocopiers is absurd. However, our experience is that it is easier to get aid for fancy things that make good press than for routine consumables. We make the best with whatever we can get from wherever we can get it, even if it means begging for "aid". And indeed, if we can train good graduates, by whatever means, we will. Our experience is that students who get access to sophisticated technology are better motivated and are better trained.

FACULTY AND STUDENT REACTION

Once our courses were transformed to the Web, as in universities in the British system, they had to be approved by the university Senate, the highest authority on academic matters, before they could be offered. Although the entire venture began with a Senate mandate to the faculty to begin to develop course material for the Web, the overall initial reaction of the Senate was negative. The negative reaction was largely based on political fear in a system wracked by student unrest. Once it was recognised that students who own computers can study from home in a truly distant mode, while those who do not have their own machines have to come to the closest regional campus for using the computers there or be left out, there was fear that the student unions would react. There were also further fears that if there is a lightning hit or surge over the telephone lines (as is common) and the computer system components burn, error recovery can take two or more months in a system where purchase controls/processes are labyrinthine[1], and disrupt the course of study. The proposal was then amended to include every kind of technical problem that can occur and under each category of trouble how reversion to the traditional mode of teaching would occur. This is shown in Table 1. With strong support from the Dean of the Faculty of Natural Sciences, it was approved. The process took three months.

Student reaction to Web-based teaching has been extremely positive wherever the authors have tried it. It is also an opportunity for students to acquire specific computer skills that they see as making them very marketable. In particular, middle-class students have reacted very positively and are encouraged by the higher status they feel by participating in this project. Two serious problems that need addressing are a) students without the requisite computer skills enrolling out of eagerness to learn computing and then having difficulties with the subject being taught. This has been addressed through a preceding computer literacy course with no credit, but it still proves inadequate because of the large enrollments in such programmes, and b) computer-based studies, at least on first appearance, being a limitation with many women students. We believe that it is because computer skills are acquired less from classroom

Table 1: Problems foreseen and Corrective Measures Proposed to the Senate by the Instructor

	Methodology	Problems/Corrective measures
Enrollment	By personal advertisement and direct requests to students before and at registration to participate in the on-line course. This effort will be handled by me.	At least ten students will be required. If no students are found, the on-line offering will be deferred for the following year.
Course material	The material will be hosted on the OUSL web for off campus access. On Personal Web-server on LAN access from regional centres. CDs will also be given for use at home.	a) Failure of network: A local area network in the Director Regional Educational Services' lab can be used for simulating a network-like situation. b) Worst case: Can revert to printed course material.
Day-schools/ Tutor contact	By e-mail and responses through e-mail list. Courtesy accounts will be provided for those without accounts.	Breakdown of e-mail: Face-to-face contact as usual until the problem is rectified.
Assignments	Assigned by web and answers will be by e-mail and the use of attachments of Word documents.	Regular response by mail allowed for those who have difficulties with equations – Note learning to type set equations is part of the training.
Labs	A half as conventional at the Regional Centres. Web-material with home-based lab kits are being developed under National Science Foundation funding. A set of six experiments for doing at home is ready for the analytical chemistry course.	
Records of assignments/ tests/exams	Stored on hard disk of instructor's PC.	Can be printed if necessary.
Tests/Exams	By normal mode is proposed and envisaged. But I would like Senate authority to do these also on-line for students who can type if the e-mail assignment experiment is a success. This would involve the student sitting at a terminal under supervision. The idea is to decentralise exams to the Regional Centres if this works. A possibility is for the exam to be e-mailed to the centres where they do it under supervision. This will obviate the problems we have in transporting exams to all centres under tight controls.	A question bank of multiple choice questions from a random selection for each student and giving the marks immediately. Since eligibility is determined immediately, that is a popular alternative.

instruction than through peer interaction in computer labs going into the late hours of the night. In conservative societies, women cannot put in the required time outside the home.

These issues are being formally studied by the authors, but it is premature and outside the scope of this chapter to delve into them here.

CONCLUSIONS

Web-based education offers many advantages, especially in distance education, but demands costly infrastructure. Third World educators must create innovative arguments for funding. One such means is by creating an MIS with a decentralised architecture as done at OUSL.

ENDNOTES

[1] The process is of necessity labyrinthine not because Third World people are more corrupt but the temptations are much larger. For instance, a 15% cut on a PC purchase is a junior lecturer's monthly salary in Sri Lanka but only a restaurant meal for a family in the U.S.

REFERENCES

Ceylon Daily News, (1998). Dons meet to Discuss Teaching over the Web, 30 Nov., 3.

Hoberg, J. (1993). Can Computers Really Help Students Understand Electromagnetics? in Hoole (1993b).

Hoole, D. (1998b). Using the Web in Distance Education (Keynote address), *Proc. National IT Conference*, 5-7 June, 1998, Colombo: Computer Society of Sri Lanka.

Hoole, D. (1999) Chemistry Web Pages. [http://www.ou.ac.lk] April. *IEEE Spectrum*, 1998

Hoole, S.R.H. (1988). Teaching Electromagnetics Through Finite Elements; Part I: The Rationale. *Int. J. for Elect. Eng. Educ.*, 25, 33-49, Jan.

Hoole, S.R.H., (Guest Editor), 1993a, Special issue on "Computers and Computing in the Electrical Engineering Curriculum". *IEEE Trans. Educ.*, 36(1).

Hoole, S.R.H., (1993b). Special issue "Computational Electromagnetics in the Classroom." *IEEE Trans. Educ.*, 36 (2).

Hoole, S.R.H. (1998a). *The Ceylon Daily News*, (Op-ed Piece), IT, Computer Networks and Distance Education. Aug. 11, 15.

Rajapakse, P., Jayawardene, L., Cumaranatunge, G. and Hoole, S.R.H. (1997). Information Technology and what it can do for Sri Lanka, Annual Sessions of the Sri Lanka Association for the Advancement of Science, paper C11.

Vanderplaats, G.N. (1993). Teaching Design through Computation. In Hoole (1993a).

Chapter 7

Cognitive Effects
of Web Page Design

Louis H. Berry
University of Pittsburgh, USA

INTRODUCTION

The advent of Web-based instruction, which relies upon hypertext models of interaction and design, reemphasizes the need for a clear understanding of how learners process and encode information presented in Web sites intended for instructional purposes. The unique nature of Web page design, mandated by constraints in the technology which limit student interactivity, and yet which support divergent exploration, necessitates a deeper consideration of how learners interact with various Web site design factors. The purpose of this chapter will be to address the cognitive implications of those factors. This chapter will not focus on specific graphic layout and design criteria or visual display specifications that have been extensively covered in the research literature on computer screen design. The intent, rather, is to review and discuss the major theoretical and design issues impacting contemporary instructional Web page design. It is essential however, to understand the basis for much of the Web page design that occurs currently, and that stems from much of the earlier work in computer screen design.

History and Research in Screen Design

The history of computer screen design has been scattered across disciplines and has addressed questions of need rather than of cognition. The vast majority of early research studies addressed the perceptual aspects of how

Previously Published in *Instructional and Cognitive Impacts of Web-Based Education* edited by Beverly Abbey, Copyright © 2000, Idea Group Publishing.

users viewed and interacted with data on the screen (Galitz, 1989). In most cases, these studies were technology driven, that is to say, they were conducted to test out or validate new screen display technologies such as higher resolution monitors and the utility of pointing devices such as the mouse (Card, English & Burr, 1978; Lu, 1984; Buxton, 1985; Foley, Wallace, Victor & Chan, 1984). The end result of this work generally reflected an attempt to answer the question of "How can we most effectively display data on the screen given the current or newest technology?" (Heines, 1984).

Of particular significance, however, was the research conducted at the Xerox Palo Alto Research Center (PARC) which led to the innovation of the Graphical User Interface (GUI) (Smith, Irby, Kimball, Verplanck & Harslem, 1982; Herot, 1984) which has come to dominate computer interfaces.

Research in some of the parent technologies has also been applied to the field of screen design, particularly in the area of visual perception. In many of the early studies, the act of interacting with the computer screen was seen as almost solely being one of maximizing visual perception (Heines, 1984). Clarity of image and recognition of display elements were the primary variables investigated (Rubinstein & Hersh, 1984; Brown, 1988). Little consideration was given to how the viewer used the information that was presented, or to how it was encoded into memory. Some of this research was useful, particularly that which was done in the area of visual complexity (Dwyer, 1978; 1987). While these studies were focused on other types of media rather than computer screens, the findings have become important to the design of screen displays and interfaces.

In a similar way, research into the perception of printed copy has contributed significantly to our understanding of how text is perceived and interpreted on the computer screen (Gropper, 1991; Gillingham, 1988; Jonassen, 1982). This research has worked almost at cross-purposes, however, to inform us on computer text display. In one sense, a good deal of the text-based research has enabled designers to specify optimum text size, font, style, and layout, but it has also made it quite apparent that the computer screen differs substantially from hard copy in important aspects (Garner, 1990; Hartley, 1997), a fact that many Web page designers fail to recognize.

When the research in computer screen design is viewed from a historical perspective, it becomes readily apparent that little attention has been given to the cognitive effects of screen design and even less to the educational implications of such design. A review of the work done previously is a useful place to start.

The Cognitive Aspects of Screen Design

Those aspects of computer screen design which are of most interest to educators are related to the ways in which information displayed on the screen is perceived and encoded into memory. Typically the processing of information has been viewed, from the perspective of cognitive theory, as falling into two general areas. The first of these is the perception and pattern recognition of information. The second is the processing and encoding of information into long-term memory. Earlier work in screen design was strongly oriented around the former, while the more recent studies focus on the latter. Hannafin and Hooper (1989) have defined screen design as "... the purposeful organization of presentation stimuli in order to influence how students process information" which is much more related to the semantic aspects of screen design than to solely perceptual aspects.

It has been suggested by Norman, Weldon, and Schneiderman (1986) that computer information is organized in three different "modes of representation". These include the machine layout which describes the internal data representation in the computer, the surface layout which describes the physical organization of objects on the screen, and the cognitive layout which describes the mental model of the information developed by the user. Of these, the latter two are of most interest to screen or page designers because they represent the two aspects of screen design which impact on students. The surface layout is analogous to the traditional view of screen design which specifies the nature and layout of objects on the screen as well as the visual and perceptual characteristics of them. The cognitive layout is analogous to the encoding and representation of knowledge in memory.

Perceptual aspects. Screen layout and the relative salience of visual elements constitute the most relevant studies in screen design. The focus of researchers, particularly in education, is the role of such elements in gaining and maintaining the user's attention (Rieber, 1994). Other studies address the importance of directing the user's attention to the more relevant aspects of the display while de-emphasizing the less relevant attributes (Hannafin & Hooper, 1989; Grabinger, 1989). The role of color and type characteristics has also been studied in the context of attention and in terms of text readability or recognition (Galitz, 1989).

It is important to recognize that the perceptual aspects of screen design, while of concern to designers, is not the only component that Web page designers should consider. The task of organizing the perceived information into coherent and encodable units is of equal importance, as well as promoting the building of mental models of the knowledge by the user. These may be considered the semantic aspects of screen or Web page design.

Semantic aspects. Research directed specifically at the encoding and retrieval of screen information has been less frequent, but in those instances where researchers proposed theory, it was of significant impact.

The ROPES Model, introduced by Hannafin and Hooper (1989), is an approach describing the various activities associated with the learner's interaction with a computer-based instructional presentation. The model addresses both the perceptual/attentional and semantic encoding aspects of screen design and represents one of the first attempts to provide guidelines for screen design that move beyond purely graphical specifications.

Another cognitively-based orientation is the Syntactic-Semantic Model of Objects and Actions (SSOA) described by Schneiderman (1992). In this model, Schneiderman discusses the different components of processing which occur as the user interacts with the computer. Syntactic knowledge deals with the device-dependent details of the computer and represents the most basic of cognitive processing. Semantic knowledge in Schneiderman's view consists of two parts, that which he refers to as computer concepts or knowledge about the interface and how it is accessed, and the second part, task concepts which he suggests relate to the task to be completed. It is this part of the processing that we can interpret as the domain knowledge that is the object of instruction. In the Syntactic-Semantic Model, Schneiderman recognizes that different types of cognitive processing and learning activities are related to the different concepts or tasks, an important point when determining how the user should be interacting with a given screen or Web page.

THE NATURE OF WEB-BASED INSTRUCTION

The term Web-based instruction has been used to describe a number of informational uses of the World Wide Web. Among these are the use of Web sites as purely deliverers of information. In these instances the Web site is not designed with any particular educational intent other than making specific information available to the visitor. In the case of an informational site, there is no intended objective of promoting learning, but rather a "use the informa-tion if you want" reasoning. An educational Web site, on the other hand, has generalized educational goals or objectives much like public or educational television. In this case the intent is that the visitor will gain some more specific knowledge, but no attempt is made to assess whether or not learning occurred. In other, instructional sites, specific instructional objectives are developed and the act of instruction is more structured and the degree of learning is carefully assessed. Instructional sites such as these are used in many on-line courses today.

Web-based instruction can be all of the above, but in every case, the means whereby the user interacts with the Web site is very different from more traditional forms of informational, educational, or instructional media.

The differences between Web-based media and the familiar types of media fall into three distinct areas: technological differences, pedagogical differences, and variations in the way users interact with the information or instruction.

Technology

The technology of the Web site is a strong determiner of how users will interact with the site. The World Wide Web is based on a hypertext model of interaction which emphasizes a search and browse method of access. The use of clickable buttons, images or hot text reduces the user's behavior to rapid hand movements which occur only slightly behind the visual scanning of text and images. The fact that the decisions to select and click can be made quickly minimize the reliance on detailed reading of text or even interpretation of pictures. A consequence of this behavior is the reliance of the user on small bytes of information which can be scanned, read, and acted upon quickly and often without reflection. Additionally, the knowledge that the site can be revisited encourages even more cursory browsing behavior.

Pedagogy

Web-based instruction is very different from traditional instruction in that knowledge is often contextualized in an effort to make it real or, more significantly, more interesting and attention maintaining. While contextualized learning is important, it does not constitute the majority of instructional strategies that can or should be employed to promote learning.

A second pedagogical criticism leveled at Web-based instruction is that much of the content delivered to the screen is of questionable validity or depth. While the question of validity is probably best debated in other forums, the matter of depth of knowledge is significant. Knowledge representation on the Web has been described by one colleague as being "like Swiss cheese, broad, thin and full of holes."

The last pedagogical difference in Web-based instruction is inherent in the hypertext environment, particularly when encountered by novice users or learners with unsophisticated search strategies. In these cases, the visitor may form erroneous conceptualizations of the content presented and may even become disoriented, experiencing the state of "hyperchaos" described by Marchionini (1988).

Interactivity
While one might expect browsing on the World Wide Web to be a highly interactive experience, this is true only to the degree that the visitor can select and access a particular site. As the technology stands today, limited two-way interaction can be achieved between the instructor and the student. In instances of on-line courses, use is frequently made of e-mail, drop boxes, threaded discussions and occasionally chat rooms, but for the most part these are rare in most informational or educational sites.

The limited two-way interactivity results in consequent limits on instructor guidance and coaching. The ability to carry on a dialogue with the instructor while interacting with the information presented in the site is simply not possible on today's Web.

Focus of this Chapter
The characteristics of the World Wide Web described above make it a very unique instructional medium with great potential. On the other hand, however, it is essential that these characteristics are understood and factored into any design of computer screens or Web sites.

While much of the research and theory related to screen design is widely known and used, it is not always applicable to the design of Web sites, and it often does not inform us as to how Web-based information is most effectively processed by learners. This chapter will focus on selected cognitive factors which appear to be significant areas for research and application in the design and development of educational Web pages and sites.

COGNITIVE FACTORS IN WEB PAGE DESIGN
The primary intent of this chapter is to identify and discuss the major theoretical and design issues impacting contemporary instructional Web page design. These can be organized into two areas: those which relate to the physical design of the message and presentation, and those which are derived from how the learner interacts with the pages or site.

The selection of relevant factors was determined by a review of current research literature as well as other popular and professional literature related to Web page design and utilization. Of particular value is the Web site maintained by Jakob Nielson (1997) at http://www.usit.com/alertbox/. It is important to note that many of the factors have not been identified in the education literature, but rather from sources in computer and information science, graphic design, and psychology.

Message Design Factors

The first of these, message design as defined by Grabowski (1995) consists of two components: message design for instruction and message design for learning, both of which are critical to the integration of knowledge into an individual's cognitive structure. Message design for instruction is defined as "...planning for the manipulation of the physical form of the message" (Grabowski, 1995). This definition fits much of what has been termed screen design. Concern has been concentrated on how to graphically lay out the screen for maximum perceptual efficiency. The definition of message design for learning according to Grabowski (1995) "...involves the planning for the inductive composition of the message which induces the learner to meaningfully relate the target information to the old." It is precisely this view that reflects the more contemporary approach to screen and Web page design.

Three significant areas of research have become important to the design of instructional Web sites, particularly with regard to the cognitive aspects of the process. These evolved from either screen design research or the "parent" technology, visual learning research. These seem to be relevant specifically to the design of Web pages or sites because they deal with some of the physical attributes of site design, but are much more closely related to how Web visitors process the information obtained from the Web site. The three most frequently referenced areas include text presentation and text density, the implications of windowing environments, and visual complexity.

Text presentation and density. The first of these factors addresses text characteristics, text formatting and text density on the screen as well as the screen density of text. In each of these instances, the early research was drawn from typography, under the assumption that text on the computer screen was identical to text on the printed page. Research (Hartley, 1997) has refuted this assumption however. Recent research into the presentation of text in Web pages further suggests that Web page displays may differ substantially from other computer displays such as those employed in computer-based instruction (Nielson, 1997).

The earliest research on computer screen design was primarily related to typographical characteristics such as font size, type, style, and color and frequently was reflective of the sophistication of the computer display technology in existence at the time, rather than associated with a *pure* standard related to the viewer's visual perception (Grabinger, 1989). Secondly, these principles were often simply a reflection of earlier research in print typography. While useful guidelines can and have been derived from such research, it should probably be considered an evolving science, dependent on the resolution and display characteristics of the technology at any given time.

Of greater significance to educational designers are the concepts of text density and screen density. Of particular significance is the work conducted by Morrison, Ross, and O'Dell (1988) and Ross, Morrison, and O'Dell (1988). These researchers have defined two variables which relate to the organization of textual information on the screen both quantitatively and qualitatively. The first construct is termed text density and represents the richness of contextual detail presented on the screen. The second is the concept of screen density which refers to the amount of expository information presented on an individual screen.

Research in the area of text density has suggested that low density text is a viable technique for presentation of lengthy text. This is congruent with the suggestions of Nielson (1997) that text should be presented on Web pages in short chunks and should be edited to simplify content.

Conversely, research on screen density has suggested that users prefer higher density screens as opposed to those with quantitatively less information. This may, however, merely reflect the fact that most users prefer to move quickly through text, and accessing a greater number of screens is more work for the amount of text obtained.

A number of contemporary writers have suggested that the browsing experience is unique in terms of reading text (Nielson, 1997; Lynch and Horton, 1999) and that users may not even read text, but rather skim it, looking for comprehensible key words and shoulder headings. Such a process may indeed be used by the casual browser, but this may not be the case when users are attempting to gain more detailed content. The sophistication of the user and their intentions may be the most critical factor dictating how text should be displayed. The degree of domain knowledge the user brings to the site visit has been described by Dillon and Zhu (1997) as being critical to the amount of textual and contextual detail preferred. Those users with a high degree of domain knowledge will prefer higher density information screens, while those users with little domain knowledge will prefer less information and more explanations (Dillon, 1996).

Clear and concise organization is important in any instructional transaction, but the current research implies that Web-based materials could profit from particularly wel- edited textual material, supported by frequent and meaningful headings and other organizational pointers. Research is less clear with regard to the prose style most effective, although concise, newspaper styles appear to be indicated (Lynch and Horton, 1999).

Windowing environments. The second set of factors related to the design of the message is one of organization of information on the screen. The cognitive layout theory proposed by Norman, Weldon and Schneiderman (1986) was formulated to describe how information can be represented in different ways on the screen. This was not a new concept, because as early as 1984, Heines described functional areas on the screen. These areas represented the consistent dedication of specific screen areas to standard informational tasks. This concept is similar to the notion of windows and windowing environments. Windows are defined by Card, Pavel and Farrell (1984) as "areas of the screen which provide a particular view of some data object in the computer". Windowing environments therefore consist of the windows, palettes, icons, buttons and tools associated with a particular interface which enable the user to interact with and potentially reorganize the various information sources available. The use of these objects has been a standard feature of computer screen design since the advent of the Graphical User Interface and exists in Web pages in the form of frames or even individual pages themselves. Of particular importance is the concept, noted by Norman, Weldon and Schneiderman (1986), that the cognitive layout is a complex representation of the elements and the relationship between elements that appear on the screen.

All windows are used to represent or display information and may be used to expand the amount of information available to working memory. In some cases, this information is presented directly on the screen, while in others, the information is implied or understood to exist in some other, non-visible, location in the memory of the computer.

Windows can be defined by form, function, or whether they are explicit or implicit. The physical forms of windows relate to their spatial design and layout on the screen. The functions of windows refer to the information representation inherent in the window or intended by the designer. The degree to which the window is explicit or implicit is determined by the user's ability or need to physically view the contents of the window, i.e. computer clipboards are implicit whereas work areas or documents are explicit.

Windows serve a variety of functions, many of which are noted by Jonassen (1989). Among those described are: *navigational*, in which windows serve as directional or browsing aids; *organizational*, in which the windows help the user spatially relate or organize information; *explanatory*, which help the user by providing guidance or substantive coaching; and *metaphorical* which employ a metaphor to represent or symbolize an operation or informational concept. In each of these functions, the window(s) aid the user in developing a mental image or organization of the knowledge being presented. Furthermore, windows can be placed under designer control to represent or model some previously determined organization, or they may be placed under user control, in which case the window can be reorganized to conform to a specific user's own mental model of that information.

In hypertext environments such as the World Wide Web, multiple pages and frames within a single page serve the same function, implying to the user that different information exists in different locations in the site or on the Web. In this manner, the user's personal representation of the organization of available knowledge forms an idiosyncratic mental model of the information which is used by the visitor to aid in processing and encoding knowledge into long-term memory, as well as holding that knowledge in working memory for subsequent use. This interpretation of the information by the user can function as a powerful cognitive tool which may be used to facilitate deeper processing of new knowledge.

Windows can also serve a negative function if they are used in a disorganized or casual manner. Research (Gaylin, 1986) has shown that the display of too many windows may be distracting, especially for inexperienced users, and suggests an average of 3.7 open windows at any time.

Visual complexity. The popular literature on Web page and site design consistently suggests that the World Wide Web is essentially a visual medium and that designers should rely primarily on visual displays to communicate their message, at the same time de-emphasizing lengthy text passages. The classic literature in instructional message design is abundant with supporting research to the effect that visuals are equivalent and frequently superior to text in communication effectiveness. Early theoretic orientations (Dale, 1946; Morris, 1946; Gibson, 1954) have all suggested that the more complex or realistic an instructional visual is, the more effectively it will facilitate learning, presumably because it will provide more meaningful cues which assist in encoding.

Other classic research and theory originally proposed by Travers (1964) contradicted this orientation in suggesting that the human information processing system is of limited capacity and, in times of increased information transmission, some information may block the processing of other, more relevant information. This information overload position has received substantial empirical support, but the debate has largely been unresolved (Dwyer, 1978; Dwyer, 1987). The fact remains that most computer applications rely heavily upon visual-based information, which not only appeals to many users, but seems to provide a good deal of the primary information which is communicated.

The extent to which complex or realistic visuals are incorporated into Web pages and sites seems to be much more a function of the image download time for larger, more complex (bit depth wise) files. This may for the present make the decision to rely strongly on realistic visuals more of a technical rather than a design decision.

The fact remains, however, that learners appear to differ with regard to the amount of time and cognitive effort required to read a visual (Dwyer, 1978). Research has shown that visual details are processed at successive levels with more basic information related to form and location being analyzed first, and more contextual elements such as color and tonality being processed later and possibly in different ways (Berry, 1990). Without engaging in a detailed discussion of the complicated field of visual processing, it can be said with reasonable assurance that more complex, realistic and detailed visuals require a correspondingly greater processing time to be effectively analyzed (Dwyer, 1978).

Web sites and pages are no exception to this rule, and the act of browsing, which may entail more cursory examination of visual materials, may increase the discrepancy between the amount of information presented and the amount that can be effectively processed. The nature of Web-based instruction may represent an important instance of the high information transmission described by Travers in 1964.

The potential of information overload due to the combination of browsing forms of interaction and complex visualization may result in imperfect or incomplete processing by students, particularly those who have not developed an adequate mental map or structure of the knowledge being presented (Norman, 1983). Visuals which have not been related to the accompanying text may not be understood and may actually work to confuse or disorient the learner. Research has not addressed this issue as yet. One research-based guideline which may be useful is to relate visual material to textual material in a meaningful manner. This will require careful organization of the information on the page as well as the use of additional cueing devices such as arrows, highlighting and spacing to direct the user's attention. Other actions which slow down the student's interaction with the visual materials can provide more processing time and make distinctive aspects of the visual salient for more detailed encoding. The incorporation of visual materials in Web sites is essential, but requires additional planning on the part of the designer to ensure that the materials are fully processed and furthermore that they do not represent an element of confusion in interpreting the site information.

Learner Factors

There are those factors which are more related to how the Web site visitor or learner views or perceives the information presented rather than to how the site designer has organized the site. These aspects of the interaction process that occurs between the student and the site may be related to individual differences across students or they may be related to the unique ways in which the student interacts with Web-based materials. To some extent, this is a function of the materials and how they are designed, but in a larger sense, these aspects are tied to the perception by the user of how the information should be approached. Student perceptions may not be accurate however and may result in misconceived strategies for gaining and processing target information. It is these concerns that are discussed in this section.

Browser mentality. The very nature of hypertext, as it has been described over the years, is one of nonlinear, searching activity (Lynch and Horton, 1999), and the technology has encouraged this type of behavior with the familiar point-and-click graphical interface. Decisions are made based more on recognition of options or paths rather than on recalled information or choices. All of this encourages a quick decision-making type of interaction augmented by an increased anticipation of the next choice or option. Researchers have not addressed these types of behaviors in any but the most mechanical ways. Substantial research has focused on such variables as menu search times, data selection and entry, and scanning times for screen targets (Galitz, 1989; Tombaugh, Lickorish and Wright, 1987). Few if any of these have, however, been related to the intentional behavior exhibited by learners as they browse Web sites.

Only recently have researchers noted that hypertext browsing engenders a different type of instructional strategy or intent (Campbell, 1998). This phenomenon may be termed browser mentality because it reflects the intentional strategies employed by individuals in browsing or searching the Web. It is described by such characteristics as skimming rather than reading text

(Nielson, 1995), rapid visual search and selection of buttons or hyperlinks, and an undefinable impatience to move on to the next page. Virtually no empirical support for these descriptions is yet available, but all one needs to do is spend an hour or two observing students interacting with the Web to recognize the effects. The technology of hypertext and the Web is based upon and obviously supports this type of interaction. This does not mean to say that interaction of this type is bad or that it is inherently counterproductive to learning, particularly when creative and divergent thinking is desirable. The difficulty arises when this form of interactivity is applied to instructional settings or content where deeper interaction with the content is desired or required. The user who simply skims over the contents of a Web page may identify terms and general concepts, but the conceptual base and elaborative aspects of the material will be lost (Nelson, 1991).

Cursory browsing may also have significant implications for the processing of information in that students cannot (or do not) take the time to reflect on the content presented. In so doing, less effort is directed at employing particular cognitive or generative strategies which have been shown to be effective in encoding new knowledge (Jonassen, 1988; Weinstein and Mayer, 1985; Rigney, 1978).

These effects will be compounded if designers adhere to the text criteria suggested by contemporary design guides (Lynch and Horton, 1999;) or include text with a low degree of text density as described earlier in this chapter (Morrison, Ross, O'Dell, Schultz and Higginbotham-Wheat, 1989).

Navigation and wayfinding. One of the earliest identified effects of hypertext navigation, user disorientation, was described by Marchionini (1988). He attributes this effect to the large amount of relatively unstructured information inherent in most hypertext environments as well as to the corresponding high level of user control provided by the system. The two of these characteristics can work together to increase the amount of cognitive load imposed on the user, resulting in what Marchionini refers to as "hyperchaos". Those Web sites that provide a rich hypermedia environment do so at the risk of overloading the novice user with navigation and informational choices that can easily overwhelm or confuse the student (Turoff, 1995).

Research has been as supportive of hypermedia environments as one might expect. Studies reported by Nelson and Joyner (1990) and Jonassen and Wang (1991) favored linear presentation of material over hypermedia formats because they provided less disorientation and provided more structure.

Wayfinding is a term that has emerged from the research on how individuals traverse a hypertext environment. As the term implies, wayfinding means the ability to move through a physical or (in terms of hypertext) information environment without becoming lost (Jones, 1988). Effective wayfinding is dependent not only on knowing where one is going, but also on knowing where one has been, which suggests that not only should designers provide consistent and intuitive navigation tools, but also clearly defined maps of the information space that constitutes any instructional Web site.

Wayfinding is strongly dependent upon the learner's cognitive skills, particularly those that relate to spatial orientation. Spatial visualization ability was studied by Alonzo and Norman (1998) to determine the degree to which one's ability to mentally manipulate spatial information is related to the ability to navigate through an information space. They found that by increasing interface apparency through graphical cues or map structures, all users could be aided, but particularly those with lower spatial abilities.

Cognitive overhead. The concept of cognitive overhead has been identified by researchers for a number of years, but was first addressed in terms of complex cognitive functioning by Sweller (1988) and Sweller and Chandler (1991). Cognitive load refers to the demands placed on the learner's working memory during instruction. In the case of computer-based instruction or Web-based instruction, the term covers both the mental processing necessary to access and interpret the screens, icons and objects, and the cognitive processing devoted to processing the actual content of the instruction. The goal is, of course, to reduce the amount of processing directed at interacting with the system and maximizing the processing of knowledge being taught.

Cognitive load is an ever-present factor in the design of computer screens and interfaces because each of the screen elements or objects must be interpreted by the user and consequently occupies some of the user's mental energy. A complex or unconventionally designed screen which uses different fonts, objects, navigation tools, and layout patterns will generally have a high procedural or functional cognitive load because each component will need to be perceived and interpreted by the learner. A screen which uses standard conventions in text, graphics, navigation, and layout will be more easily interpreted and consequently have a much lower cognitive load. One of the reasons many screen and interface designers have, for years, advocated the use of consistent screen design conventions is to reduce the cognitive load of interacting with the screen (Heines, 1984; Schneiderman, 1997).

Web sites and pages frequently (and unfortunately) are haphazard design attempts which combine a vast number of different and often incomprehensible screen elements in a format which is awkward and difficult to follow. In those instances where the design is planned, the intent is usually to make the site bright and flashy in an effort to gain and hold the attention of the learner. In most of these sites the design elements are difficult to interpret easily and consequently make high demands on the learner's cognitive resources (Tauscher and Greenberg, 1997).

It is difficult to train learners to devote less cognitive effort toward processing system related activities, but it is relatively simple to design Web sites that display information in a consistent and transparent manner. Transparency describes Web sites or computer pages that require minimal cognitive resources to perform system-level tasks. The term transparency means that the functions of relating to the system requirements are only peripherally obvious to the user and consequently involve minimal cognitive effort (Berry & Olson, 1992). This can be achieved through the use of accepted symbolic standards for screen elements and through explicit labels or icons which describe choices or tasks. The key aspect of transparency is that the user should not have to think about his or her actions, but simply respond in an intuitive manner.

FUTURE DIRECTIONS IN WEB PAGE DESIGN

Based upon this review of the most frequently noted cognitive factors in screen and Web page design, a number of speculative recommendations can be made regarding the future directions for research and theory building. Of course, many of these factors may change in relative importance or interest depending upon changes and innovations in the technology.

Further research is called for in regard to the development of mental models of knowledge that can be generated via Web site or page structure. Some researchers have even suggested that training in creating such models may increase the limits of memory and processing (Mayhew, 1992).

Other researchers have described complex symbol systems (such as windowing environments) that are learned, over time, by users and may indeed be useful in modeling cognitive processes (Salomon and Gardner, 1986). Research attention should focus on the cognitive effects of these more complex page design features.

The phenomenon of browser mentality needs to be studied more deeply, not only to understand how users interact with and extract information from hypertext/hypermedia systems such as instructional Web sites, but also to assess any transfer of the same effects to other study and learning situations.

If, indeed, this type of browsing behavior is learned and pervades other instructional activities, then it will have significant implications for the design of many different instructional materials and experiences.

Researchers are only beginning to look at how screen design criteria affect deeper processing of knowledge, although some fairly comprehensive guides have been published to aid designers. The question of greatest interest here, however, is whether this knowledge can transfer to the medium of Web page and site design given the unique nature of the medium. In the highly user-controlled environment of Web-based instruction students may not be inter-acting with the same screen elements or in the same manner as they have traditionally done in CBI applications. In a similar way, the newer technolo-gies of Web-based instruction may exert different priorities or capabilities on users which could influence the usability of the instruction.

As the technologies evolve, newer and different interfaces emerge. The means of navigating through information spaces which employ these inter-faces tend to change also and this will necessitate an alteration in how we view the act of navigation. To reduce the cognitive load imposed by navigating and interacting with Web-based instruction, we need to understand how to maximize the degree of intuitiveness that is inherent in the materials.

Additionally, research must address the need for effective wayfinding strategies that orient any user at any time, even in complex information environments. We also need to explore, in much greater depth, the role of user cognitive variables such as spatial ability and cognitive style in terms of how they relate to wayfinding.

CONCLUSION

This chapter has addressed only some, although perhaps some of the most significant cognitive aspects or problems related to the design of pages and sites for Web-based instruction. The list of topics is certainly not exhaustive, nor will it remain exclusive for long, because as the technology changes, there will be a corresponding change in design capabilities and instructional needs. Web-based instruction is only beginning to show its potential and researchers are just becoming aware of the problems or benefits of the new medium. It has been said that designers tend to view new technologies in terms of older, yet similar technologies, particularly with regard to design methods (Rieber and Welliver, 1989). A substantial block of knowledge exists with respect to computer screen design, but it is yet unclear just how valid much of this will be in the design of Web-based materials and particularly those intended for instruction. The World Wide Web is an exciting and powerful tool for learning, but only if we know how to make it effective.

REFERENCES

Alonzo, D. L. & Norman, K.L. (1998). Apparency of contingencies in single panel and pull-down menus. *International Journal of Human Computer Studies*, 49, 59-78.

Berry, L. H. (1990). Effects of hemispheric laterality on color information processing, *Perceptual and Motor Skills*, 71.

Berry, L. H. & Olson, J. S. (1992). *Hypermedia: Cognitive factors in screen design*. Paper presented at the annual convention of the Association for Educational Communications and Technology, Washington, DC: February, 1992.

Brown, C. M. (1988). *Human-computer interface design guidelines*. Norwood, NJ: Ablex.

Buxton, W. (1985). There's more to interaction than meets the eye: Some issues in manual input. In Norman, D. A., & Draper, S. W. (Eds.). *User centered system design: New perspectives on human-computer interaction*. Hillsdale, NJ: Lawrence Erlbaum Associates.

Campbell, R. (1998). HyperMinds for hypertimes: The demise of rational, logical thought? *Educational Technology*, January-February, 24-31.

Card, S. K., English, W. K., & Burr, B. J. (1978). Evaluation of mouse, rate-controlled isometric joystick, step keys, and task keys for text selection on a CRT. *Ergonomics*, 21(8), 601-613.

Card, S. K., Pavel, M. & Farrell, J. E. (1984). Window-based computer dialogues. In B. Shakel (Ed.), *Human-computer interaction - INTERACT R84*, Amsterdam, NL: Elsevier.

Dillon A. (1996). Myths, misconceptions and an alternative perspective on information usage and the electronic medium. In J. Rouet et al. (Eds.), *Hypertext and cognition* (pp. 25-42). Mahwah, NJ: Lawrence Erlbaum Publishers.

Dillon, A & Zhu, E. (1997). Designing Web-based instruction: A human-computer interaction perspective. In B. H. Khan (Ed.)*Web-based instruction*. (pp. 221-224) Englewood Cliffs, NJ: Educational Technology Publications.

Dwyer, F. M. (1978). *Strategies for improving visual learning*. State College, PA: Learning Services.

Dwyer, F. M. (1987). *Enhancing visualized instruction; Recommendations for practitioners*. State College, PA: Learning Services.

Foley, J. D., Wallace, V. L., & Chan, P. (1984). The human factors of computer graphics interaction techniques. *IEEE Computer Graphics and Applications*, 4(11), 13-48.

Galitz, W. O. (1989). *Handbook of screen format design* (Third Edition). Wellesley, MA: Q.E.D. Information Sciences

Garner, K. H. (1990). 20 rules for arranging text on a screen. *CBT Directions*, 3(5), 13-17.

Gaylin, K. B. (1986). How are windows used? Some notes on creating an empirically-based windowing benchmark task. *Proceedings CHI T86 Human Factors in Computing Systems*, (pp. 96-100).

Gillingham, M. G. (1988). Text in computer-based instruction: What the research says. *Journal of Computer Based Instruction*, 15(1), 1-6.

Grabinger, R. S. (1989). Screen layout design: Research into the overall appearance of the screen. *Computers in Human Behavior*, 5, 175-183.

Grabowski, B. L. (1995). Message design: Issues and trends. In G. J. Anglin (Ed.) *Instructional technology: Past, present, and future* (pp. 222-232). Englewood, CO: Libraries Unlimited.

Gropper, G. L. (1991). *Text displays: Analysis and systematic design.* Englewood Cliffs, NJ: Educational Technology.

Hannafin, M. J., & Hooper, S. (1989). An integrated framework for CBI screen design and layout. *Computers in Human Behavior*, 5, 155-165.

Hartley, J. (1987). Designing electronic text: The role of print-based research. *Educational Communication and Technology Journal*, 35(1), 3-17

Heines, J. M. (1984). *Screen design strategies for computer-assisted instruction.* Bedford, MA: Digital Press.

Herot, C. F. (1984). Graphical user interfaces. In Y. Vassiliou (Ed.), Human factors and interactive computer systems (chap. 4). *Proceedings of the NYU Symposium on User Interfaces*, New York, May 1982. Norwood, NJ: Ablex.

Jonassen, D. H. (1988). Integrating learning strategies into courseware to facilitate deeper processing. In D. H. Jonassen (Ed.) *Instructional designs for microcomputer courseware.* Hillsdale, NJ: Lawrence Erlbaum Associates, Publishers.

Jonassen, D. H. (1989). Functions, applications, and design guidelines for multiple window environments. *Computers in Human Behavior*, 5, 183-194.

Jonassen, D. H. & Wang, S. (1991, February). *Conveying structural knowledge in hypertext knowledge bases.* Paper presented at the annual meeting of the Association for Educational Communications and Technology, Orlando, FL.

Jones, M. K. (1989). *Human-computer interaction: A design guide.* Englewood Cliffs, NJ: Educational Technology Publications.

Lynch, P. J. & Horton, S. (1999). *Web style guide.* New Haven, CT: Yale University Press.

Marchionini, G. (1988). Hypermedia and learning: Freedom and chaos. *Educational Technology,* November, 8-12.

Mayhew, D. (1992). *Principles and guidelines in software user interface design.* Englewood Cliffs, NJ: Prentice-Hall.

Morrison, G. R., Ross, S. M., & O'Dell, J. K. (1988). Text density level as a design variable in instructional displays. *Educational Communications and Technology Journal,* 36, 103-115.

Morrison, G. R., Ross, S. M., O'Dell, J. K., Schultz, C. W. & Higginbotham-wheat, N. (1989). *Computers in Human Behavior,* 5, 167-173.

Nelson, W. A. & Joyner, O. J. (1990, February). *Effects of document complexity and organization on learning from hypertext.* Paper presented at the annual meeting of the Eastern Educational Research Association, Clearwater, Fl.

Nielson, J. (1997). *Alertbox: Jakob NielsonUs column on Web usability.* Internet. Available: http://www.usit.com/alertbox/.

Norman, D. A. (1983). Some observations on mental models. In D. Gentner & A. Stevens (Eds.), *Mental models.* Hillsdale, NJ: Lawrence Erlbaum Associates.

Norman, K. L., Weldon, L. J. & Shneiderman, B. (1986). Cognitive layouts of windows and multiple screens for user interfaces. *International Journal of Man-Machine Studies,* 25, 229-248.

Rieber, L. P. (1994). *Computers, graphics, and learning.* Dubuque, IA: Wm. C. Brown.

Rieber, L. P. & Welliver. P. W. (1989). Infusing educational technology into mainstream educational computing. *International Journal of Instructional Media,* 16(1), 21-32.

Rigney, J. (1978). Learning strategies: A theoretical perspective. In H. F. O'Neil (Ed.), *Learning strategies.* New York, NY: Academic Press.

Ross, S. M., Morrison. G. R., & O'Dell, J. K. (1988). Obtaining more out of less text in CBI: Effects of varied text density levels as a function of learner characteristics and control strategy. *Educational Communications and Technology Journal,* 36, 131-142.

Rubinstein, R. & Hersh, H. (1984). *The human factor: Designing computer systems for people.* Burlington, MA: Digital Press.

Salomon, G. & Gardner, H. (January, 1986). The computer as educator: Lessons from television research. *Educational Researcher,* 13-19.

Shneiderman, B. (1992). *Designing the user interface: Strategies for effective human-computer interaction*. Reading, MA: Addison-Wesley Publishing Company.

Schneiderman, B. (1997). *Designing the user interface: Strategies for effective human-computer interaction* (Third edition). Reading, MA: Addison-Wesley.

Smith, D. C., Irby, C., Kimball, R., Verplank, B. & Harslem, E. (1982, April). Design the star user interface. *Byte*, 242-282.

Sweller, J. (1988). Cognitive load during problem solving: Effects on learning. *Cognitive Science*, 12, 257-285.

Sweller, J. & Chandler, P. (1991). Evidence for cognitive load theory. *Cognition and Instruction*, 8(4), 351-362.

Tauscher, L., & Greenberg, S. (1997). How people revisit Web pages: empirical findings and implications for the design of history systems. *International Journal of Human-Computer Studies*, 47, 97-137.

Tombaugh, J., Lickorish, A., & Wright, P. (1987). Multi-window displays for readers of length texts. *International Journal of Man-Machine Studies*, 26, 597-615.

Travers, R. M. W. (1964). The transmission of information to human receivers. *Educational Psychologist*, 2, 1-5.

Turoff, M. (1995). *Designing a virtual classroom*. International conference on computer assisted instruction. National Chiao Tung University, Hsinchu, Taiwan (http://www.njit.edu/njIT/Department/CCCC/VC/Papers/Design.html).

Weinstein, C. E., & Mayer, R. E. (1985). The teaching of learning strategies. In M. C. Wittrock (Ed.), *Handbook of research on teaching* (3rd Ed.), New York, NY: Macmillan.

Chapter 8

Distance Education in the Online World: Implications for Higher Education

Stewart Marshall
Central Queensland University, Australia

Shirley Gregor
Australian National University, Australia

In this chapter, the authors identify forces leading to change in industries in the online world, including increasing global competition, increasingly powerful consumers and rapid changes in technology. In the higher education industry, outcomes are evolving, but include the formation of alliances, outsourcing and re-engineering of systems and work practices. The communication and information technologies that created the online world also link lecturers, tutors, and teaching resources to create the possibility of networked education. The authors outline a "glocal" networked education paradigm that separates out global and local resource development and global and local learning facilitation. By embracing this separation, it is possible to develop ways of working that allow the creation of a flexible model of education delivery that is scalable and hence globally competitive. In this model, the work of the university academic is changed considerably. The functions traditionally performed by a single university academic are differentiated and are performed by a network of learning facilitators. In this scenario, university academics may find themselves responsible for the learning of hundreds of students, but they may never find themselves face-to-face with a single student.

Previously Published in *The Design and Management of Effective Distance Learning Programs* edited by Richard Discenza and Karen Schenk, Copyright © 2002, Idea Group Publishing.

INTRODUCTION

As the world moves online, pressure increases on industries and organizations to change the way they do business. According to Turban, McLean and Wetherbe (1999), pressures acting on industries and organizations result from: the market, technology, and society. *Market pressures* include global competition and consumers who are becoming more demanding; *technological pressures* include the use of e-commerce to lower the costs of production and transaction costs; and *societal pressures* include government regulations and economic conditions (for example, through the use of subsidies, tax policies, and import/export regulations).

The higher education industry and universities are subject to the same pressures as other industries and organizations in the online world. For example, in Australia, enrollment of foreign students was the country's eighth largest export earner during 1997/8 earning A$3.1 billion [the larger ones being: coal (A$9.5b), tourism (A$8.0b), transport (A$6.7b), gold (A$6.2b), iron (A$3.7b), wheat (A$3.6b) and aluminium (A$3.2) (AVCC, 2000)]. Because of the Internet, Australian universities must now *compete* with universities from other countries offering online programs to those students in their own countries. So universities must change the way they do business.

> *Those institutions that can step up to this process of change will thrive. Those that bury their heads in the sand, that rigidly defend the status quo - or even worse - some idyllic vision of a past that never existed, are at very great risk. ...The real question is not whether higher education will be transformed but rather how and by whom?*
>
> (Duderstadt, 1999, p.1)

To understand how universities need to be transformed, it is necessary to look at the impact of distance education in the online world on higher education organizational structures and work groups, including organizational roles, workgroup dynamics, and communication. It is also necessary to examine which structures and processes are needed to allow a university to exist and prosper in an age of globalization and rapid changes in the information technology underlying remote education and work. This chapter tackles these issues using a model based on Giddens' (1977) theory of structuration in which process (activity) and structure are reciprocally constitutive, and the application of this theory to information technology by Orlikowski and Robey (1991). Central to this model is the view that change is not solely "technology led" or solely "organizational/ agency driven." Instead, change arises from a complex interaction between technology, people and the organization.

The authors then consider, as a case study, Central Queensland University (CQU), which is a university in Australia that is responding to the challenge of remote education and operation on a national and international basis. CQU has been a distance education and on-campus education provider since 1974 and is now Australia's fastest growing university. Inherent in all CQU's operations is a model in which the organization, its members and its partners are all constituents of a "glocal" network of learning facilitators.

IMPLICATIONS OF THE ONLINE WORLD FOR STRUCTURE AND PROCESS IN INDUSTRIES AND ORGANIZATIONS

In considering the implications of the online world for industry, it is necessary to consider both *structure* and *process,* where process includes *change processes* (Gregor & Johnston, 2000; 2001; Johnston & Gregor, 2000). For example, one defining characteristic of an industry structure is the degree to which vertical integration has occurred. Vertical integration and alliances are formed by negotiation over periods of time. The result is a structure that becomes formalized to some extent. Further activities and processes are needed to maintain the alliance and modify it as needed.

In Giddens' theory of structuration, process (activity) and structure are reciprocal (Giddens, 1977, 1984, 1991). As Giddens (1977, p. 121) states, "Social structures are both constituted by human agency, and yet at the same time are the very *medium* of this constitution," or as Rose (1999, p. 643) puts it, "Agents in their actions constantly produce and reproduce and develop the social structures which both constrain and enable them."

This link between process and structure is also important at the organizational level. In order to develop technology and systems to survive in the online world, an organization must engage in certain processes, such as business process re-engineering. These processes are of great importance – many information systems fail and exhibit the *productivity paradox* (Brynjolfsson & Hitt, 1998). This paradox refers to the fact that investment in Information Technology appears to be unrelated to increased outputs. One explanation of the productivity paradox is that some organizations do not pay sufficient attention to processes within their organization when introducing new technology. If organizational change is not implemented well, and work processes not redesigned, the new systems do not lead to gains in productivity. Organizations that gain in productivity appear to be those in which there is a restructuring of the organization and flatter, less hierarchical structures with decentralized decision-making.

Thus, it is necessary to consider change and processes of change as well as structure. The authors have a particular view of organizational change. This view is that change is "emergent." Change is not solely "technology led" or solely "organizational/agency driven." Change arises from a complex interaction between technology and the people in an industry or organization (Markus & Robey, 1988).

The conceptual model developed here is based on the structurational theory of information technology of Orlikowski and Robey (1991). This model posits four relationships: (1) information technology is a product of human action; (2) information technology is an influence on human action; (3) organizational properties are an influence on human interactions with information technology; and (4) information technology is an influence on the organization. The model is extended to include the market, technological and societal influences from the external environment that affect an organization.

So what are the implications of the online world for industry structure and process? Barriers to participating in electronic transactions are decreasing. Rather than having networks only link existing trading partners in a tightly coupled environment, new electronic markets can easily include larger numbers of buyers and sellers (Malone, Yates & Benjamin, 1987).

On the other hand there is evidence for hierarchical arrangements supported by electronic networks, with firms in many industries reducing the number of their suppliers, and entering into contractual arrangements for the supply of goods. These arrangements constitute *supply chain management*. The arguments from economic theory for the changes in market structures are complex. Holland and Lockett (1994) propose an *"anything goes"* or mixed-mode hypothesis where firms develop different forms of market and hierarchical relationships that are maintained simultaneously. The interrelationships and interdependencies of governance structure, asset specificity, market complexity and coordination strategy will determine interorganizational arrangements (Klein, 1998).

A value chain consists of the movement of components through various stages of production and distribution as they are transformed into final products. A firm can decide to produce each of the goods and services needed along the value chain in-house or to outsource it. There is a view that greater use of interorganizational networks will lead to vertical disintegration and greater outsourcing. For example, instead of an organization having its own IT department, it may outsource this function to a specialist IT service provider. However, evidence to support this view is still being collected (Steinfeld, Kraut & Chan, 1998). Some expect disintermediation to occur, where intermediaries are removed because of the ease with which they can be bypassed on electronic platforms. For example, retailers and wholesalers can be bypassed by the customer placing orders online directly with the manufacturers. It is not clear, however, that disintermediation will always occur. Instead, different forms of intermediaries may emerge; e.g., a cybermediary such as Amazon.com which to some extent replaces the traditional intermediaries, namely, book shops.

It appears that maximum benefit is obtained from e-business when it is integrated with other applications in the organization. This integration can require re-engineering of the way in which the organization does business. E-business reduces the costs of handling paper-based information. For example, the cost to the U.S. Federal government of a paper check was 43 cents compared to two cents for an electronic payment (Turban, McLean & Wetherbe, 1999). Small companies can use the Internet for marketing and compete against firms globally at comparatively little expense. Employees can work from home or from different parts of the globe. Teams can be linked with electronic communication.

To summarize, the implications of the online world for industry include: market transformations, the need for alliances, changes in outsourcing behavior, and changes in the role and type of intermediaries. In addition, the need for re-engineering and the manner in which organizational change is approached must be considered carefully.

What are the implications for higher education?

CHANGING UNIVERSITIES

Universities and the higher educational sector face similar challenges to other industries in the online world.

Universities are due for a radical restructuring. After centuries of evolutionary changes, they are faced with carving out new roles and methods to get there. Today the predominant model is still the combination of traditional teaching and academic research as mapped out by Wilhelm von Humboldt in the last century. The guiding principles of Humboldt's vision of the university are forschung und lehre *(research and teaching) and of professors,* einsamkeit und freiheit *(solitude and freedom). But change is unavoidable and pressure for change is increasing from the public, the media, and political groups. This change is mainly driven by the new technological possibilities and the new learning environments they enable.*

(Tsichritzis, 1999, p.93)

Specific implications for universities can be drawn from the conceptual model based on the structurational theory of information technology of Orlikowski and Robey (1991):

- Organizational change arises from a complex interaction between technology and the people in the organization. For example, information technology makes possible new learning environments and changed work practices for university staff.
- Information technology can influence changes in organizational structure. The improved communication options offered by advances in information technology support the formation of alliances and the "unbundling" of the functions of the university (content, packaging and presentation). This vertical disintegration, in which functions are differentiated and either outsourced or dealt with by partners in strategic alliances, creates new intermediaries in the learning/teaching network.

There is evidence of organizational change arising from the interaction of technology and people in some universities. In Australia, online and videoconferencing systems are being developed as alternatives to face-to-face communication where the people are physically dispersed. These methodologies require both staff and students to change existing work practices and to acquire new literacies (Wallace & Yell, 1997). The new technological possibilities (and new learning environments that arise from the interaction between technology and the people) include: the Internet (facilitating synchronous and asynchronous interactions between learners); videoconferencing (facilitating tutorials comprising distributed groups of students, and also remote access to live lectures); digital libraries (as knowledge repositories); computer simulation (substitutes for laboratories); etc. Overall, the interaction of these new technologies with the people creates a learning environment in which learners, tutors and learning resources can all be networked.

These same technological possibilities also permit new working environments for those responsible for the facilitation of learning. Thus lecturers can use the Internet for synchronous and asynchronous communication with colleagues, videoconferencing for meetings, digital libraries for research. The interaction of these new technologies with the people creates a teaching environment in which lecturers, tutors and teaching resources can all be networked.

There is also evidence of changes in organizational structure that have been influenced by information technology. Traditionally, universities have carried out all the functions relating to the provision of higher education: content production; packaging content; credentialing programs; presentation to students; marketing; registration, payment and record keeping; and assessment. In the online world, these functions can more readily be "disintegrated" and the university can specialize in those functions which it regards as its "core business," forming alliances for other functions or outsourcing to new intermediaries in the value chain.

The marketing of a university's programs can be outsourced to a company that specializes in researching the market and promoting the university. Recruitment can be better accomplished close to the student, and in the case of international students, in the student's mother tongue by agents overseas. Library facilities could be provided by new intermediaries close to the students or provided online by cybermediaries. Fee payment, especially online payment, can similarly be outsourced to a cybermediary. If an institution is offering on many sites and many countries, then outsourcing invigilation and related examination administration is necessary. Sylvan Learning Systems (2001) is an example of an organization specializing in the function of assessment in the education value chain. Based in the USA, it offers computer-based testing services to educational institutions, for example the Graduate Management Aptitude Test (GMAT) and the Test of English as a Foreign Language (TOEFL).

Research, of course, can be conducted by others outside universities, so there is really no reason why this activity couldn't be outsourced. But it could be argued that there is a nexus between research and teaching in universities that is essential for higher education.

The functions of course development and materials development are perhaps the ones seen as most likely to remain with universities. But there are those who even suggest the need for outsourcing and alliances for the performance of these functions. Gibbons (1998, p.61) predicts that universities "will learn to make use of intellectual resources that they don't own fully. This is the only way that they will be able to interact effectively with the distributed knowledge production system."

In the higher education industry there is an increasing number of instances of institutions delivering the content of others. UNext is an internet-based distance learning 'university' which utilizes content developed by the London School of Economics, the University of Chicago, Colombia, Stanford and Carnegie Mellon Universities, and delivers Master of Business Administration (MBA) degrees to the corporate sector. UNext also handles the global marketing and management of the programs (UNext, 2001). Western Governors University (WGU) was formed in 1996 by the governors of the western USA to share higher education distance learning resources. It offers online access to over 500 distance education courses from over 40 higher education institutions. It assesses students and awards degrees, but its programs are produced and delivered by the participating institutions (WGU, 2001).

Gibbons (1998, p.61) suggests that a university should be regarded as "a sort of 'holding institution' in the field of knowledge production, perhaps limited to accrediting teaching done primarily by others while in research doing their part by forming problem-solving teams that work on fundamental issues." This view sees the core business of the university as participating in knowledge production and credentialing the teaching programs of others. But if so many functions are outsourced, then an important new function must be added to the work of the university – the function of organizing the learning space – bringing all the outsourced functions together to facilitate learning by the students. Indeed, one could say that the organization of the learning space perhaps becomes the central function of the university.

As the various functions of the higher education process are differentiated, so too the *nature of work* and the *workforce* change (Coaldrake & Stedman, 1999). The authors now consider a case study that illustrates this change.

CASE STUDY OF CENTRAL QUEENSLAND UNIVERSITY IN AUSTRALIA

Central Queensland University (CQU) is a regional university in Australia that is responding to the challenge of the online world. With 15,000 students, CQU is now Australia's fastest growing university in terms of international students. Only 25% of its students were in grades 11 and 12 in Australia during the last two years; the remainder are mature-aged or international students. In other words, CQU has a diverse student population quite unlike that of "traditional" universities.

In Central Queensland, CQU's traditional catchment area, Rockhampton is the location of the main campus; Mackay campus 350 kilometres to the North; Gladstone campus 120 kilometres to the South; Emerald campus 280 kilometres to the West; and Bundaberg campus 330 kilometres to the South. A key component of this integrated network of campuses is the Interactive System-Wide Learning (ISL) system – a synchronous video link that facilitates networked learning. Thus, on these campuses, classes are taught using combinations of synchronous video delivery of live lectures, videoconferencing to connect distributed groups of learners, web-delivery, synchronous and asynchronous computer-mediated discussions, and face-to-face classes.

CQU has been a distance education provider since 1974. Distance education students are serviced with a combination of printed, CD-ROM and web-delivered material, as well as electronic asynchronous communication for class discussion and mailing lists.

CQU formed an alliance with a commercial partner, Campus Management Services, to establish campuses at Sydney in 1994, Melbourne in 1996 and more recently in Brisbane and the Gold Coast. At these campuses the students are mostly of international origin. In addition, there are campuses operating in Singapore, Hong

Kong and Fiji. At all these campuses, the CQU programs are tutored by locally appointed academic staff, specifically employed for teaching rather than research. The mode of delivery is face-to-face for tutorials and lectures, supported by the distance education resource materials produced by the CQU academic staff in Central Queensland.

Inherent in the CQU educational partnership with Campus Management Services is a model in which the function of content production has been detached from other functions traditionally carried out by the university (for example, lecturing). This vertical disintegration, in which functions are differentiated and either outsourced or dealt with by partners in strategic alliances, creates new intermediaries in the value chain.

For both on-campus and distance education modes, CQU has moved to a networked learning paradigm, using communication and information technologies to link learners and learning resources. But it has also moved to a networked teaching paradigm that links lecturers, tutors and teaching resources.

There are inherent dangers, however, in globalization coupled with the facility to network all teachers and learners. Inappropriate structures and processes for this global network have the potential to create stress for the individuals at the CQU campuses. When becoming more global, it is important to take care that the models used for teaching are scalable—for example, one coordinator in Rockhampton should not be dealing with a mailing list comprising one thousand students from all over the world.

There are also fears that the globalization of higher education could lead to a global western academic homogeneity—yet another wave of cultural imperialism. But the fear that global higher education will destroy indigenous cultures fails to acknowledge that other forms of communication between cultures have existed for hundreds of years, and the fact that cultures survive such transculturation is evidence of cultural 'resistance' and 'adaption' (McQuail, 1994).

> *The intensifying of worldwide social relations sets up dialectical ties between the global and local, such that what happens in any particular milieu is an expression of, but also can often stand in contradistinction to, distanciated social forms.*
>
> (Giddens, 1991, p. 210)

So, when becoming more global, it is important to take care to create a system which does not seek to undermine cultural 'resistance' and 'adaption,' but which instead is responsive to the knowledge, culture and needs of the local learners. One aspect of this process is the "internationalising" of the curriculum to allow local knowledge and culture to be incorporated and valued.

Figure 1: The "Glocal" model of networked learning

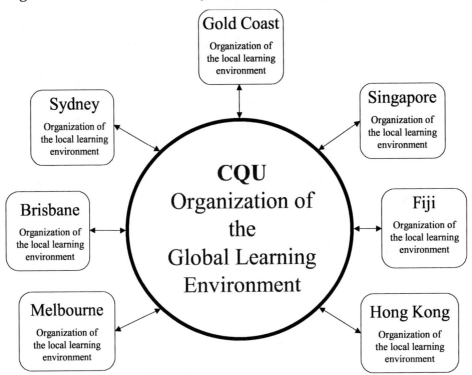

To overcome the dangers mentioned above, it is important to move to a "glocal" meta-model in which the staff in each faculty of CQU are responsible for the organization of the global learning environment whilst the educational partners are responsible for the organization of the local learning environment (see Figure 1). Hence the portmanteau expression "glocal" – it is global and local at the same time.

CASE STUDY OF THE "GLOCAL" META-MODEL: CQU GOING ONLINE IN SINGAPORE

Let us consider the specific example of CQU facilitating learning in Singapore.

CQU was originally offering programs in Singapore using distance education (DE) materials together with local tutorial support – a sort of "supported DE delivery." This was the original "glocal" model, viz., global learning resources with local learning support/mediation provided by local tutors employed by our Singaporean partner. The penetration of communication and information technology in Singapore is considerably higher than in most of the other CQU learning locations and so it was natural to make this the first location for CQU to offer its programs online.

The first, and perhaps most important point to make about the Singapore online project is that it was the result of emergent change. In an evolutionary fashion, CQU added online interactivity and support to what it was already offering in Singapore. Thus, the online programs in Singapore are not offered in a pure online mode of delivery – instead they are offered in "supported online mode," i.e., with some printed DE materials, some face-to-face tutorials and other campus-based support. This "supported online mode" is simply an example of the flexible learning paradigm embraced by the University, or more specifically, an example of the "glocal networked learning paradigm."

The communication and information technologies which enable us to create the networked learning environment for the student also enable us to create a networked education system in which lecturers, tutors and teaching resources are all linked. In the CQU/Singapore network, a CQU academic development team is responsible for the collection of the resources, the creation of the materials and the development of the "global core" for the supported online course. The global core is then electronically delivered to the local partner in Singapore.

The local partner in Singapore is responsible for adding the local education interface to the global core (see Figure 2). Thus, the online component of the global core is mirrored on our partner's server in Singapore and the local partner then creates a website with the required local online "look and feel." The CQU academic development team works electronically with the local development team to maintain quality control of this locally added component.

As regards the facilitation of learning during the running of a particular course, a lecturer on one Central Queensland campus is designated as the coordinator of a particular unit (course), and that person, together with the administration multi-campus support team, coordinates the activities of the learning facilitators/tutors on all the other campuses on which that particular course is taught. Thus, rather than dealing directly with a thousand students on campuses all over the world, the CQU coordinator deals with the in-country tutors who in turn facilitate the learning of the students. The local campus/centre acts as a hub – a local network – as shown in Figure 3.

Through the coordinator, CQU is responsible for quality control of the facilitation of the learning process. The usual quality control mechanisms are used, including moderation of assignments, marking of examination scripts, and site management visits.

Figure 2: The "Glocal" resource development process

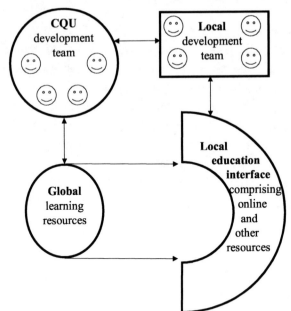

Figure 3: The local learning network linked to CQU

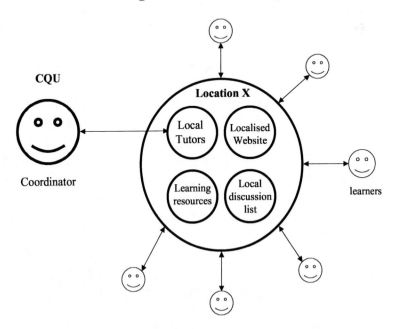

CONCLUDING REMARKS

In this chapter, the authors have identified forces leading to change in industries in the online world, including increasing global competition, increasingly powerful consumers and rapid changes in technology, especially those related to telecommunications. Implications for industry include market transformations, the need for alliances, changes in outsourcing behavior, the need for re-engineering, and changes in the role and type of intermediaries.

In the higher education industry, pressures for change include global competition and technology-facilitated learning. Outcomes are evolving, but include the formation of alliances, outsourcing and re-engineering of systems and work practices. In particular, the communication and information technologies that facilitate networked learning also link lecturers, tutors, and teaching resources to create the possibility of networked education.

The particular "glocal" networked education paradigm that the authors have outlined separates out four functions:

1) Development of the global core of learning resources;
2) Development of the local education interface;
3) Coordination of the learning facilitation on a specific occasion; and
4) Local learning facilitation.

An important distinction here for CQU is the separation of the development and the teaching functions. By embracing this separation, CQU has been able to develop ways of working which allow the creation of a scalable and flexible model. In this model, however, the work of the university academic is changed considerably.

The authors have shown how the online world tends to lead to vertical disintegration in universities and results in the differentiated functions being performed by alliance partners or being outsourced. In the same way, the functions traditionally performed by a single university academic are differentiated in the CQU "glocal" networked education paradigm and are performed by a network of learning facilitators. The distinction between academic and nonacademic university staff blurs as both take on more "learning management" roles, for example, management of learning facilitators and management of learning resources. In this scenario, university academics may find themselves responsible for the learning of hundreds of students. They may never, however, find themselves face-to-face with a single student.

REFERENCES

AVCC. (2000). *Australian Vice Chancellors Committee: Key Statistics Internationalisation.* Canberra: AVCC. Available on the World Wide Web at: http://www.avcc.edu.au/australias_unis/statistics/internationalisation/.

Brynjolfsson, E. and Hitt, L. M. (1998). Beyond the productivity paradox. *Communications of the ACM,* 41(8), 49-55.

Coaldrake, P. and Stedman, L. (1999) Academic Work in the Twenty-first Century: Changing roles and policies. *Department of Education, Training and Youth Affairs (DETYA)*, Commonwealth of Australia: Canberra. Available on the World Wide Web at: http://www.detya.gov.au/highered/occpaper.htm.

Duderstadt, J. J. (1999). Can colleges and universities survive in the information age? In Katz, R. N. & Associates (Eds.), *Dancing With the Devil-Information Technology and the New Competition in Higher Education.* San Francisco: Jossey-Bass.

Gibbons, M. (1998). Higher education relevance in the 21st century. *UNESCO World Conference on Higher Education*, Paris, October 5-9.

Giddens, A. (1977). *Studies in Social and Political Theory.* London: Hutchinson.

Giddens, A. (1984). *The Constitution of Society.* Cambridge: Polity Press.

Giddens, A. (1991). Structuration theory: Past, present and future. In Bryant, C. and Jary, D. (Eds.), *Giddens' Theory of Structuration: A Critical Appreciation.* Chapter 8. London: Routledge.

Gregor, S. and Johnston, R. B. (2000). Developing an understanding of interorganizational systems: Arguments for multi-level analysis and structuration theory. In Hansen, H. R., Bichler, M. and Mahrer, H. (Eds.), *Proceedings of the 8th European Conference on Information Systems,* Vienna, 3-5 July, 1, 575-582.

Gregor, S. and Johnston, R. B. (2001). Theory of interorganizational systems: Industry structure and processes of change. *Thirty-Fourth Hawaii International Conference on System Sciences (HICSS-34).* January. To appear.

Holland, C. P. and Lockett, G. (1994). Strategic choice and interorganizational information systems. In Nunamaker, J. F. and Sprague, R. H. (Eds.), *Proceedings 27th HICSS, vol IV, Collaboration Technology, Organizational Systems and Technology.* Los Alamitos, CA: IEEE Computer Society Press, 405-413.

Johnston, R. B. and Gregor, S. (2000). A structuration-like theory of industry-level activity for understanding the adoption of interorganizational systems, In Hansen, H. R., Bichler, M. and Mahrer, H. (Eds.), *Proceedings of the 8th European Conference on Information Systems,* Vienna, 3-5 July, 1, 567-574.

Klein, S. (1998). The diffusion of auctions on the Web. In Romm, C. and Sudweeks, F. (Eds.), *Doing Business Electronically.* London: Springer, 47-63.

Malone, T., Yates, J., and Benjamin, R. (1987). Electronic markets and electronic hierarchies: Effects of information technology on market structure and corporate strategies, *Communications of the ACM,* 30(6), 484-497.

Markus, M. L. and Robey, D. (1988). Information technology and organizational change: Causal structure in theory and research. *Management Science,* 34(5), 583-598.

McQuail, D. (1994) *Mass Communication Theory: An Introduction.* 3rd ed., London: Sage.

Orlikowski, W. J. and Robey, D. (1991). Information technology and the structuring of organizations, *Information Systems Research,* 2(2), 143-169.

Rose, J. (1999). Frameworks for practice: Structurational theories of IS, *Proceedings of the European Conference on Information Systems.*

Steinfeld, C., Kraut, R. and Chan, A. (1998). The impact of interorganizational networks on buyer-seller relationships. in Romm, C. and Sudweeks, F. (Eds.), *Doing Business Electronically,* Springer, London, 7-26.

Sylvan Learning Systems. (2001). Sylvan Learning Systems. Available on the World Wide Web at: http://sylvanlearning.com/home.html.

Tsichritzis, D. (1999). Reengineering the university, *Communications of the ACM,* 42(6), 93-100.

Turban, E., McLean, E. and Wetherbe, J. (1999). *Information Technology for Management,* Wiley, New York.

Unext. (2001). Unext.com. Available on the World Wide Web at: http://www.unext.com/.

Wallace, A and Yell, S. (1997). New literacies in the virtual classroom. *Southern Review,* 30(3). Available on the World Wide Web at: http://www.infocom.cqu.edu.au/Staff/Susan_Yell/Teaching/fmctl/liter.htm.

WGU. (2001). Western Governors University. Available on the World Wide Web at: http://www.wgu.edu/wgu/index.html.

Chapter 9

The Consequences of e-Learning[1]

Henry H. Emurian
University of Maryland Baltimore County, USA

It is time for realism regarding the applications of information technology to education and training[2]. People learn; electrons do not. Accordingly, the dust will eventually settle from the flurry of activity related to "e-Learning," in all of its manifestations, and the foregone conclusion will stand out: learning is hard work. There is value in remembering this conclusion because in this Internet era, there is sometimes the impression gained that all the human effort involved in learning and in the achievement of excellence has been removed by information technology and knowledge management.

Since the inception of the world-wide web, nothing has changed about the ways that people learn (Bransford, Brown, and Rodney, 1999). In fact, there is nothing electronic about learning. Learning is a process that includes the actions of study and practice (Swezey and Llaneras, 1997), sometimes for years (Ericsson and Lehmann, 1996), and the assessment of effectiveness as a change in the learner (Skinner, 1953, 1954), a change that might be observed and documented by others or even by the learner as a self-evaluating authority. And one important advantage of a book as a repository of managed knowledge for learning is that it is easy to use (Brock, 1997). The impact of web-based instructional delivery and assessment of competence, however, will have a profound consequence on pedagogy, particularly as the art and science of teaching are tailored to the needs and status of the individual learner. The consequence will be a rational pedagogy that most of us only dreamed about as students ourselves. This is evidenced by the volume of emerging commen-

Previously Published in the *Information Resources Management Journal, Vol.14, No.2,* Copyright © 2001, Idea Group Publishing.

tary that addresses the current and potential impact of the world-wide web and automated instructional delivery on education and training (Eamon, 1999; Hodgins, 2000; Krantz and Eagley, 1996; Lange, 1999; Tennyson, 1999). A common denominator within this stream of important and timely discussion is the attempt to cope with individual differences among learners and to overcome them.

Those of us who now write editorials for our colleagues to read and ponder were once students ourselves. We sat there in large classes. We listened to lectures that were sometimes inspiring, more often not. We took notes as the professor spoke, and we studied a textbook. We managed our learning under the strict temporal constraints of a course. We sometimes experienced "just-in-time" learning on the night before an examination. We recited on objective tests, usually, and these evaluations gave rise to grades, typically a distribution of letter grades that intended to show our intellectual competence in a subject matter relative to the competence displayed by our student colleagues. Indeed, the mission of the academy was to present information in a constant format and then to document individual differences in the use of that information. Even though many of us excelled academically under such circumstances, we all harbored a nagging suspicion that something was fundamentally flawed and unfair about the whole thing. That was the correct feeling to have.

All of us knew then that the impact of the instructional delivery media, typically lectures and books, and the assessment methods, typically objective tests, would differentially affect the members of a diverse group of students taking a particular course. All of us knew then that the students in a class were not equally advantaged in academic background, motivation, maturity, study skills, and available energy to undertake learning within a competitive academic context. There was a tacit failure by the academy to adopt course admission criteria and course exit standards of excellence that would address individual differences as a factor to be solved *by the academy*. Instructional delivery media, together with organizational constraints, failed to accommodate those differences and to overcome them. We now look with fascination at the applications of information technology in education and training, and some of us may wonder how our own careers, and those of our students, might have developed differently if we had used the world-wide web, simply because this technology has occasioned an enlightened and compassionate understanding of individual differences among learners.

It will no longer be business as usual within academe, and the transformation will produce a global, egalitarian, shared, and ultimately optimistic sociological context for education and training. The reason is that the conditions that promote efficient and effective learning will be made increasingly accessible to public scrutiny, debate, and evaluation. Students, as newly empowered consumers of education and training products and services, will not be complacent in the face of inferior alternatives, whether provided by public, private, or commercial sectors of society. The consumer of education and training products and services now has so many options available that a constructive competition among providers is responding to a consumer-generated evolution of intellectual products and services. This evolution favors a better match between the individual student and the process of learning. This evolution will occasion a reconsideration of the significance of traditional accreditation and credentialing authority, and most importantly, the reconsideration will be driven by the student consumer, not by elitist organizations.

These developments have not escaped the attention of the professoriate (Eamon, 1999), especially as the time-honored recognition of general intellectual achievement and merit (*i.e.,* academic degrees) continues to lose force, and as the arbitrary, if not increasingly anachronistic, degree milestones continue to support the needs of the academic organization, not the student. But organizations, to include formal and accredited educational institutions, are being propelled to address the needs of the student in ways that have long been known to benefit the individual learner (Bloom, 1984). Where is it written that the pace of a life must be controlled by an academic institution? Where is it written that a course grade must be frozen in time forever? Where is it written that a student must be limited to only a single evaluation occasion, without the opportunity for additional learning to achieve an intellectual criterion of excellence? Where is it written that the scale of an intellectual unit must be a traditional semester-long course? A new unit of measure is required, an intellectual metric of learning that is quantifiable without regard to these customary constraints (Greer and McDonough, 1999). The evolution to a rational pedagogy is evidenced by relationships between commercial online-instruction enterprises and major academic institutions (e.g., UNext.com) in which the products are downscaled for effective information resource management on the Internet, rather than in the classroom. The reduction in the size of the units of mastery and the elimination of arbitrary timelines for completion are constructive developments in the effective management of individual differences among learners.[3]

The results of public dissemination and discussion of education and training strategies, via the world-wide web, will produce an informed learner who will shop, comparatively, for the optimal learning strategy to achieve a specific competency objective. Hardly a day goes by without reading the news of yet another Web-based learning opportunity with subject matter ranging from Java[4] to conflict analysis and management[5]. In many ways, e-Learning approaches are best suited to knowledge domains where the steps to mastery and the assessment of competence are precise and non-controversial. Mastering the arts of critical analysis, reflection, and synthesis, however, may sometimes require a mentor – a person – because the judgments involved may not always lend themselves to precise specification. Neglecting fundamental learning parameters in favor of a preoccupation with information technology and with making e-Learning systems more and more human-like could drive the "Turing test" to gratuitous philosophical discourse that will not advantage a learner's acquisition, retention, and use of knowledge. Finally, a rational pedagogy, in addition to fostering mastery of a particular knowledge domain, also teaches learning discipline to those students who lack it, and e-Learning and mentoring strategies may be separate or synergistic at different occasions in a lifelong process of intellectual development and contribution.

The diffusion of a rational pedagogy will require change management initiatives that will extend beyond the academic organizational level and even societal level. A rational pedagogy, recognized and practiced by the global community, will require enlightened thought on the sources and consequences of individual differences. And the traditional milestones and certificates of intellectual achievement and merit will fall away because they will no longer be useful.

A totally effective education and training environment, when applied to information technology instructional strategies that are enhanced by the world-wide web, will include factors that have long been identified as contributing to an optimal and multi-dimensional learning context – a personalized system of instruction (Keller, 1968). The ingredients of such a system have long been known to contribute to an optimal learning environment for the individual student (Ferster and Perrott, 1968). Today, these ingredients might include the following instructional tactics and resources, in combinations that depend on the knowledge domain and the objectives of learning: programmed instruction modules, web-based delivery and management of information, supervised laboratory exercises, interactions with peers and experts, mentoring, individual student research, traditional textbooks, industry certification training, lectures, and the library, to name just a few. The integration of e-Learning information technology into this framework, together with the evolution toward a rational pedagogy, bodes well for the universal acceptance of an enlightened perspective on the sources of individual differences and the availability of opportunities for all students, everywhere and at any age, to reach their potential throughout their life span.

In a universally accepted rational pedagogy, evaluation outcomes will be entry points to progress for all, not end points for some. This is long overdue.

REFERENCES

Bloom, B.S. (1984). The 2 sigma problem: The search for methods of group instruction as effective as one-to-one tutoring. *Educational Researcher*, *13*, 4-16.

Bransford, J.D., Brown, A.L., & Rodney, R.C. (1999*). How People Learn: Brain, Mind, Experience, and School.* Washington, D.C.: National Academy Press.

Brock, J.F. (1997). Computer-based instruction. In G. Salvendy (Ed*.), Handbook of Human Factors and Ergonomics* New York: Wiley, 578-593.

Eamon, D.V. (1999). Distance education: Has technology become a threat to the academy? *Behavior Research Methods, Instruments, & Computers*, *31*, 197-207.

Ericsson, K.A., & Lehmann, A.C. (1996). Expert and exceptional performance: Evidence of maximal adaptation to task constraints. *Annual Review of Psychology, 37*, 273-305.

Ferster, C.B., & Perrott, M.C. (1968). *Behavior Principles*. New York: Appleton-Century-Crofts.

Greer, R.D., & McDonough, S.H. (1999). Is the learn unit a fundamental measure of pedagogy? *The Behavior Analyst, 22*, 5-16.

Hodgins, H. (2000). Into the future: A vision paper. Prepared by the Commission on Technology and Adult Learning for the American Society for Training & Development (ASTD) and the National Governors' Association (NGA). http://www.astd.org/

Keller, F.S. (1968). Goodbye teacher... *Journal of Applied Behavior Analysis*, *1*, 79-89.

Krantz, J.H., & Eagley, B.M. (1996). Creating psychological tutorials on the world-wide web. *Behavior Research Methods, Instruments, & Computers, 28*, 156-160.

Lange, M. (1999). Museum of perception and cognition website: Using JavaScript to increase interactivity in Web-based presentations. *Behavior Research Methods, Instruments, & Computers, 31*, 34-45.

Skinner, B.F. (1953). *Science and Human Behavior*. NY: The Free Press.

Skinner, B.F. (1954). The science of learning and the art of teaching. *Harvard Educational Review, 24*, 86-97.

Swezey, R.W., & Llaneras, R.E. (1997). Models in training and instruction. In G. Salvendy (Ed.), *Handbook of Human Factors and Ergonomics*. New York: Wiley, 514-577.

Tennyson, R.D. (1999). Goals for automated instructional systems. *Journal of Structural Learning and Intelligent Systems, 13*, 215-226.

ENDNOTES

[1] The writer appreciates the comments by Ashley G. Durham, Angela Kaan, and Roy Rada about the opinions expressed here, for which I assume sole responsibility.

[2] The debate regarding "education" and "training" occasions uproarious discussions within the professoriate. Somehow, teaching vocationally oriented skills within a university setting is perceived as less intellectually meritorious than teaching the arts of knowledge assimilation, reflection, and generation. In this e-Learning era, however, many students seek the former, and all students need the latter. The question is this: who has the wisdom to dictate the balance and the timing of the two? Perhaps that is best left to the consumer. But both objectives should be honored, and many academic organizations, to include research universities, are taking steps to ensure quality in both areas of intellectual development. At UMBC, for example, an industry certification center (http://continuinged.umbc.edu/IT/) provides authoritative instruction in many areas of information technology that prepares the student to pass industry certification examinations. In both undergraduate and graduate degree programs, moreover, a student who successfully passes an industry certification examination may receive limited academic credit when a non-credit "value-added" academic course accompanies the former. Since the industry certification courses are taught by technical experts, this approach relieves the research professoriate from the impossible task of maintaining both research productivity and technical competence in information technology sufficient to offer authoritative and effective instruction in the latter. This is very good news, indeed, for the research professoriate. At UMBC, Professor Kip Canfield (canfield@umbc.edu) has provided the initiative for the development of these important interrelationships between scholarship and skill.

[3] An example of a competency-based degree program offered by an academic institution is evidenced by UMBC's "flexible masters" degree program in Information Systems that will be available online in 2001. Under the directorship of Professor Roy Rada (rada@umbc.edu), this e-Learning program will provide the student with access to modularized units of knowledge in a progressive fashion where demonstrated competence is required across successive knowledge modules. The student may

complete successive modules in a self-paced progression of study to the terminal degree objective, and competency evaluations may be repeated until they are passed at a standardized criterion of achievement. This approach is "flexible" because it adjusts to the needs and status of the individual student, while maintaining academic rigor, and it is an exemplar of a rational pedagogy.

[4] http://www.jobsuniversity.com/
[5] http://modules.royalroads.ca/

Chapter 10

Student Perceptions of Virtual Education: An Exploratory Study

Anil Kumar, Poonam Kumar and Suvojit Choton Basu
University of Wisconsin-Whitewater, USA

Over the years instructors and administrators have worked together to provide education to students in academic institutions. The role of the participants in this educational system were well-defined. Instructors and administrators were responsible for the dissemination of knowledge and the methodology used was simple: the instructor transferred the knowledge to the students. The merging of computers and communications technology is transforming the way we teach and learn. Physical classrooms are being replaced by electronic classrooms. The roles of the participants are being redefined where the instructor is becoming a facilitator in the electronic classroom and students are participating in these classes from anywhere and at anytime. Questions that arise for universities include: Is this the future of higher education? Will electronic classrooms replace traditional classrooms? In this study we explore and discuss the perceptions of students in a mid-western rural university regarding virtual education. Implications for the participants in the educational system are also discussed.

Previously Published in *Managing Information Technology in a Global Economy* edited by Mehdi Khosrow-Pour, Copyright © 2001, Idea Group Publishing.

INTRODUCTION

The rapid advancements in computers and telecommunications technology in recent years is impacting "where" and "how" instruction is taking place. It is changing the concept of a classroom with physical boundaries, as well as pedagogical approaches. Technological advances are making it possible for education to be delivered electronically anywhere at anytime. The Internet provides access to courses, teachers, resources, and educational institutions for students who are located in different parts of the world. Educational and commercial institutions are using the Internet to deliver courses over the World Wide Web. These institutions store and transmit data digitally in different forms, e.g., text, voice, graphics, video, etc., across geographical boundaries, over the Internet. Web-based technologies are also enhancing the potential for two-way communication between students and teachers. This increases the richness of data that is transmitted over the Internet and helps in providing students an environment that promotes learning in real time.

In the March 10, 1997 issue of *Fortune* magazine, Peter Drucker predicted that "universities won't survive" thirty years from now. Already there are several schools that have begun offering courses over the Internet. Online training or courses are becoming a big business worldwide. Many institutions are experimenting with electronic delivery of courses or entire academic programs and considering whether to make major investments in this technology. For example, the University of Phoenix is the largest private university delivering online degree courses to 56,000 students. The traditional institutions of higher education are also moving towards virtual instruction. Penn State (World Campus), the University of Minnesota, UCLA (Home Education Network), Lansing Community College, and Florida's Gulf Coast University are other examples of institutions delivering instruction electronically (Gladieux & Swail, 1999). California has developed its own California Virtual University, which offers about seven hundred courses online, but no degrees. Virtual education has become a billion dollar industry that will continue to grow in the future.

Higher education institutions are also forming partnerships with the private sector to support their move towards virtual classrooms. Western Governors University (WGU) which was formed by the governors of seventeen states in partnership with Microsoft, Sun Systems, IBM, and AT&T, started as the nation's first exclusively virtual university in 1998 (Blumenstyk, 1998). WGU offers three degree programs and certificate programs. Cardean University, an online "academy" established by UNext, an Internet education company includes as its partners Columbia University, the University of Chicago, Stanford University, and the London School of Economics and Political Science. The Jones Education Company College Connections Online is a partnership of colleges and universities around the nation, including the George Washington University, the University of Colorado, and the University of Delaware. It provides ten degree programs and two certificate programs in the areas of educational technology, business administration, communications, nursing, and hotel management. Instruction is provided via videotape and satellite feed, with Internet and email support.

Given the growing popularity of virtual education, in this paper we attempt to explore student perceptions about virtual education and their willingness to enroll in a virtual education degree program. It is important to note that we are determining student perceptions about a "degree program" and not just a few courses offered via virtual education. In this paper, virtual education is defined as "knowledge or skill transfer that takes place using the World Wide Web as the distribution channel. In a virtual education environment there are no traditional classrooms. Students are not required to come to the classroom. All instruction and interaction takes place over the World Wide Web." Other characteristics of virtual education include the following:

- The student has the choice to participate in the best program offered anywhere in the world, without being constrained to a specific geographical region.
- Knowledge dissemination is by way of computers and communications technology.
- The World Wide Web is used extensively for knowledge dissemination and to enhance the learning process. The students are provided the opportunity to interact with instructors, peers, and business professionals. The interaction is not subject to geographic and time limitations, unlike in a traditional classroom.
- The technologies utilized include, among others, computer hardware and software (e.g., video conferencing, GroupWare, email, etc.), communications technology (e.g. computer networks with access to the Internet), multimedia tools and virtual reality, etc.

The study seeks to explore the following research question: "Will students be willing to enroll in a virtual degree program?" Most of the studies so far have determined student opinions about a particular course they had taken to evaluate the course; this study takes a proactive approach and seeks to determine student opinions before a university spends millions of dollars to create the necessary infrastructure for virtual education. With all these advancements, the question is whether or not virtual universities supplant traditional universities. If virtual education is so alluring, flexible, and student-centered, as claimed by the proponents, then why do we find students enrolling for traditional programs? The students being the customers, it is important to consider what they feel or perceive about the value of this "product." We believe that it is critical to identify issues and identify student's perceptions before actually implementing or developing virtual degree programs. These perceptions can help the administrators and faculty members to use technology and develop programs that address these issues so that students are more willing to enroll for such programs.

The paper is organized as follows: in the next section we provide a review of the literature, in section 3, we discuss the methodology used for the study, and section 4 presents the results and discussion. Finally, we conclude the paper by discussing implications for the future for universities that plan to start virtual education degree programs.

LITERATURE REVIEW

Technological advancements have necessitated a pedagogical paradigm shift from "teaching" to "learning" and from the traditional "teacher-centered" to a constructivist "student-centered" teaching approach. Traditionally, the instructor's role was to transfer knowledge to the students, and the primary method of delivering the course content was lectures and handouts. The very concept of teaching is changing from knowledge dissemination to knowledge creation (Leidner and Jarvenpaa, 1995) and the instructor is not considered the sole source of knowledge but rather a facilitator of students' learning.

Virtual classrooms, where students and teachers located in different places communicate electronically in cyberspace without actually meeting each other, are replacing the traditional classrooms with blackboard, chalk, students and the instructor. The "web is being used as tool for learning, as opposed to a medium for predetermined content" (Owston, 1997, p 29). Classrooms are linked to the outside world using computers and communications networks, and instructors are able to bring the "world" into the classroom in real time. Knowledge is not transmitted from the instructor to the student, rather the students construct and create their own knowledge by solving problems, experimenting, discovering and working on hands-on projects.

Proponents of virtual education claim that it is learner-centered as it is flexible and students can choose where, how and when they want to learn (Gladieux and Swail, 1999; Owston, 1997). In a virtual classroom setting, the text, lessons, assignments, product demonstrations and other course materials can be made available on the Web for easy access any time of the day or night. This allows the students to learn at their own convenience and at their own pace. So in a way, teaching and learning become ongoing or perpetual in nature, rather than being confined to pre-specified hours in a week (Hiltz, 1995).

The Internet is also changing the nature of student-student and student-teacher interactions. In virtual environments, there are no geographical boundaries, so students can interact and collaborate with students from all over the world. There is no face-to-face interaction among students and teachers. Class discussions take place at an electronic 'chit-chat' center at times convenient to each individual. A separate web site can be dedicated for this purpose. All such discussions made at different times throughout the duration of a course can be grouped by topics, dated, and linked to related topics for easy reference (Peha, 1997). Guest speakers can join in class discussions easily, regardless of where the speaker lives or works. Further, instead of just one class session, he/she is able to participate for several weeks (Burgstahler, 1997).

Virtual education learning environments provide opportunities for students to interact and collaborate with other students from all over the world, work on real life projects, and use the information available on the Web to search for answers and engage in ongoing learning. Technology can also be effectively used to promote collaborative learning as it makes it possible for students to interact and work with students in different places (Alavi, Wheeler and Valacich, 1995).

Several studies have examined student perceptions in an attempt to evaluate the effectiveness of Web-based technologies. Usip and Bee (1998) determined undergraduate student perceptions about Web-based distance learning after they had taken a statistics course at Youngstown State University in which Web-based instruction was integrated into the traditional environment. Students who had used technology before found integrating the Web was useful in obtaining information and improving their performance in class. The nonusers did not feel that using Web instruction would improve their performance. In another study, Gifford (1998) examined the perceptions of graduate students who took a course in research on curriculum and instruction taught entirely via the Web. Students felt that self-discipline and self-motivation were needed to complete a course on the Internet and more time was spent on a web-based course compared to a traditional class.

There is no doubt that Web-based technologies have the potential of enhancing the student learning, but there is no empirical data to prove that students learn better in virtual environments compared to traditional classrooms (Owston, 1997; Phipps and Merisotis, 1999). Most of these benefits are based on assumptions or perceived benefits as research has not proved that students learn better in virtual environments compared to the traditional environments. Phipps and Merisotis (1999), in a review of the current research on distant education, contend that most of the research so far has focused on studying the effectiveness of individual courses rather than a complete degree program. They further note that research has not taken into consideration individual student characteristics such as gender, age, student experience, motivation, etc. These characteristics may impact students' willingness to enroll in a virtual degree program. In our study we explore student perceptions on virtual degree programs rather than a single course.

METHODOLOGY

This study was conducted in a rural mid-western university with approximately 10,000 students. The university has four colleges: education, business, arts and communications, and letters and sciences. The majority of the students enrolled in the university come from neighboring counties and cities within a 250-mile radius. The study was conducted in two phases. Phase I was a pilot study conducted to derive a list of questions that could be administered to students for the final survey. Fifty-nine undergraduate students in the business school (30 male and 29 female) were asked to respond to the following open-ended questions:

"Virtual education has been defined as the process of knowledge or skill transfer that takes place using the World Wide Web as the distribution channel.
- What would be the impact of virtual education on the future of the education system?
- What in your opinion are the pros and cons of this approach?
- If given a choice would you be willing to enroll for a virtual education-based program? Give reasons for your answer."

These students were not picked at random. Access to students as they were enrolled in a class being taught by one of the authors was the main criteria. Student responses were examined for common themes, which were used to develop a 15 item survey (Appendix) for phase II.

In phase II of the study, the common themes identified in phase I were structured in the form of a statement on a 5-point Likert scale. Respondents were asked to provide their responses, ranging from strongly disagree (1) to strongly agree (5). Demographic questions were added to the 15 item survey from the previous phase. The final survey was administered to 431 students across campus from the four colleges. The sample was not randomly selected. Instructors from the four colleges were selected by the authors on the basis of acquaintance and requested to distribute the survey in class. Student participation was voluntary.

RESULTS AND DISCUSSION

Of the 431 respondents, 219 (50.8%) were male and 208 (48.3%) were female. Four respondents (.9%) did not provide a response for the gender question. Approximately 9.3% (N=40) of the respondents were graduate students and 89.5% (N=386) students were undergraduate students. Five respondents (1.2%) did not answer the question about their graduate/undergraduate status. Forty students were part-time and 385 students were full-time. Six students did not provide a response to this question.

When asked if they would be willing to register for a virtual education degree program, 158 respondents (38.07%) replied in the positive. The total respondents for this question were 415. Sixteen people did not respond to this question. More than half (61.9%) of the respondents were not willing to enroll in a virtual education degree program. This result indicates that though students seem to be interested in virtual education they are not willing to enroll in virtual education degree programs at this point. What is interesting over here is the fact that a higher percentage of undergraduate students (39.57%) responded in the positive compared to graduate students (23.07%). This implies that universities with a predominantly undergraduate student body in similar settings should consider the option of providing virtual education degree programs in addition to the traditional programs. It would be interesting to find out if undergraduate standing (freshman, sophomore, etc.) and/or major has an impact on this choice.

Of the 415 respondents, 214 were males and 201 were females. 44.39% (N=95) of the male respondents and 31.34% (N=63) of the female respondents said yes, they would be willing to enroll in a virtual education degree program. A possible explanation for this can be the fact that women in general do not feel comfortable using technology. In a recent study (Proost et. al., 1997) it was found that women compared to men have a negative perception of computer-based technology and indicate a preference for traditional methods of learning. This fact is also reflected in the results of a study conducted by the American Association of University Women Educational Foundation (*Information Week*, April 2000) where it was found out that women constitute less than 20% of the IT workforce.

In the following paragraphs we explore the reasons that may provide further insights for the students' response to this question. Table 1 provides a summary of these results.

An overwhelming number of respondents agree that virtual education degree programs increase flexibility for students to take classes at anytime from anywhere. When comparing the means, this result is consistent for male/female, graduate/undergraduate, and full-time/part-time respondents. The flexibility provided by virtual education programs is supported in the literature (Daugherty and Funke, 1998) and is a possible explanation for 38.07% of the respondents willingness to register for such programs.

Approximately two thirds (67.5%) of the respondents strongly disagreed/disagreed with the statement that virtual education increases interaction among students and more than half (58.9%) of the respondents strongly disagreed/disagreed with the statement that virtual education increases one-on-one student teacher interaction. In both of these cases the percent of respondents that agreed with these statements is less than fifteen. This result indicates that student-teacher and student-student interaction is an important criterion for respondents and they perceive that virtual education does not provide these interactions. Lack of interaction in a virtual education degree program, as perceived by respondents, possibly explains why 61.9% of respondents were not willing to register for such programs.

Respondents (65.6%) strongly agreed/agreed that virtual education will be more effective for motivated and self-disciplined students. This result should be interpreted with caution and, in our opinion, the fact that the majority of the respondents of this study were undergraduate students explains their perception. Undergraduate students, generally speaking, need structure, direction, and guidance in their education, which may not be adequately provided in a virtual degree program. Further, the fact that respondents perceive virtual education to lack student-teacher interaction, activities such as student advising, may explain the respondent's opinions.

Table 1: Overall Mean Scores and Frequency Percent

Individual Survey Items	Overall means (N=431)	Strongly agree/agree (%)	Neither agree nor disagree (%)	Strongly disagree/disagree (%)
Virtual education increases flexibility for students to take classes at anytime.	4.29	92.1	5.6	2.3
Virtual education increases flexibility for students to take classes from anywhere.	4.37	93.8	3.9	2.3
Virtual education increases quality of education by allowing students to learn at their own pace.	3.00	31.3	36.2	32.5
Virtual education increases quality of education by providing access to more knowledge on the Web.	3.11	35.5	36.7	27.8
Virtual education increases ongoing learning by providing availability to resources on the Web.	3.50	57.1	27.8	15.1
Virtual education will increase understanding of concepts and issues as there will be no need to take notes.	2.57	17.0	30.6	52.4
Virtual education increases the diversity in a classroom by allowing students from other parts of the world to enroll in classes.	3.44	55.4	22.3	22.3
Virtual education changes the role of teachers to a facilitator rather than an instructor.	3.61	59.2	32.0	8.8
Virtual education will be more effective for motivated and self-disciplined students.	3.73	65.6	16.5	17.9
Virtual education increases "free time" for students to develop skills.	3.24	42.9	34.1	23.0
Virtual education increases one-on-one student-teacher interaction.	2.33	14.4	26.7	58.9
Virtual education increases interaction among students.	2.16	10.0	22.5	67.5
Students will learn more effectively using the Web.	2.60	14.4	41.2	44.4
Virtual education increases the thinking process of students.	2.84	22.5	42.0	35.5
Virtual education reduces the cost of education for students.	3.51	48.5	40.1	11.4

A surprising result was the respondents perception, only 14.4%, that in a virtual education program students will learn more effectively using the Web. A possible explanation for this response can be the fact that there is a tremendous amount of information available on the Web. Information overload caused by excessive data that needs to be scanned before a student can find relevant information may reduce the effectiveness of the Web as a learning tool.

CONCLUSION

In this study we tried to find out if students in a predominantly undergraduate rural university would be willing to register for a virtual education degree program. One of the key findings of this study was the fact that there is an interest, though limited, in virtual education degree programs. Students perceive flexibility to take classes anytime and anywhere as a key reason to register for virtual education degree programs. However, there is strong evidence that students perceive interaction, student-to-student and student-to-instructor, to suffer as a result of virtual education. Further, students perceive that virtual education programs place a heavy demand on students to be self-motivated and disciplined. Students also perceive that learning is not more effective using the Web.

Universities need to be proactive in determining the need for virtual education degree programs in their regions and then prepare them selves for developing such programs. Care must be taken to ensure that these programs are designed and developed keeping in mind the social needs of students. A significant part of learning for students in a university environment comes from the interaction that takes place among themselves and with teachers. Students that are educated in isolated environments where interaction with peers and teachers is limited may be deprived of "true education." Education for students is a holistic experience and means more than an electronic package.

Designing and developing virtual education degree programs requires a collective effort with all participants in the educational process contributing. There is a need for a champion at the highest level, such as the chancellor, who provides the motivation and incentives for faculty to be involved with this project. All faculty members should be involved willingly in this process and contribute their skills towards the success of this project. Finally, universities should conduct studies on their campuses to determine the needs of students to ensure that their concerns are addressed and that they are willing to register for such programs.

In this paper we discussed the perceptions of students regarding virtual education. This study is unique as it is proactive, unlike other studies where student perceptions are based on courses that have already been delivered electronically. Also in this study we focused on degree programs rather than individual courses that are offered online. Some of the factors that we believe can help explain the student's perceptions, such as their majors, individual experience with the use of technology before starting college, and educational standing, need to be investigated in future studies. This would enable universities to develop a framework that can guide the implementation of virtual education degree programs.

APPENDIX

Virtual education increases flexibility for students to take classes at anytime.
Virtual education increases flexibility for students to take classes from anywhere.
Virtual education increases quality of education by allowing students to learn at their own pace.
Virtual education increases quality of education by providing access to more knowledge on the Web.
Virtual education increases on-going learning by providing availability to resources on the Web.
Virtual education will increase understanding of concepts and issues as there will be no need to take notes.
Virtual education increases the diversity in a classroom by allowing students from other parts of the world to enroll in classes.
Virtual education changes the role of teachers to a facilitator rather than an instructor.
Virtual education will be more effective for motivated and self-disciplined students.
Virtual education increases "free time" for students to develop skills.
Virtual education increases one-on-one student-teacher interaction.
Virtual education increases interaction among students.
Students will learn more effectively using the Web.
Virtual education increases the thinking process of students.
Virtual education reduces the cost of education for students.

Chapter 11

Online Student Practice Quizzes and a Database Application to Generate Them

Gary B. Randolph
Purdue University – Anderson, USA

Dewey A. Swanson
Purdue University – Columbus, USA

Dennis O. Owen
Purdue University – Anderson, USA

Jeffrey A. Griffin
Purdue University – Kokomo, USA

Online practice quizzes are a popular way for students to test their readiness for a classroom exam. The authors have developed a quiz database application that stores potential test questions and exports selected subsets of questions to a web-based Javascript program. Feedback from students has been very positive. Students indicate that the question-feedback cycle helps them learn the material and prepare for the real exam. This paper will discuss how the database application works, explain how educators can obtain and use the application for use in their own classes, and provide general guidance for constructing quiz questions that make the quiz a positive learning experience.

INTRODUCTION

With the growth of the Internet, educators have begun using on-line practice quizzes to help students prepare for in-class exams (Brooking and Smith,). Online practice quizzes have the advantages of allowing students to access the practice quiz at

Previously Published in *Managing Information Technology in a Global Economy* edited by Mehdi Khosrow-Pour, Copyright © 2001, Idea Group Publishing.

any time, allowing students to progress at their own pace, providing instant feedback, and allowing information to be constantly updated (Ng and Gramoll, 1999). Students using online quizzes report that they appreciate the immediate feedback on their performance as well as the "anytime/anyplace" capability (Crepeau, 1998).

Javascript is a simple non-compiled programming language for webpages (Reynolds, 1996) that is used in many Internet applications, including creating online quizzes (Aylor, 1998). Because Javascript is non-compiled, the questions and answers are not secured. Any user who knows how to view the source code of a webpage can see all the questions and the answers. Therefore, Javascript is not an acceptable technology for graded exams. But for the purpose of a nongraded practice quiz, Javascript is a simple way to build practice quizzes so students can gauge their knowledge and prepare for an exam.

TAKING THE QUIZ

When students start the practice quiz program they will first see a welcome screen telling them what to expect. When they click on the Start button they will then begin seeing questions as shown in Figure 1. The program is set up to select a random group of questions for presentation from a larger universe of possible questions. This encourages students to take the practice quiz several times in a "drill-and-practice" approach.

Students can click on any of the three answers. Their selection will lead them either to a "Wrong Answer" screen or a "Correct Answer" screen as shown in Figure 2. In either case they will be told what the correct answer is and why.

Figure 1. Sample question

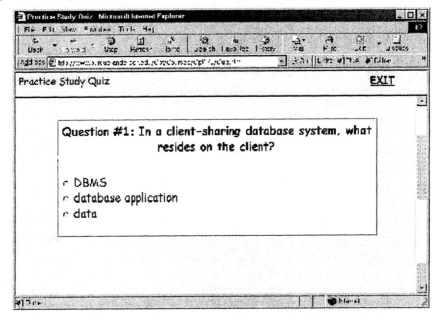

Figure 2. "Correct Answer" screen

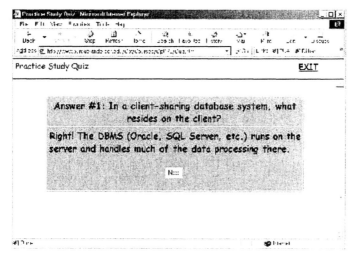

When students finish the practice quiz, they will be shown a summary of their performance. They will also be given an opportunity to take the practice quiz again with a different random selection of questions.

QUIZ GENERATOR DATABASE APPLICATION

These practice quizzes can be generated by instructors with the proverbial click of a button from a Microsoft Access 2000 database. The database allows instructors to store a ready list of questions. When it is time to generate the practice quiz, the instructor simply selects the questions to use and clicks a button to create the quiz file to the appropriate data path.

Care was taken to make the database application as user-friendly and foolproof as possible. The application shields the user from the intricacies of Microsoft

Figure 3. Database startup screen

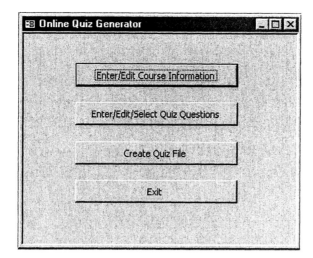

Access. The discussion below covers general questions about the application. No attempt has been made here to document Microsoft Access. Instructors can learn Access from a number of books and tutorials.

When the application is launched, it automatically comes to a startup screen shown in Figure 3. It has four buttons that control all the functionality of the program. Each of these (except Exit) will be discussed below.

ENTER/EDIT COURSE INFORMATION
The Enter/Edit Course Information screen shown in Figure 4 is used to enter general information about each course. For each course, the instructor/user should enter a new record and identify the course by some ID. The "Page to Exit to" should be the course homepage or any other exit page. The "Path to write files to" is the location of the course website on the web server or a local folder from which the website is later posted.

ENTER/EDIT/SELECT QUIZ QUESTIONS
This is the main screen for the application as shown in Figure 5. Instructors using the system should create a record for each question. For each question, instructors can enter the text of the question followed by text for three possible answers. Instructors should be sure to select the "Correct Answer" from the dropdown box.

The "Explanation" is displayed as part of the feedback after each question (see Figure 2). It provides an opportunity for the instructor to extend teaching into the "teachable moment" right after a student has been told that his or her answer is wrong. It should explain the concept being assessed in the question and explain why the wrong answers are wrong.

Instructors can click on "Use this question for the current quiz" to select that particular question for the practice quiz currently being generated. This allows the

Figure 4. Enter/Edit course information

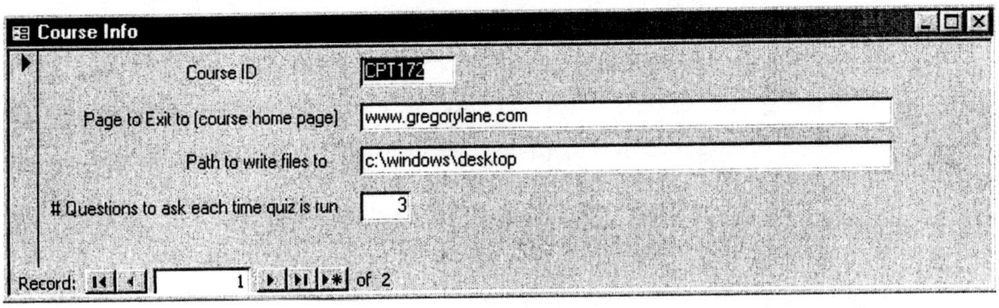

Figure 5. Enter/Edit/Select quiz questions

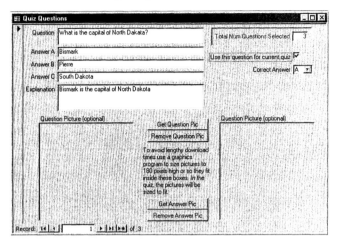

instructor to keep a semester's worth of questions on file and use them when appropriate. The total number of questions currently selected for the quiz is shown in the upper right corner of the screen.

Pictures can be displayed while the student is taking the quiz. One picture can be shown when the question is asked and a different picture shown when the answer is given. This allows instructors to ask questions about a picture or diagram that is shown with the question. Miscellaneous pictures, such as a question icon, could also be displayed with each question. The pictures must be in a web-compatible format, either .gif or .jpg. To add a picture to either the question or answer page for a question, click on the "Get Question Pic" or "Get Answer Pic" buttons. A standard Windows dialog box will open, allowing the instructor to select a picture file. The "Remove Question Pic" and "Remove Answer Pic" buttons are used to clear out the pictures. The quiz will scale the picture from any size to fit into the webpage. However, transmitting large pictures over the Internet can be time consuming, and scaling can result in distorted images. For best results, pictures should fit inside the display boxes.

CREATE QUIZ FILE

After all questions to be used on the current practice quiz have been entered and selected, this option allows instructors using the system to export those questions to an HTML/Javascript file. Instructors will see the screen shown in Figure 6. At first, only the course designation is shown. The instructor selects the course he or she wants to create the quiz for (see Enter/Edit Course Information on page 40). After making that selection, the other information will be displayed. The instructor can change that information "on the fly" or just click on OK to create the file.

Figure 6. Create Quiz File

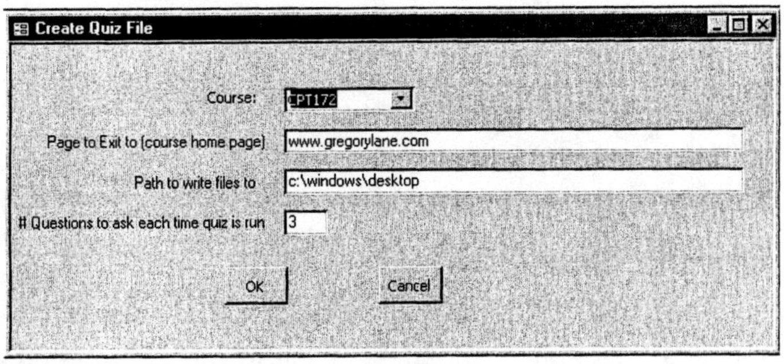

The program will then create an HTML file called Quiz.htm in the specified directory. It will also copy all picture files specified in the selected questions to that same directory. When the process finishes, the screen will close.

RESULTS

Informal feedback from classes in which the quiz has been used indicates that it is popular with students. One of the authors surveyed students twice during the Fall 2000 semester. One survey came after using the quiz to prepare for the first exam. The second survey came after using the quiz to prepare for the final.

The first survey found that fourteen out of fifteen students in the class used the quiz, running it an average of eight times. The number of times the quiz was run ranged from one student running it just once to one student running it twenty times. Thirteen out of fifteen students ran the quiz five or more times. Students were asked if the quiz was easy to run. Using a seven-point Likert-type scale with 7=Very Easy, the average score was 6.29. In other words, they found the quiz extremely easy to run. Students were also asked if they believed the quiz helped them understand the material. Using a seven-point Likert-type scale with 7=A Great Deal, the average score was 5.07. Students were asked if they believed the quiz helped them prepare for the exam. Using a seven-point Likert-type scale with 7=A Great Deal, the average score was 4.86.

One survey question that led to a change in the use of the quiz was how the students felt about the repetition of the questions. Because the quiz selects questions at random each time it is run, questions are often repeated from run to run. Four out of fourteen students found the repetition "annoying." Six out of fourteen students said the repetition was "useful in drilling me on concepts." Because of this, for later exams the instructor had the quiz ask the entire bank of questions (generally twenty) each time the quiz was run.

Thirteen out of fourteen students remaining in the class at the time of the final took the quiz an average of four times. This was half the amount of quiz taking from the first exam, but students were then getting all twenty questions instead of just seven as with the first exam's quiz. Students reported higher levels of belief that the quiz helped them understand the material (5.69) and prepare for the exam (6.00) using the same seven-point Likert-type scale. Eight of the thirteen students preferred the quiz asking the entire bank of questions, while five said they would rather have the quiz ask just some of the questions.

One author, who previously created study guide sheets for students, now just uses the online practice quizzes. The data can be entered and the quiz generated in no more time than it previously took to prepare a study guide. Anecdotal evidence indicates that the results are better. Students who would simply skim through a study guide without really mastering the material quickly discover their level of mastery using the online quiz. The possibility of further explaining concepts in the "Explanation" entry allows study time to be a true learning experience – not just an exercise in memorization.

IDEAS FOR IMPROVEMENT

As the application has been used, various ideas have been suggested for improving it. One idea would be to better implement the use of True/False questions. True and False can be used in the current version as answers A and B. However, when the quiz is run, a selection circle for the nonexistent answer C will also appear. It should be possible to modify the underlying Javascript to hide that. Some students have requested the inclusion of fill-in-the-blank questions, but those are much harder for a computer program to evaluate. The database application could use a few more features to automatically clear the "use this question" check marks or to store and sort questions by class, chapter, or topic.

As mentioned above, some students running the quiz found that the random assignment of questions repeated many of the same questions each time they ran the quiz and would like that repetition eliminated. However, using random questions encourages students to try the quiz again and again and also drills students on key concepts. The best way to keep repetition to a minimum with the current version of the program is to have a large bank of questions (30-40) and ask small numbers of them (6-8) each time. With only 15-20 questions it seems to be best to ask them all each time. A future update might allow students to select how many of the questions they want asked.

DESIGNING GOOD QUIZ QUESTIONS

Online practice quizzes will be a learning experience for students if questions are designed for learning. A few principles for designing good multiple choice questions follow (Gronlund, 1997; Wiggins, 1998):

1. Make a list of major learning goals for the material being covered by the practice quiz. Then ask: What would students have to do to convince me they had met that learning goal? Some of these mechanisms cannot fit within the structure of a multiple choice quiz, but many "knowing" and "thinking" goals will fit.
2. Create a two-dimensional grid with course topics down the side and the following column headings: Recall, Analysis, Problem Solving, and Evaluating. Create an appropriate number of questions for each cell in the grid.
3. Some questions need to focus on "recall" knowledge, but questions can be written that require a student to analyze and interpret. In these questions, provide students with information or a case followed by a question that calls for students to analyze, interpret, or make choices about that information.
4. Make your answer choices straightforward, unambiguous, and plausible.

OBTAINING THE APPLICATION

Instructors can run a sample version of the practice quiz program using a web browser and the address: http://www.purdue.anderson.edu/download/jquiz/quiz.htm. To download a copy of the database application, go to http://www.purdue.anderson.edu/download using a web browser and click on "Quiz Generator Database Application." Microsoft Access 2000 is required for the program to run. A copy of the Winzip program (available from www.winzip.com) will be needed to unpack the file.

REFERENCES

Aylor, S.E. (1998). *A look at asynchronous learning network courses as used at Kettering University*. Retrieved from ASEE Annual Conference Proceedings, CD-ROM.

Brooking, C. J., & Smith, D. A. (?). Simulation and Animation of Kinematic and Dynamic Machinery Systems With Matlab. *Computers in Education Journal, 9,* (2), pg. 2-3.

Crepeau, R. G. (1998). *Student Assessment with Internetquiz*. Seattle, WA: American Society for Engineering Education, pg. 3. Retrieved from ASEE Annual Conference Proceedings, CD-ROM.

Gronlund, N. E. (1997). *Assessment of Student Achievement*. Boston: Allyn & Bacon.

Ng, A., & Gramoll, K. (1999). *On-line Review and Practice Tests for the Fundamentals of Engineering Exam*. Retrieved from ASEE Annual Conference Proceedings, CD-ROM, pp. 13.

Reynolds, M. C. (1996). *Special Edition Using JavaScript*. Indianapolis: Que.

Wiggins, G. (1998). *Educative Assessment: Designing Assessments to Inform and Improve Student Performance*. San Francisco: Jossey-Bass.

Chapter 12

Classroom Component of an Online Learning Community: Case Study of an MBA Program at the University of St. Gallen

Julia Gerhard, Peter Mayr and Sabine Seufert
University of St. Gallen, Switzerland

GOALS AND MOTIVATION

The Internet not only affects various fields of business but also the educational sector increasingly. The impact of Internet technologies on the way of learning are immense. New learning scenarios arise; learning processes shift; learning methods are technologically better supported (Reeves, 1992). On a content side, it is possible to present knowledge in a network in the form of hypertexts. In addition, the participants of an educational program can benefit from a personal network developed in online supported learning communities (Paloff and Pratt, 1999).

This development challenges educational institutions to find successful ways of integrating the emerging learning scenarios and learning processes. To overcome disadvantages like isolation of students, slower learning progress because of missing team spirit, or low involvement of students in the learning material, educational institutions should not just use the Internet as a new distribution channel of old learning methods, but employ the Internet's chances to provide students with the knowledge required for a successful professional life as well as to prepare them for lifelong learning and a continuing education.

Previously Published in *Managing Information Technology in a Global Economy* edited by Mehdi Khosrow-Pour, Copyright © 2001, Idea Group Publishing.

This contribution wants to:

- show a way of designing an online learning environment, and
- design a possible classroom component of a specific online learning community.

We will first introduce the concept of online learning communities. We will then briefly describe the reference model for learning communities, which allows us to model a medium for the learning community. The reference model is applied to a concrete MBA program, and the design of the classroom component of this MBA learning community is introduced. Finally, we will give a brief outlook.

CONCEPT OF AN ONLINE LEARNING COMMUNITY

An online learning community can offer the basis for lifelong learning and intensify students' learning experiences immensely. Mutual, thus mostly deeper, examination of learning materials and the exchange between the group members deliver more aspects and different points of view on a topic and help to assess and enlarge the members' knowledge. On an interpersonal level, mutual studying creates a feeling of affiliation, which is maximal when considering formal learning goals as well as common social interests.

After defining the term "online learning community," we will give an overview of our proposed design for an online learning community.

Definition of an Online Learning Community

An online learning community unites the concepts of the (online) community and of the new learning paradigm:

A *community* is a group of actors (Armstrong and Hagel, 1996) who are connected by a common interest, common goals, or common actions in a commonly used channel system (Schmid, 1997). The channel system is part of the medium through which the exchange between the group members is maintained. According to Schmid, a medium is a system consisting of these components: logical space (semantics and syntax of a common language), channels, and organization (the structure with definitions of roles and their rights and obligations, and the process with protocols and processes) (Schmid, 1997; Schmid, 1998). A community can be called an Internet-based community (online community), if it uses the Internet as its "channel system" for exchange between the members (Lechner and Schmid, 1999; Mynatt, Adler, Ito, and O'Day, 1997; Rheingold, 1993).

A learning community (Harasim, 1995; Paloff and Pratt, 1999) has learning as its common interest. Actors involved can take on certain roles and the resulting rights and obligations in the community such as the role of a student or teacher or, less restricted, of alumni or project partners. The membership in the community

Figure 1: Emergence of Internet-based (Online) Learning Communities

Online Learning Communities

heavily depends on the learning environment, the kind of community, and its goals. The community develops a common language that is understandable for all members.

The *new learning paradigm* (Roblyer and Edwards, 1997) implies that studying is not product but process oriented (Dubs, 1996), shifting the focus from the result to the way the learning process takes place. Group-oriented learning, meta-cognitive learning strategies ("learning how to learn" and reflection of one's own learning process), and the possibility for knowledge exchange in the learning network as a basis for a lifelong learning concept are emphasized.

Connecting those concepts (Figure 1), an online learning community can be understood as a group of humans who share, on a pedagogical level, a common language, a common world, and common values, and who communicate and cooperate through electronic media during the learning process (Seufert, Lechner, and Stanoevska, 2000).

The Internet's characteristics, as opposed to the traditional channels, can increase flexibility in the design of the community: independent of time and place, both synchronous and asynchronous learning over long distances is possible (Seufert and Seufert, 1999). Individual preferences of community members in learning can more easily be considered, and students, as members of a global learning community, can work on assignments or group projects in a flexible manner.

Internet-based learning is not necessarily "distance learning." An Internet-based learning method can be utilized although all group members are at the same location. Respectively, an online learning community can support a "traditional" learning community partially. In this case, we speak of media-supported learning rather than of media-conducted learning (Euler, 2000).

Design of an Online Learning Community

Most successful in the development of an online learning community in order to support its members optimally seems to be the combination of the advantages and approved methods of the traditional university and the flexibility of online media. A successful online learning environment, for example, would be the depiction of a university on the online learning platform, including a classroom community and a campus community.

- The *classroom community*, the community within the course or in the "classroom," is mainly determined by learning objectives and methodological goals of the class; it supports the "formal" learning community. It follows a didactically structured course design (e.g., a study program or training course), allowing the formation of several sub-communities (e.g., student groups, project teams).
- The *campus community* characterizes a campuswide, more informal community and reflects the "campus life" that takes place beyond the didactically planned study offers; it is designed comprehensively and is long-term oriented (in the sense of "life-long learning" concepts), focusing on informal exchange of knowledge and experience. Community members are tied together by social interaction and other common interests.

The depiction of a university on the Internet platform allows for the program to portray online, in a comprehensible and user-friendly way, most of the typical processes that occur during a study program. It should also support the cohesion between students and the community. Taking over such an important role, the platform as the learning community's channel system has to be designed diligently in order to fulfil the community's needs. We will now introduce a reference model for learning communities that suggests a design for such a platform, as well as the other components (organization and logical space) of a learning community.

A REFERENCE MODEL FOR LEARNING COMMUNITIES

Platforms of Internet-based learning communities can be modeled – referring to the media reference model for communities of Schmid (1998; 2000) – in four designs (derived from four views). We separate the design for the campus community from the design for the classroom community, since those two communities have different focuses and different functions (see Figure 2).

- The *Organizational Design* shows the community view. It defines the structure of the community, the community interests, the actors and roles, their common language and the process with protocols and guidelines for the community. Differing focuses and goals of campus and classroom community require different roles, languages, and protocols. The organizational design is also adapted to the needs of a specific online learning community.
- The *Interaction/Process Design* is seen from the viewpoint of the implementation view and connects the preceding organizational design with the subsequent service design. Based on the organization of learning communities and

Figure 2: Reference Model for Online Learning Communities (Seufert et al., 2000)

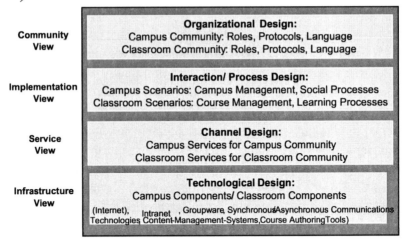

supported by the services offered by the platform for learning communities, the processes and scenarios are depicted. The (media-supported or presence) phases of particular learning processes are designed. Considering campus and classroom situations, each community will have special interactions and processes.

- The *Channel Design* represents the service view; the channel systems and services offered to the different communities and their members are described, and the web interface is determined.
- The *Technological Design* is presented from the perspective of the infrastructure view (technological aspect). In this part, the decision about where to develop which new technological tools and where to use which standard tool is made. For spotlighting the user needs, not the technology, this level is only performed after the community, its interactions and processes, and the required services are specified.

The reference model can be used to design learning communities which perform all their communication and learning processes on the Internet, as well as to model the design of communities combining attendance classes and online phases, using the Internet for certain functions and selected learning processes only. We now utilize the reference model to support an MBA learning community that combines online and presence elements.

MODELING THE MBA CLASSROOM COMMUNITY
The Executive MBA in New Media and Communication

The Masters program "Executive MBA in New Media and Communication," offered at the University of St. Gallen by the Institute for Media and Communications Management (=mcm*institute*), combines competence of business administration, knowledge about technological and economical components of new media, and the interaction of new media with sociological aspects. The use of new media is imparted to students through a combination of theory and practical application, supporting the goal "learning new media through new media." To enhance the employment of new media, predominant face-to-face classes in the beginning are increasingly supplemented by Internet-based elements. The MBA community is tied together by the common interest in the topic "new economy" and the related topics in the field of media and communications management.

The Internet platform is target group-oriented to allow students, alumni, business partners, and sponsors direct access to sections of their special interest. The MBA community and its platform are developed following the four design steps of the reference model. As a pioneer, this community uses the NetAcademy (www.netacademy.org), which was originally developed as a platform for knowledge exchange, publications, and discussions in research communities (Schmid, 1997) and is currently used by members of five research communities in the field of media and communications management Lincke, Schubert, Schmid and Selz, 1998).

The NetAcademy is designed as a "generic" platform. A new research or learning community can choose and combine existing services of the NetAcademy according to its needs and also add other required services. Numerous services already offered by the NetAcademy (e.g., the digital libraries and the glossaries) will be used by the MBA learning community. Additional services, such as curriculum catalogs or teaching templates, will be developed specifically for this community "type." An overlap with the research communities connects MBA community members to and enlarges their network with interesting researchers.

The MBA Community

Pursuing the idea of lifelong learning and a strong affiliation to the MBA community, the MBA team strives to create a close cohesion between students from the very beginning by following the campus-classroom approach mentioned above.

The MBA *campus community* holds the roles "student," "business," "faculty," "alumni," and "guest" and serves as platform for social interaction and networking. Services of the campus community therefore include a meeting point, an information desk, and a "networkers' guide" for finding former study colleagues or experts on different topics.

Figure 3: Roles in the Classroom Community

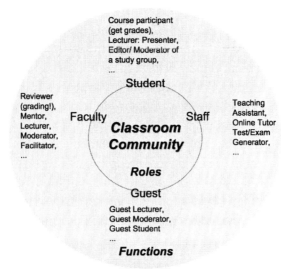

The MBA *classroom community* is not an exceptional online community, but supplements initially predominant face-to-face classes. The Internet platform plays a critical role as coordination platform and as communication and collaboration instrument in different learning methods of the MBA program. In the following section, we use the reference model for learning communities to model a classroom community for the MBA program in the NetAcademy environment.

Community View: Organizational Design. From a community view, the classroom community is structured in terms of roles and rules/ protocols, the common language, and the channel system. The classroom community, due to its formal character, is well-structured and has specific goals. The common interest lies in mastering the learning materials and succeeding in the assignments.

Actors in the classroom community can take the roles "student," "faculty," "staff," and "guest". Their functions vary depending on the learning method employed (e.g., faculty as lecturer, reviewer, or discussion leader (see Figure 3)).

In addition to general rules for interacting on the online platform, there are special rules for successful interaction in the classroom community, such as guidelines for courses (course management: e.g., planning of courses, self assessment of students or course evaluation) and design of classes or learning arrangements (Seufert, 1999) ((didactic) guidelines for teaching/ learning methods (Jonassen, 1992)).

The NetAcademy creates a common language (logical space) through glossaries and interlinked contents (links to glossary entries, links to authors and their roles in the community, etc.). The definition of a specific terminology for the classroom community creates a common understanding and the uniform use of terms and, thus, allows a better exchange and better communication among the members. The common understanding should not only refer to contents but furthermore to the structure of and the processes in the community, such as learning goals, key takeaways, or learning methods.

Implementation View: Interaction/Process Design. The implementation view concentrates on the processes and interactions in different learning scenarios. Every scenario encounters several phases, not all of which necessarily have to be media-supported. Structured interaction protocols can be generated for some processes that are highly automated; other phases may be structured only basically.

The interaction design includes the class management, which has a more administrative character, as well as the design of the learning processes, which deal with imparting contents. In order to determine the design of learning scenarios, we will briefly introduce our teaching framework depicted in Table 1.

The MBA program uses learning methods according to the study categories (contact study, self study, context study) introduced by the University of St. Gallen in the tide of restructuring its study programs (1999/2000). *Contact study* (Becker and Carnine, 1980), as a first category, contains of face-to-face events, ranging from "traditional lectures" to interactive lectures, in which the direct contact between the participants plays an important role. The second category, *self study*, includes student-centered methods. These can vary from highly controlled self study integrated in lectures to completely independent self study tutorials. As a last category, reflection or *context study* focuses on a broader context of learning content and mostly combines team-centered methods and complex, practical assignments of interdisciplinary fields (Jonassen, 1992; McDermott, 1999).

A teaching/ learning method may be explained by two dimensions. The *social form* distinguishes between class events, group work and individual work according to the dominant part of the lesson. The *activity form* indicates the kind of the learning task and knowledge achievement of the students. Whereas during a lesson based on "frontal teaching" prepared knowledge and thinking structures are imparted, during lessons based on case methods, project-based methods, or scientific work, the emphasis lies on the learner's own creation of knowledge.

Not every combination of social form and activity form is possible or recommendable. A faculty dominant approach to scientific work would not be successful, neither would be frontal teaching for group work or self study. The challenge lies in combining different methods for the greatest possible learning success.

Service View: Channel Design. The services in the service view are used to execute the processes of the implementation view. We identify four basic services for the classroom community which are learning community specific, thus new on the NetAcademy. Faculty and staff have very similar roles using the services in the classroom community and are conglomerated here. Guests have the same rights as students, but are restricted in their access to single courses.

- A *managing tool* serves as a course planner for all members, for (administrative) preparation of courses by faculty/ staff, and for evaluation of courses by students/ guests.

Table 1: Teaching Framework for the MBA Program

Study Categories	Appropriate for: ☑ Contact Studies ☐ Self-Studies ☑ Context Studies	Appropriate for: ☑ Contact Studies ☑ Self-Studies ☑ Context Studies	Appropriate for: ☐ Contact-Studies ☑ Self-Studies ☑ Context Studies
Social Form / **Activity Form**	1. Class Events Dominant: Faculty	2. Group Work Dominant: Group	3. Individual Work Dominant: Student
1. **Frontal Teaching** (New Theories and Concepts)	Examples: • (Online) Lecture • Q&A-Sessions • (Online) Guest Lecture, Mentoring • (Online) Symposium • Dinner Speech • Excursion		
2. **Preparation / Revision "Wrap Up"**	Examples: • Lecture: Instructor-led Preparation and Wrap up	Examples: • Homework in Groups • Group Presentations: What's new, Tech Talk, Lessons Learned	Examples: • Homework • Presentation: What's new, Tech Talk, Lessons Learned
3. **Training / Practice** • Tutorials/ Exercises, • Computer Lab Sessions	Examples: • (Online) Tutorial: Instructor-led • Computer Lab Session: Instructor-led	Examples: • (Online) Tutorial: Group-led • Computer Lab Session: Group-led	Examples: • (Online) Tutorial: self-paced • Computer Lab Session: Student-led
4. **Case Methods:** • Case Studies, • Web Quests, • Case Writings	Examples: • Lecture: Presentation of Cases • Guest Lecture: Presentation/ Demonstration of Business Cases	Examples: • "Classic" Case Study • Self-Study Case	Examples: • Case Study • Self-Study Case
5. **Projects:** • Media Venture • Real Life Projects • Students' Projects		Examples: • Integration Seminar • Project Seminar • Task Forces/ Expert Groups	Examples: • Student Project • Experiment • Field Study
6. **Scientific Work:** • Working Reports/Analysis • Thesis		Examples: • Group Reports • Group Thesis	Examples: • Reports • Thesis

- A *reporting tool* allows students/ guests to assess individual course progress and their own grades; faculty/ staff can overview class progress and the grades of all students.
- Using a *content repository tool*, faculty/ staff can provide materials for class events, group work, self studies and self tests; students/ guests can get class materials and assess their knowledge in self tests.
- A *cooperation tool* supports faculty/ staff in preparing team work or group projects, provides team spaces for group projects of students/ guests, and serves as a discussion forum for all members.

Depending on the learning method, one or more basic services can be integrated into new, more complex services. The following example illustrates how the online community is supported in the activity "thesis" by a "thesis marketplace service":

The starting hurdle of writing a thesis can be choosing a suitable topic or finding a supervisor for a self-selected topic. A "thesis marketplace service" (see Figure 4) offers a platform for trading topics and finding supervisors or students interested in working on specific topics. Later on, the service can provide support in phases of tutoring. In the cooperation tool, students can place a topic proposal and search for a supervisor, a tutor, and writing partners. Faculty members can provide topics and search for students interested in those topics, and they can respond to students who require tutoring services. Materials can be exchanged in the content repository tool. Administrative issues are covered in the managing and reporting tool.

Figure 4: "Thesis Marketplace Service"

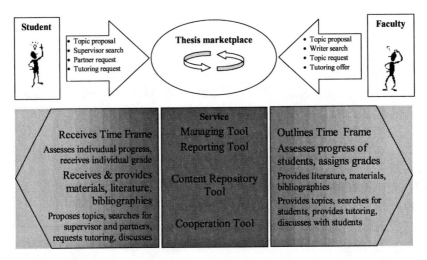

Technological Design. The technological design of the classroom community includes the supply of discussion databases for team work, synchronous chat
tools, asynchronous discussion tools, and content databases for class materials,
cases, and assignments. It also includes the graphic design of the platform, managed in a separate design repository to allow quick adaptations independent of
the technological design.

Not only the three layers above determine the decision about the way of
implementing the infrastructure, but also other circumstances (already existing technological framework, financial and personal resources, time frames, etc.). Considering those prerequisites, a tradeoff between choosing a lowcost standard service solution and a highcost customized service solution or even development of
new services has to be reached.

The MBA classroom community is implemented as a combination of standard software and individual software solutions.

CONCLUSION

We have described how a learning environment can be depicted, we have
used the reference model for learning communities to design an example classroom component for a specific learning community, and we have illustrated a
sample community service.

We are convinced that the design of this online learning community, according to the media reference model, considered all important factors of the learning
community. The critical factor for acceptance and use by the community members, however, will be the fulfillment of their needs. We therefore see the diligent
observation and critical investigation of student, faculty, staff, guest and business
partner needs as our everlasting challenge to lead the MBA online learning community to success.

REFERENCES

Armstrong, A., and Hagel, J., III (1996, May-June). The real value of on-line
    communities. *Harvard Business Review*, pp. 134-41.
Becker, W. C., and Carnine, D. W. (1980). Direct instruction: An effective ap-
    proach to educational intervention with the disadvantaged and low performers.
    Advances in Clinical Child Psychology, *3*, pp. 452-68.
Dubs, R. (1996). Betriebswirtschaftliche ausbildung in der herausforderung., *Die
    Unternehmung*, *5*, pp. 305-24.
Euler, D. (2000). Neue Medien - alte Pädagogik? Multimediales und
    telekommunikatives Lernen zwischen Potenzialität und Aktualität, in: *Wirtschaft
    und Erziehung*, pp. 251-57.

Harasim, L. (1995). *Learning networks: A field guide to teaching and learning online*. The MIT Press: Cambridge.

Jonassen, D. H. (1992). Evaluating constructivistic learning: T. M. Duffy and D. H. Jonassen (Eds.), *Constructivism and the technology of instruction: A conversation*. Lawrence Erlbaum: Hillsdale, NJ, pp. 137-48.

Lechner, U. and Schmid, B. F. (1999, January). Logic for media. The computational media metaphor. In *Proceedings of the 32nd Annual Hawaii International Conference on Systems Science (HICSS)*.

Lincke, D. M., Schubert, P., Schmid, B. F., and Selz, D. (1998, January). The NetAcademy: A novel approach to domain-specific scientific knowledge accumulation, dissemination and review. In *Proceedings of the 31st Annual Hawaii International Conference on Systems Science (HICSS)*.

McDermott. Learning Across Teams (1999). *Knowledge Management Review*, 3, (8), pp. 32-36.

Mynatt, E.D., Adler, A., Ito, M., and O'Day, V.L. (1997). Design for Network Communities. *Online Proceedings of CHI'97*, www.acm.org/sigs/sigchi/chi97/proceedings/edm.html.

Paloff, R. M. and Pratt, K. (1999). Building learning communities in cyberspace: Effective strategies for the online classroom. *The Jossey-Bass Higher and Adult Education Series*, Cambridge.

Reeves, T. (1992). Effective dimensions of interactive learning systems. In *Proceedings of the Information Technology for Training and Education Conference (ITTE '92)*, Brisbane, Australia: University of Queensland.

Rheingold, H. (1993). The virtual community: Homesteading on the electronic frontier. New York: Addison-Wesley.

Roblyer, M. D., and Edwards, J. (1997). Integrating technology into teaching. Merill, pp. 50-53.

Schmid, B. F. (1997). Das NetAcademy Projekt: I Die Idee, II Kontext und Ziele. Working papers mcm-1997-01, Institute for Media and Communications Management, University of St. Gallen.

Schmid, B. F. (1997, September). The concept of media. Ron Lee, et al.: Proceedings of the EURIDIS Fourth Research Symposium on Electronic Markets, Maastricht: Negotiation and Settlement in Electronic Markets, Erasmus Universiteit Rotterdam, The Netherlands.

Schmid, B. F. (1998). Elektronische Märkte – Merkmale, organisation und potentiale. Sauter, M. and Hermanns, A.: *Handbuch Electronic Commerce*, Franz Vahlen, München.

Schmid, B. F. and Lindemann, M. (1998, January). Elements of a reference model electronic markets. In *Proceedings of the 31st Annual Hawaii International Conference on Systems Science (HICSS)*.

Seufert, S., Lechner, U., and Stanoevska, K. (2000). A reference model for online learning communities. mcminstitute-Working Paper-2000-05, St. Gallen.

Seufert, S. and Seufert, A. (1999, January). The genius approach: Building learning networks for advanced management education. In *Proceedings of the 32nd Hawaiian International Conference on System Sciences (HICSS)*, Hawaii.

Seufert, S., PLATO (1999, August). "An electronic cookbook" for Internet-based learning networks. In *Proceedings of the 8th International Conference on Human-Computer Interaction (HCI 99)*. Munich, Germany.

Stanoevska, K. and Schmid, B. F. (2000, January). Community supporting platforms. In *Proceedings of the 32nd Hawaiian International Conference on System Sciences, Hawaii (HICSS)*.

University of St.Gallen, Jahresbericht (1999/2000). Universität St. Gallen, 2000, http://www.unisg.ch/hsgweb.nsf/c2d5250e0954edd3c12568e40027f306/452344e2a7bffc18c12568fd0026fca9/$FILE/Uni-Jahresbericht.pdf.

Chapter 13

Using Lotus Learning Space to Enhance Student Learning of Data Communications

Michael W. Dixon
Murdoch University, Australia

Johan M. Karlsson
Lund Institute of Technology, Sweden

Tanya J. McGill
Murdoch University, Australia

Online delivery of courses has become a viable option because of the Internet. This paper describes how we deliver and manage part of a postgraduate degree in telecommunications. We aim to foster learner-centered education while providing sufficient teacher centered activities to counter some of the known concerns with entirely learner-centered education. We use the Internet as the communication infrastructure to deliver teaching material globally and Lotus LearningSpace to provide the learning environment.

INTRODUCTION

Computer-based packages have increasingly entered the higher education curriculum. Many provide a useful supplement to students studying conventionally by illustrating aspects of the curriculum. Other packages are directed at aspects of course administration such as automated assessment (Oakley, 1996). Until recently, such packages have played only a supplementary role in course offerings,

Previously Published in *Challenges of Information Technology Management in the 21st Century* edited by Mehdi Khosrow-Pour, Copyright © 2000, Idea Group Publishing.

but this is rapidly changing. For example, Coleman, Kinniment, Burns, Butler and Koelman (1998) describe a successful attempt to replace all lecturing with computer-aided learning. Remote delivery of courses has also become a viable option because of the advent of the WWW on the Internet. For example, Petre and Price (1997) report on their experiences conducting electronic tutorials for computing courses.

Hiltz and Wellman (1997) report on a study comparing student learning and satisfaction between virtual learning and traditional classroom teaching across a large range of courses. They found that mastery of course material was equal or superior to that in the traditional classroom and that virtual learning students were more satisfied with their learning on a number of dimensions. In particular, they found that the more students perceived that collaborative learning was taking place, the more likely they were to rate their learning outcomes as superior to those achieved in the traditional classroom. They did, however, identify some disadvantages to virtual learning. These included ease of procrastination and information overload.

The different types of teaching and learning activities that are made possible by the Internet are shown in Figure 1. Harasim and Hiltz (1995) divided these activities into two categories: learner or teacher centered. There is, however, no common agreement about which category is the best, and many researchers argue for a mixture of learning activities emphasising group learning. At the moment there still seems to be an overemphasis on the teacher centered approach, which hopefully will slowly change as a better knowledge of online learning develops.

Figure 1. Categories of online activities

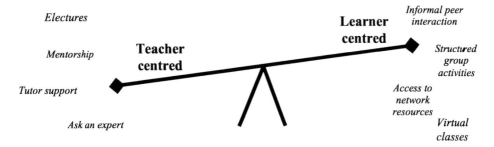

AIM AND IMPORTANT ISSUES

This paper describes how we deliver and manage part of a postgraduate degree in telecommunications management. We aim to foster learner-centered education while providing sufficient teacher-centered activities to counter some of the known concerns with entirely learner-centered education. We use the Internet as the communication infrastructure to deliver teaching material globally and Lotus LearningSpace to provide the learning environment.

While the primary aim of our approach is to enhance the student learning process, there are also other incentives to go along with this approach. From the university's point of view, it makes it possible to attract an entirely new group of students, such as industry professionals and tentative students, who due to other difficulties have problems undertaking traditional university education.

As always, there are two sides to everything. In proclaiming the advantages of online education above, we also have to be well aware of the potential drawbacks. It is even more important to have tight quality assurance of students due to the limited personal interaction between the students and teachers and the mostly unsupervised work the students produce and submit. There is also the issue of at which level to teach the course, i.e., what background knowledge is required? In face-to-face teaching the teachers usually have a feeling for the difficulties the students experience, but this is much harder to obtain with online education. These problems are compounded by the fact that students studying in a more flexible manner also often have a much wider diversity than traditional university students do. Letting students set some of the direction for the class isn't always an easy task. When students are afforded the opportunity to define some of the course objectives, the role of the instructor shifts from the pedagogical model of the instructor as "keeper of knowledge" to that of a guide and supporter. The instructor must ensure that the competencies and skills required for moving to the next level of learning and those necessary for meeting program objectives, and in our case also industry certifications, are included in the course goals.

At a more basic level there are issues, such as the fact that reading from the screen slows down reading speed by about 25% and most people prefer paper for long works (Nielsen, 1995). We also have to be aware that courses that require hands on experience limit the number of courses suitable for online education, although on-campus attendance one or a few times per semester can provide a solution to this problem.

REQUIREMENTS FOR A COURSE DELIVERY SOFTWARE PACKAGE

After defining the requirements for a software tool for developing and delivering courses online, we evaluated various software packages on the market. The requirements that we identified included:

- Instructors should not have to program and debug HTML code;
- All courses should have the same professional look and feel without having to hire computer programmers to write special software, and students should always be presented with the same interface for all their courses;
- The software needed to be fully integrated (one software package should allow the instructor to do everything required, such as course development and course management); and
- Professional support.

After evaluating various alternatives, we chose Lotus LearningSpace (LS), as it fulfilled all of our requirements. It contains tools to develop the curriculum that do not require the instructor to code in HTML. This allows the instructor to focus on the learning of the students rather than on creating and debugging HTML and on unit administration. LS provides instant feedback to the students and instructor and enables progress and problems that students encounter to be monitored as they go through the curriculum. Students can also have a discussion area where they can ask questions and communicate with the instructor as well as with other students.

LS allows us to create distributed learning courses that students and instructors can access whether they are online or offline. Students are able to download all the material for the course onto their machine so they can go through the curriculum without having to have a direct Internet connection. Using the offline access method makes it easier for students to learn whereever they are located and for instructors to develop and manage course material and reduce critical network bandwidth requirements.

Features that facilitate student learning include:

- *Schedule* – provides students with a structured approach to assignments, materials, and assessments. Through the schedule, students can link to everything required to complete their course.
- *MediaCenter* – allows immediate and searchable access to all materials for the course as the instructor makes them available.
- *CourseRoom* – provides a discussion group facility, which hosts collaborative interchange between student groups and/or students and instructors.
- *Profiles* – helps students and instructors get to know their classmates to form productive teams and to network outside the course.

Features that facilitate course management include LS Central for course management and the Assessment Manager for setting up and tracking of students' progress in their courses.

USE OF LS TO DELIVER ONLINE COURSES

In 1999, half of the courses in the Masters of Science in Telecommunications Management were offered online. We offered more courses online in 2000 to compliment the six existing online courses so that students could complete the full Masters degree online (some of the online courses have on campus requirements).

Students can access LS with a Lotus Notes Client or through a web browser. The Lotus Notes Client allows students to work offline by placing an image of what is on the LS server on their laptop or PC at home. This allows students to work while they travel and can reduce the amount of time they are required to be connected to the Internet (some countries have timed local calls). When they connect up to the Internet they can resynchronize their copy with the master copy located on a Lotus Notes Server.

LS has been used to integrate course material from a variety of sources. For example, in several of the courses students study material that contributes to different industry certifications, such as the Cisco Certified Network Associate certification (CCNA). This kind of external material must be integrated seamlessly with local content so that students see a totally integrated system when it comes to the delivery of each course. Students also have a consistent learning environment across the courses so that no time is wasted learning a new system as they start a course.

All quizzes are done online and all assignments (including group assignments) are submitted electronically and returned to students electronically. The online Cisco exams are done on separate assessment servers, as they are part of the certification process. The Cisco Networking Academy results of all the students around the world are maintained in a database in Arizona so that instructors can analyze how their class has answered questions and compare the results of their students with those of students in other institutions around the world.

Students get immediate feedback when they submit their quizzes and exams for grading online. Assignments are graded locally and returned with the instructor's personal comments and grade. The final exams for each course are taken locally in a more traditional way. The students may actually get two final exams, one to pass the university course and one administered by an independent testing center to pass the industry certification. Students could fail or pass both as well as pass one and fail the other. The integration of the two curriculums gives the students their credits in the university degree as well as the opportunity to pass the industry certification as a "bonus".

We use LS to monitor the progress of on-campus and off-campus students in courses and to identify the areas where students are having problems. This allows instructors to cover the material again as necessary to make sure that the students do understand the material. Testing and checkpoints with built in repetition are important for long term retention and understanding of the material. Students also use LS to track their own progress and performance in the courses.

As mentioned above, the intention is to be able to offer the same courses to the students irrespective of their location. However, a few practical things and student attitudes towards some of the features differ slightly. For example, on-campus students tend not to use the online CourseRoom facility that contains threaded discussions as much. However, the off-campus students tend to rely heavily on this for interaction with other students and the instructor. The instructors tend to try and only answer questions in the discussion groups, because this reduces students sending emails to the instructor asking the same questions. The instructors will usually refer students back to the CourseRoom. This requires a well working discussion group with some kind of search engine to be effective.

AN EXAMPLE OF THE ONLINE APPROACH

Depending on course content, the migration to online teaching can be more or less laborious. There are differences within as well as between disciplines, and there are differences in the goals set by those introducing online education. We have chosen one course in the Telecommunication Management degree to provide an example of how online teaching was implemented. Appropriately, this course is about networking technology.

The Data Communications Systems course provides an introduction to networking and networking devices, focusing on Local Area Networks (LANs) and Wide Area Networks (WANs). Network design, Ethernet, ISDN, Frame Relay, and TCP/IP are introduced, including IP addressing and router protocols. There is a strong practical context that provides the students with the opportunity to build, configure, and problem solve in a multi router network environment. This course also includes the first part of the Cisco Certified Network Associate (CCNA) curriculum. The second half of the CCNA curriculum is covered in a second course, the Advanced Data Communications course. The Data Communications Systems course provides a good example of a difficult class to integrate with LS because of the external curriculum, which is contained on a separate web server, and the external assessment requirement for students.

Students are required to login to LS once they have selected the Data Communications Systems course. The students use LS schedule to follow the schedule for the course. Through the schedule, students can access the external curriculum, which resides on a separate web server.

Theory is presented to students in the form of online topics (web-based), mini lectures, and laboratories. The online teaching material combines web-based text and graphics to explain concepts. Short movies, shown on their screen, are also used to illustrate concepts that are difficult to communicate with just static text and graphics. The students are given aims and objectives at the start of each topic. The teaching material covers these topics in detail, and at the end of each topic students have optional self-assessment quizzes that allow them to gauge their understanding of the material. Students are required to have gone through the online material and additional reading before class.

Instructors also use these online quizzes in LS to measure the understanding of the students before the students attend the class. As students work through the curriculum, they are required to pass formal quizzes for each module (eighty modules in total). This allows students and the instructor to receive important feedback. The instructor is able to identify students who are not keeping up to date with their work and also areas that students are having problems with. The questions in the quizzes are directly linked to objectives for each module. Students have to achieve a pass of 80% on each quiz, otherwise they are required to repeat the quiz until they achieve 80% or better. Detailed answers to the questions are not made available, so students are required to go through the curriculum again to make sure they understand all the material, not just the questions they missed.

The instructor is able to compare how each student has performed on the quizzes, so this allows them to identify areas where students are having problems. The mini lectures for on-campus students can then focus on the areas where these students are having problems. The instructor can also discuss areas where students are having problems in the discussion group. Students are required to participate in the discussion group because part of the total grade is based on participation. There are two Cisco online exams for the course, and students are required to pass these exams with a minimum score of 80%. Students are allowed to take the exam more than once. All students must also take a separate supervised written final exam to meet University requirements.

The philosophy used in the practical labs is to prepare students to solve real world networking problems. Students work in groups during the practical lab sessions. Students are given timed practical exams at the end of each major component, and some of these practical exams are groups exams. Students are allowed to take these exams as many times as they like but are required to pass all these exams. Distance education students are required to attend an on-campus part of the course. During this time they are required to design and implement networks and troubleshoot network problems and take the practical exams. The distance education students also take the two required Cisco online exams during this on-campus part of the course for supervision reasons.

The factors discussed above all contribute to facilitating student learning. Faster and more frequent feedback on the material keeps students more in touch with their progress. The facility to continue to work with the teaching material until an 80% pass is achieved enhances performance. Students see important material three times so that their learning is reinforced and students are able to study wherever they are and still be part of the student community. The use of a virtual discussion group will enhance the sense of community among the students and teachers. Combining a learner-centered approach with LS allows us to achieve a quality course online.

CONCLUSIONS

This paper discussed an approach used to adopt a learner-centered environment within an Internet-based degree. We do not believe that online teaching and computers are a substitute for a human interaction, but rather that technology can provide flexibility of learning and hence enrich the learning experience and diversify the student mix. As the courses used to illustrate the issues in the paper are about telecommunications, the Internet is a very appropriate medium for instruction. Students learn about telecommunications while accessing information through the Internet. There are, however, a number of important issues to take into consideration while setting up an online course. For example, just converting teacher-centered material to electronic form doesn't work. It doesn't make use of the technology available today in an optimal way. The opportunity to adopt a more learner-centered approach should be taken by including, among other things, well-structured group activities and virtual discussion groups. The electronic classroom challenges instructors and students to move beyond the traditional boundaries of learning and presentation. Online education projects may in many ways be the motivational tool that instructors have sought for a long time, for both on and off-campus students.

REFERENCES

Coleman, J., Kinniment, D., Burns, F., Butler, T., and Koelmans, A. (1998). Effectiveness of computer-aided learning as a direct replacement for lecturing in degree-level electronics. *IEEE Transactions on Education*, *41*, pp. 177-84.

Harasim, L., and Hiltz, S. R. (1995). *Learning networks: a field guide to teaching and learning on-line.* Cambridge, USA: The MIT Press.

Hiltz, S. R., and Wellman, B. (1997). Asynchronous learning networks as a virtual classroom. *Communications of the ACM*, *40*, (9), pp. 44-49.

Nielsen, J. (1995). *Multimedia and hypertext: The Internet and beyond.* Boston, USA: AP Professional.

Oakley, B. (1996). A virtual classroom approach to teaching circuit analysis. *IEEE Transactions on Education*, *39*, pp. 287-96.

Petre, M., and Price, B. (1997). *Programming practical work and problem sessions via the Internet.* ITiCSE 97 Working Group Reports and Supplemental Proceedings, pp. 125-28.

Chapter 14

Development of a Distance Education Internet-Based Foundation Course for the MBA Program

James E. LaBarre
University of Wisconsin-Eau Claire, USA

E. Vance Wilson
University of Wisconsin-Milwaukee, USA

Course development is a task that requires a methodology if it is to result in a cohesive, well organized unit. This paper details the procedures to develop a distant education foundation course for the MBA program. All MBA courses using this methodology are delivered to students enrolled in several universities within the Wisconsin System.

INTRODUCTION

In the University of Wisconsin system, several institutions have been designated as non-doctoral institutions. Of the twelve institutions in this category, several provide an MBA program. Even though all of these institutions have been engaged in distance education media such as compressed video, two-way audio/video, and Internet delivery, they were basically functioning as independent institutions. Looking to provide efficiency and effectiveness in education, five of the institutions formed a consortium to supply foundation courses leading toward the MBA program. It was the intention of the consortium to allow each institution to continue to provide the MBA as they had envisioned it and, at the same time, to allow students to obtain prerequisite educational background prior to entering the MBA without eating up the resources needed to administer the graduate program. In addition, the administration at each of these institutions wanted to have the

Previously Published in *Challenges of Information Technology Management in the 21st Century* edited by Mehdi Khosrow-Pour, Copyright © 2000, Idea Group Publishing.

flexibility of providing enrolled students in the respective MBA programs the opportunity to take courses from another institution if they so desired.

NEEDS ANALYSIS

The increasingly volatile business environment that students face when they graduate drives the need for ongoing curricular improvement. Alumni report that their familiarity with technology and their ability to use it for self-training have enhanced their position in the business world. Integrating the use of learning technologies into the curriculum can provide students hands-on experience in using both the Internet and groupware applications, such as Lotus Notes.

By using both synchronous and asynchronous technologies, the institutions sought to achieve the goal of providing students throughout Wisconsin with access to quality educational opportunities while lessening the need for costly duplicate investment in educational resources. Through a careful mix of faculty and technology, consortium participants felt the quality of course offerings could be enhanced.

BACKGROUND LITERATURE

Asynchronous, computer-based courses have been offered for more than a decade, and research findings have been reported concerning several aspects of learning in asynchronous versus traditional classroom environments. These findings include:

- *Higher satisfaction.* Asynchronous students feel that the system is a valuable part of their learning (Wilson and Whitelock, 1998), that they have better access to professors, that classes are more convenient overall, and that they took a more active part in their courses (Hiltz and Wellman, 1997).
- *Greater learning.* Students take advantage of the extra time, course resources, and problem examples that are available (McIntyre and Wolff, 1998), and they frequently work harder to keep up with their classmates (Hiltz and Wellman, 1997).
- *High enthusiasm.* Asynchronous students are more enthusiastic, at least initially, and this frequently leads to production of an overwhelming amount of communication during the first few weeks of an asynchronous course at a pace which falls off later in the course (Hiltz and Wellman, 1997). This problem may be mitigated through system design, which can be used to structure message volume and, potentially, student enthusiasm to more sustainable levels (Stoney and Wild, 1998; Warren and Rada, 1998).
- *Fewer interpersonal interactions.* Asynchronous students find it more difficult to socialize (Wilson, Morrison, and Napier, 1997). They interact less and develop substantially fewer new friendships in class (Hiltz and Wellman, 1997).

- *Lower information confidence and motivation.* Students have less confidence in information received via electronic communication than face-to-face (Trushell, Reymond, Herrera, and Dixon, 1997), and asynchronous students are more likely to stop attending class if they get busy with other activities (Hiltz and Wellman, 1997).
- *Individual, task, and context dependencies.* One line of research indicates that asynchronous communication systems offer qualitatively different levels of support than traditional media for students with certain individual characteristics (Wilson, 1998), for certain tasks (Wilson and Morrison, 1999), and for certain educational contexts (Wilson and Morrison, In Press).

In summary, the literature suggests that asynchronous distance education is a complex process that has both intrinsic benefits and intrinsic detriments in comparison with traditional instruction methods. It is particularly important to note the studies that find association between system design elements and specific outcomes, as these suggest that asynchronous delivery can be "fine tuned" beyond its current capabilities. In total, the literature suggests that new development and testing of asynchronous distance education programs, such as the MBA consortium foundation project, has the potential to leverage academic productivity and use of resources.

THE MBA FOUNDATION PROJECT

A grant was written to provide funding for development of Internet-based foundation courses students need to enter consortium MBA programs. The purpose of the MBA Foundation Project was to:

- Expand cooperative efforts among colleges to offer foundation modules and MBA electives via the Internet.
- Address the educational needs of customers.
- Coordinate distributed learning services among the participating colleges.
- Enhance faculty technology development opportunities through training provided via faculty-trainer programs within each college.
- Develop a website and Internet delivery for MBA foundation courses (Lotus Notes and the academic LearningSpace software were chosen previously as the platform applications for course delivery)
- Investigate the applicability of new Internet-based learning technologies for potential use by the participating college faculties.
- Explore the possibility of developing a series of non-credit modules capable of being delivered asynchronously over the Internet to support "just-in-time-learning" students.

The project was divided into three phases. The first phase (1998-99) was designated the Development Phase. The second phase was identified as the Implementation Phase (1999-2000) and the third, the Assessment Phase (2000-01).

The Development System

In an attempt to satisfy the needs of all institutions involved, the development team for each of the foundation courses is made up of representatives from two or more colleges. The individuals serving on the team decide the extent of the course content development by each member, which is used to determine responsibilities and compensation. The development team members agree to:

- Participate in team meetings, and coordinate curriculum development via the MBA directors;
- Meet with developers and designers from the UW Learning Innovations;
- Prepare modules for conversion to a common format within LearningSpace;
- Teach the first offering of the Internet course;
- Conduct virtual office hours; and
- Provide revisions to the course.

The MBA Foundation Course Development System includes the utilization of personnel and technical assistance from the UW Learning Innovations. Learning Innovations is an organization set up to coordinate the development of the foundation courses and to ensure that uniformity and standards are met for each of the courses. Figure 1 shows the activities involved in the development of a typical course.

Figure 1. MBA Consortium Foundation System course development data flow

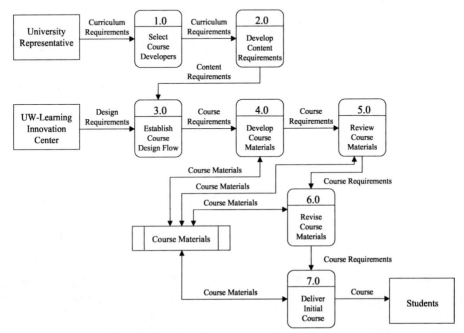

The System Defined

The development of each of the foundation courses required for entry into the MBA and elective modules that support the MBA proceed in basically the same manner. Participating institutions select the faculty representative(s) who will cooperate in the development of the course or module. These individuals meet to establish the course content, activities to be completed, the assessment techniques, etc. Once the preliminaries have been decided upon, the development team has an initial meeting with the Learning Innovations. The purpose of this meeting is to make sure that all developers have a thorough understanding of the technologies to be used for the delivery of the course. Since the Internet, Lotus Notes, and Lotus LearningSpace are the primary hardware and software tools selected for use by the consortium, the developers must understand the role of the interactive modules. LearningSpace is a popular online distributed learning technology that includes several key components (Lou, Van Slyke, & Luo, 1999). It provides a *Schedule* which allows the instructor to store the course materials, assignments, and feedback on self-administered exams. *Profile* is a database of information that faculty and students enter about themselves. The profile area can also be used for private reporting of the results of assignments and examinations. *CourseRoom* supports efforts of teams to collaborate on assignments for the course. The *Assessment Manager* is a tool used for creating and reviewing tests and surveys. Student grading is managed via this module.

Review Process

Faculty initially develop the content units of the course, which then are reviewed by the Learning Innovations to ensure that design and flow are appropriate for delivery via the technology being utilized. It is the responsibility of the personnel at Learning Innovations to modify the electronic format of course content as necessary to conform to the learning environment.

Following review by the Learning Innovations, faculty revise the course materials. The revised course materials are then put into a standard course format so the learner basically sees the "same thing" as they enroll in course after course.

Developing the Course

Faculty members developing the course content and activities need not be overly concerned about the students' hardware and software availability. They are encouraged to plan the course as they would if it were being delivered in the classroom. The developer might plan to use a video tape, software programs and/or Competency Based Training modules as part of their instruction. Learning Innovations is responsible for determining how this content is best delivered to the student. In many cases, the content is delivered via the Web, although in some cases video tapes or CD-ROMs are duplicated and sent to students.

Special Activities

Instructors are encouraged to choose activities that best assist in delivery of content to achieve the objectives of the course. For example, the faculty member who developed the Financial and Managerial Accounting foundation course set up an area in the CourseRoom entitled "Hallway" for any discussions that students may want to carry on that do not pertain to the course. This special area gives the students an opportunity to discuss issues of mutual concern without impacting any discussions pertaining specifically to the course.

Launching the Course

Students enrolled in a course complete the registration at their respective institution and are provided access codes by the instructor responsible for the course. Students from outside the state would apply as special students and register at the institution of their choice. As students initially come online on the Internet, they are given an opportunity to test their hardware capabilities in relationship to the hardware specifications required to complete the course. If they do not have the appropriate hardware capabilities, they are informed at that point. Currently, it is up to the student to obtain appropriate hardware. Planned for next year is an option whereby the student would have the opportunity to lease the appropriate hardware. Students are given the opportunity to order the textbook online, or they may print off the form and complete the purchase via postal mail.

Virtual Office Hours

When a course is delivered via the Internet and/or via supporting media, the course instructor maintains virtual office hours. Since these office hours are maintained via the CourseRoom, it is not necessary for students or instructor to meet in any specific location. Students are not required to be online during the stated office hours, but they are able to rely on the instructor being available during this period. The instructor is also generally available to support the student needs via email and voice mail if necessary.

Future Outcomes

The initial launch of our MIS foundations module is scheduled for January, 2000. Thus, by the time the IRMA conference convenes in May, 2000, the authors will be in a position to report on the trials and tribulations of developing and delivering an asynchronous Internet-based foundation course in MIS for the MBA.

REFERENCES

Hiltz, S. R., and Wellman, B. (1997). Asynchronous learning networks as a virtual classroom. *Communications of the ACM, 40* (9), 44-49.

Lou, Van Slyke, and Luo, W. (1999). Asynchronous collaborative learning: The mitigating influence of LearningSpace™. In M. Khosrowpour (Ed.), *Managing Information Technology Resources in Organizations in the Next Millenium,* pp. 874-875. Hershey, PA: Idea Group Publishing.

McIntyre, D. R., and Wolff, F. G. (1998). An experiment with WWW interactive learning in university education. *Computers & Education, 31,* 255-264.

Stoney, S., and Wild, M. (1998). Motivation and interface design: Maximising learning opportunities. *Journal of Computer Assisted Learning, 14,* 40-50.

Trushell, J., Reymond, C., Herrera, R, and Dixon, P. (1997). Undergraduate students' use of information communicated during e-mail "tutorials." *Computers in Education, 28* (1), 11-21.

Warren, K. J., and Rada, R. (1998). Sustaining computer-mediated communication in university courses. *Journal of Computer Assisted Learning, 14,* 71-80.

Wilson, E. V. (1998). Determinants of communication in student software development teams. In *Refereed Proceedings of the 1998 International Association of Computer Information Systems Conference* (pp. 353-359). Cancun, Mexico.

Wilson, E. V., and Morrison, J. P. (1999). A task-based measure of perceived effectiveness in computer-mediated communication. In M. Khosrowpour (Ed.), *Managing Information Technology Resources in Organizations in the Next Millenium,* pp. 646-653. Hershey, PA: Idea Group Publishing.

Wilson, E. V., and Morrison, J. P. (In Press). Effects of educational context on socialization in computer-mediated communication. *Journal of Computer Information Systems.*

Wilson, E. V., Morrison, J. P., and Napier, A. M. (1997). Perceived effectiveness of computer-mediated communications and face-to-face communications in student software development teams. *Journal of Computer Information Systems, 38* (2), 2-7.

Wilson, T., and Whitelock, D. (1998). Monitoring the on-line behaviour of distance learning students. *Journal of Computer Assisted Learning, 14,* 91-99.

Chapter 15

Web-Based Learning: Is It Working? A Comparison of Student Performance and Achievement in Web-Based Courses and Their In-Classroom Counterparts

Kathryn A. Marold, Gwynne Larsen and Abel Moreno
Metropolitan State College of Denver, USA

In an in-depth study of Internet and classroom students' test grades and assignment grades spanning three semesters, it was found that there is a significant difference in achievement and performance for these two types of course delivery. Although there were not significant differences in the final grades for two of the three levels of computer information systems students in CMS 1010, CMS 2010, and CMS 3270 at Metropolitan State College of Denver, there were significant differences between classroom students and Internet students when the authors examined performance—as measured by eight homework assignments and achievement—as measured by test scores. Reinforcing what many studies have found, the distribution of final grades among eighteen classes (nine Internet delivered and nine classroom delivered) did not differ significantly, but how those grades were earned did differ for two of the three sets. Internet students did better on the exams, with significant

Previously Published in *Challenges of Information Technology Management in the 21st Century* edited by Mehdi Khosrow-Pour, Copyright © 2000, Idea Group Publishing.

differences at all three levels. When performance was compared, there was a significant difference for the junior set of data. Classroom students performed better on the hands-on homework assignments for this level. The upper level course student averages differed significantly in both achievement and performance measures. The three courses examined all had the same instructor for Internet and classroom sections; all had exactly the same tests and assignments for their particular course; all three courses had a hands-on skills component.

The authors caution against generalizing about all Internet-delivered courses from the results of this study. It appears that there are significant differences in online learning experiences when one delves more deeply into how mastery of material is obtained. The sample size of 302 students provided a rich data set which showed variances according to gender, class level, past experience with Internet delivered courses, and even age. T tests were performed on three sets of matched pairs of students. The authors believe the findings support the theory that Internet delivered distance education courses require different design. More importantly, however, this research demonstrates that Web courses are working. As more research is done on achievement and performance in Internet-delivered classes, and as our instructional design for Web courses is refined, we will find the best way to design these distance education courses.

INTRODUCTION

Are web-based courses working? In the last five years, the number of classes offered via the Internet rather than in the traditional classroom setting has grown exponentially. Web-delivered courses began as basically a collection of text-based pages of information—albeit nicely formatted. Many of the courses quickly progressed to graphical and even multimedia dependent pages as the World Wide Web became more sophisticated and higher speed modems and widespread access became commonplace. Web-based classes are the newest variation of distance education, which has been around for decades. Web-delivered distance education is distinctive in several ways: the course is presented on dynamic web pages, meaning the course is often changed throughout the weeks of the term; interactive multimedia on the Web pages offers greatly enhanced student involvement; and due to the asynchronous and synchronous communication capabilities of state-of-the-art web-based classes, there is often as much, or more, teacher-student communication than in the traditional classroom-delivered course (McGinnis, Marold, and Monroe, 1998). These elements are not part of the older, more traditional distance education environment, such as the correspondence course (Larsen and Helms, 1996). The promise of "electronic tutelage," or using computers (specifically, the Internet) for learning, may have materialized (Marold, 1994). Online training and web-based training have greater value than previous distance learning methods because they can be much more interactive and results can be tracked automatically (Dager, 1998). The following paper describes the results of a statistical analysis of three courses at three levels, spanning three semesters at Metropolitan State College of Denver. Data were collected from 329 students who were taking either an Internet-delivered course or its classroom counterpart. The results reinforce past research results on final grade distribution and also reveal new findings as to achievements and performance of students taking Internet-delivered classes.

THE RESEARCH QUESTION(S)

Internet-delivered courses are now firmly established at most institutions of higher education. In the past four years, the number of courses offered online through the World Wide Web server at Metropolitan State College increased from eleven to fifty. The student enrollment exploded from 142 students to 1061. The number of students choosing to take Web-based delivery of a course is ever increasing. Student satisfaction with the Internet route grows (McCloskey, 1998). It has been found that final grades between the two environments do not differ significantly (Mawhinney, 1998). Web-based courses are here to stay (Dager, 1998).

But are these Internet courses working? Are students really learning and retaining as much in an Internet course as they would in a classroom environment? The early pioneers who developed Internet counterparts of classroom courses at institutions all over the world did so without the guarantee that this form of distance education would be as effective as the traditional lecture/lab courses that had been offered for centuries. Will this new model of electronic tutelage become the standard, or at least coexist on an equal basis with the face-to-face lecture method?

The "honeymoon" period that the novel method of Internet-delivered courses enjoys is at an end. Accountability and measures of effectiveness are indicated. Educators everywhere now insist that we measure the effectiveness of this new electronic tutelage. Are students who receive part, or sometimes all, of their college credits online performing and achieving as well as the students who choose to take all of their courses in a traditional classroom setting? Is web-based learning really working?

REVIEW OF THE LITERATURE

It is becoming obvious that we are at a turning point in higher education. Some individuals even caution that reengineering of the university is required

(Tsichritzis, 1999). The changes required are driven primarily by the new techno-logical possibilities and the new learning environments that have been established. Today's university is no longer restricted to a specific time or place. Students can take the course anytime, anyplace (ATAP). Students' demand for a complete graduate degree instead of partial credit toward a graduate degree or a certificate of training is increasing (Nixon, Leftwich, 1998). They want it easily accessible, yet they want it to be as credible as a degree obtained in the physical classroom. In this day of the part-time commuter student, it is often difficult to find a conve-nient time for instructor and student to meet. On the Internet, individual student-teacher communications can take place efficiently and easily. Burgstahler found that students participate more in class discussions when the course is delivered electronically than they would in a traditional class (1997). Forums, white board discussions, and chat rooms increase opportunities for interaction. Studies have shown that some students perceive the opportunities for communication greater in a web-based course (McCloskey, Antonucci, and Schug, 1998). In a study by Kroder, Suess, and Sachs, eight out of ten students who responded said they would take another Internet-based course, even though the same proportion said it took more time than a classroom course. A student stated, "Yes. Believe it or not, I actually felt that my asynchronous instructor was easier to approach with questions than my classroom teachers" (1998). And Mcgrath (1998) found that one of the major advantages of Internet-based learning was that you could make use of "real time" data, such as weather—say, meteorological conditions that change hourly. The same would hold for business and government classes where events change daily. Links to other subjects are so simple that a course can be changed "on the fly" as new hardware and software are introduced, making a systems analysis or hardware and software course on the Web instead of totally in the classroom preferable for some instructors (Braun, and Crable, 1999). Aside from the time factor (web-based courses take more total time for the student and for the instructor teaching them), both students and instructors have heartily endorsed them (Kroder, Suess, and Sachs, 1998).

Initial research showed that grades are substantially equivalent as well. In a 1995 study by Bowman, Grupe and Simkin, there were no statistically significant differences in student achievements and final grades using CBTs (Computer Based Training modules) rather than Web courses. And McCloskey, Antonucci, and Schug (1998) found no significant differences in Web course and classroom course grades for their students.

Yet for the business community to accept electronic tutelage as a viable alter-native to the classroom environment, the online degree needs to be proven equivalent to a degree obtained exclusively in the classroom. Even though there have been initial studies proving no grade differentiation between the two groups, more in-depth measurement is indicated. Soloway said in 1995, "Pedagogy and curriculum will need to change in profound ways in order to make effective use of the Internet" (Granger, and Lippert, 1998).

In the intervening four years, many web-based courses have progressed into very high quality interactive learning experiences. However, institutions and industrial communities alike must be assured that students who earn credits on the Internet have accomplished the learning objectives that are appropriate for those courses. Serious Internet courses strive to ensure maximum consistency between the two delivery formats. The grading criteria for the Internet courses is the same as for traditional classroom courses (Kroder et al., 1998).

If we use the established measures of effectiveness by relying on student grades, as has been noted, it has been found numerous times that the grade differences in web-based courses and classroom courses is not significant (McCloskey, 1998; Mawhinney, 1998). Final grades for Internet-delivered courses are at the same level or higher than classroom courses (Schulman, and Sims, 1999). Naturally, it is as debatable in the Web environment as in the classroom environment as to whether grades are a valid indicator of learning. And the authors of this research project are just as skeptical as to the validity of measuring learning by examining grades as many other educators. Nevertheless, this is an established norm and an accepted method of measuring effectiveness.

Uniqueness of This Research

The authors of this research project attempted to strengthen measures of effectiveness by not only looking at final grades, but also looking at interim test grades and projects submitted in the Internet courses. Achievement and performance were both examined. In this way, theory and practice could be compared between the experimental group of Internet students and the control group of classroom-based students. Student achievement was measured by test scores and performance was measured by homework assignments. The present belief that today's dominant learning style calls for hands-on practice and lab assignments in most information systems and management courses (Hanson, and Freeman, 1993) dictated a look below the surface final grades of students into the components of those grades. The idea that "you don't know it unless you can do it," or Bloom's application of theory level of mastery (Bloom, Engelhart, Hill, Furst, and Krathwohl, 1956), spurred the researchers' plan to look also at homework projects as reflection of what has been learned. Internet and classroom students should be compared as to whether the theory in the course can be accurately expressed on tests and whether the practical skills can be demonstrated by hands-on assignments and projects.

Many educators are concerned that there is no real way to know if the Internet student actually was the one who did the hands-on project, whether he/she had help doing it, and so forth. However, there are the same concerns in the classroom environment. Although the classroom group may have instructor-led lab sessions for skills introduction and practice, the homework assignment is most often done outside of this setting using a separate exercise similar to the in-lab practice. There is no guarantee that the student actually did the work unassisted in either setting. Both classroom and Internet environments for testing can be much more tightly controlled. The students in this study took their exams at the college Testing and Assessment Center, where the tests were monitored and a picture ID was required of each student taking each of the three tests.

THE HYPOTHESES

In an attempt to examine not only the final grades of students in Internet and classroom sections of the same course, but also to look at performance and achievement separately, the hypotheses were as follows:

Null

There is no significant difference in performance and achievement of students taking Internet-delivered courses and classroom-delivered courses.

Alternate

There is a significant difference in performance and achievement. When you examine levels below final grades and delve into more representative measures of learning, such as productivity and achievement, there are differences.

METHODOLOGY

Data were collected from both the classroom students and the Internet students at the beginning of each of the three semesters under study. The collection process was identical in both groups. That is, during the first week of class, or in the required Orientation session for the Internet sections, a Student Data Form was distributed, and the students completed it. (The Student Data Form used is available by contacting the authors.) The instructors kept records of each student's grades on three exams and on eight homework assignments. The data were entered in a data set by course number. There were three semesters of the *Introduction to Computers* course, with a control (classroom) and an experimental (Internet) set for each class. There were three semesters of the *Computer Applications for Business* course, a sophomore beginning information systems class, with control and experimental groups for those. Finally, there were two sets of the

Micro-based Software course, a junior advanced office skills-based course, with control and experimental groups for those as well. The junior level course had only two semesters of data available because this was the last course to be put online; the 1010 and 2010 course were the first in the department to be offered as Internet sections.

The data were entered into a *Minitab®* file and analyzed by course number. There were three sets of data, each containing control and experimental pairs. In this way, performance and achievement could be analyzed individually for each level of class. This proved to be noteworthy, since the first data analysis of the freshman *Introduction to Computers* course showed significant differences in both performance and achievement, the sophomore level course showed a significant difference in the achievement area, and the junior level showed significant differences in both areas. (The freshman course also showed a statistically significant difference in final grades of the Internet and classroom sections.) The description of the sample and the results of the study are as follows.

Description of the Sample

The data collection of 329 forms resulted in 302 usable forms. Since many forms were submitted before students officially dropped a course, a number of the data sheets were discarded. Students who failed the course but did not officially withdraw with a NC (no credit) process were initially retained in the data set. Since some students who received an F participated in the entire semester and others did not, there was a very large standard deviation in the performance and achievement scores. Therefore, prior to the final analysis, the records of students who failed the course because they had never dropped the class and stopped "attending" were removed. Thus, the records of failing students who remained were those who were actually active in the course through the majority of the semester. The researchers decided the final data set more accurately reflected the true distribution of grades.

In both the control and experimental groups, the data were self-reported. The students indicated their individual assessment of their computer literacy level, using the Bodker Computer Literacy Scale. This Likert scale has five categories, from Beginner to Novice to Competent to Proficient to Expert. Data were also collected on gender, status as full or part-time student, number of hours carried in the semester, student age, and so forth. Students also answered whether they had ever taken a distance education course before and specifically if they had taken an Internet-delivered course. Finally, the authors were interested in how many traditional hours the students were carrying. Frequency distributions were plotted for all of the demographic data. Table 1 details the breakout for the most salient demographic variables.

Table 1: Demographic distribution of the sample (n=302)

Course Level & Delivery	Female Gender	Full-time student	Age range <=25 yrs	Computer Literacy level = 2 or 3	First *Internet* course ?
C1010(n=73)	67%	72%	69%	66%	
In1010(n=54)	59%	61%	46%	67%	69%
C2010(n=34)	35%	79%	85%	85%	
In2010(n=42)	41%	54%	41%	75%	78%
C3270(n=48)	32%	87%	50%	82%	
In3270(n=51)	45%	64%	41%	48%	47%

In=Internet   C=Classroom
Bodker Computer Literacy Scale:
   1 = Beginner; 2 = Novice;3=Competent;4=Proficient;5=Expert

If one examines the frequencies, it is notable that there are more females than males in the lower level classes (sometimes twice as many), while in the upper level classes, more males were in both sections of the course. Likewise, more full-time students than part-time students took the classes being examined. Most of the students in all three levels of classes were 25 years of age or under, but when the percentage of students 40 years of age or over exceeded 5%, it was in the Internet sections. And oddly enough, the self ratings on the Bodker Computer Literacy Scales were higher for those from the freshman Computer Literacy class than the junior *Micro-based Software* class. In the junior level classroom sections, no one rated him/herself as an expert, and only six in the Internet class did so. Most said they were competent or proficient (level 2 or 3). Yet the majority of the students in the *Introduction to Computers* class rated themselves above the beginner level - as competent or novice (66% in the classroom sections; 67% in the Internet sections) - and they were taking a beginning computer course! Eight individuals rated themselves as proficient or expert in the 1010 Internet class. (Perhaps this is testimony to the adage that "the more you know, the more you realize what you don't know." Or perhaps the population in introductory computer classes has changed. Or lastly, those eight 1010 individuals were simply acquiring three hours credit and really didn't need this elective course.) At any rate, the frequency distributions of the demographic variables appear quite normal.

Experience of the Instructors

The two instructors whose students were analyzed had authored the Web courses for each level and/or had selected the texts for the courses. They had written the project assignments for the three levels. Together they had authored the textbook used in the 1010 *Introduction to Computers* class and had been on a team that produced one of the first online WBTs for the *Works* and *Office 97* applications. Both had extensive teaching experience and knowledge of educational pedagogy; they continue to teach both in the classroom and online.

THE FINDINGS

In Table 2, the results of the analysis are shown. As previously reported, the average final score obtained by students taking CMS 2010 and CMS 3270 in a traditional classroom setting was not significantly different from the average final score obtained by students taking the courses online. The average final score for students taking CMS 1010 in a classroom was, however, significantly different from that obtained by students taking it online. This result is counter-intuitive. The researchers conjecture that the difference may be due to the fact that the vast majority of the students taking the *Introduction to Computers* CMS 1010 course in the classroom are freshmen with less computer background than their peers taking the course online. Student performance, as measured by the average projects score, varied with how the course was delivered for students taking CMS 3270, but did not for students taking CMS 1010 or CMS 2010. Student achievement, as measured by the average exams score, varied with how the course was delivered for all courses considered in the study. In all cases, the Internet students on average achieved higher scores on their exams than their classroom peers. Since the testing environment was similar to that of the classroom, this again points to a different type of student who takes online courses.

Table 2: Results

Average Scores (Std. Dev.)

Course	Delivery (n)	Projects	Exams	Final Grade
CMS 1010	Classroom (73)	92.4 (11.1)	73.5 (13.8)	83.7 (11.3)
	Internet (54)	92.4 (12.8)	78.2 (9.2)	86.7 (9.2)
	t-value	-0.02	-2.02^2	-1.45^3
CMS 2010	Classroom (34)	91.8 (9.9)	70.01 (14.4)	79.2 (10.2)
	Internet (42)	90.3 (11.7)	77.5 (8.1)	81.7 (11.0)
	t-value	0.57	-2.63^1	-0.98
CMS 3270	Classroom (48)	93.8 (7.5)	67.8 (13.8)	86.4 (8.2)
	Internet (51)	87.5 (14.1)	77.7 (17.1)	86.7 (9.2)
	t-value	2.57^1	-1.48^3	-0.16

[1] p-value <0.02   [2] p-value <0.05   [3] p-value < 0.15

CONCLUSION

Based upon the results of this statistical analysis, the null hypothesis that there is no significant difference in performance and achievement for students taking web-based courses rather than classroom-delivered sections is rejected. The alternate hypothesis that indeed, there are subtle differences, can be accepted. This does not mean that all courses in all disciplines can be indiscriminately "put up on the Web" and professors can retreat to their offices, or even homes, to "teach" in virtual classrooms. There is much more to the higher education experience than simply earning credits in specific courses. The professors are still the guardians and authors of curriculum and still function as facilitators for student learning. What the research does indicate, however, is that the web-based courses are working, that students are acquiring the knowledge and skills necessary to pass the course. In addition, the findings indicate that the student who takes online courses might be a significantly different type of learner than the student who takes courses in a more traditional environment. The findings do point out a need to design web-based courses with optimum opportunity for achievement and performance in every area. The findings indicate a difference in the *way* the course material is mastered. And finally, it does point out once again that, in this arena, for this place in time, web-based learning works!

REFERENCES

Blomberg, D., Marold, K., Mawhinney, C., and Uliss, B. (1998, October). Panel discussion, Online Course Management. In *Mountain Plains Management Conference*. Denver, Colorado.

Bloom, B. S., Engelhart, M. D., Hill, W. H., Furst, E. J., and Krathwohl, D. R. (1956*). Taxonomy of educational objectives. Handbook I: The cognitive domain.* New York: David McKay.

Bowman, B. J., Grupe, F. H., and Simkin, M. G. (1995). Teaching end-user applications with computer-based training: Theory and an empirical investigation. *Journal of End User Computing, 7*, (2), 12-17.

Braun, G., and Crable, E. (1999). Student perceptions of the paperless classroom. In *Proceedings of the 27th Annual Conference of International Business School Computing Association,* July 18-21, 1999. Georgia Tech University. Altanta, Georgia.

Burgstahler, S. (1997). Teaching on the net: What's the difference? *T.H.E. Journal. 24* (9), 61-64.

Dager, N. (1998). Little web schoolhouse. *AV Video Multimedia Producer, 20,* (12), 15.

Granger, M. J., and Lippert, S. K. (1998). Preparing future technology users. *Journal of End User Computing, 10*, (3), 27-31.

Hanson, R., and Freeman, J. (1993). Learning style differences of management and computer information students. In *Proceedings of the Mountain and Plains Management Conference.* Cedar City, IA, pp. 7-9.

Kroder, S. L., Suess, J., and Sachs, D. (1998). Lessons in launching web-based graduate courses. *T.H.E Journal, 25*, (10), 66-69.

Larsen, G. and Helms, S. (1996, September). The Internet as an instructional delivery vehicle for higher education: A framework for evaluation. In *Proceedings of the International Association for Computer Information Systems.* Las Vegas.

McCloskey, D. W., Antonucci, Y. L., and Schug, J. (1998). Web-based versus traditional course deployment: Identifying differences in user characteristics and performance outcomes. In *Proceedings of the International Business Schools Computing Association Annual Conference.* Denver, Colorado.

McGinnis, D., Marold, K., and Monroe, S. (1998). Developing and delivering Internet courses. In *Proceedings of the FACT Symposium.* Glenwood Springs, CO.

Mcgrath, B. (1998). Partners in learning: Twelve ways technology changes the teacher-student relationship. *T.H.E. Journal, 25*, (9), 58-61.

Mesher, D. (1999). Designing interactivities for Internet learning. *Syllabus, 12*, (7), 16-20.

Nixon, M. A., and Leftwich, B. R. (1998). Leading the transition from the traditional classroom to a distance learning environment. *T.H.E. Journal, 2*, (6), 54-57.

Soloway, E. (1995). Beware techies bearing gifts. *Communication of the ACM, 28*, (1), 17-24.

Schulman, A. and Sims, R. L. (1999). Learning in an online format versus an in-class format: An experimental study. *T.H.E. Journal, 26*, (11). pp. 54-56.

Tsichritzis, D. (1999). Reengineering the university. *Communications of the ACM, 42*, (6), pp. 93-100.

Chapter 16

Audio and Video Streaming in Online Learning

P.G. Muraleedharan
XStream Software India (P) Ltd., India

INTRODUCTION

Online Learning Systems provide educational and training services at anytime, in any location, and often when the resources would not otherwise be available. Major technologies that have been responsible for the growth of online learning include advances in PC technologies, improved connectivity, better bandwidth capabilities of the Web, video conferencing, and the streaming of audio and video. Audio and video streaming technology will play a key role in most online learning programs of the future. In the past, audio and video files were directly accessed from the Web servers and were subjected to larger wait time for a user browsing the Web. Today, live videos can be displayed without wait time using streaming technology.

The two major players in media streaming technology are Microsoft and Real Networks. Both provide the media servers, content development tools, and streaming media players. Version 4.0 of Windows Media Technologies contains a rich suite of products and features that you can use to create, deliver, and play streaming media for applications ranging from news and entertainment to e-commerce, corporate communications, and distance learning.

Windows Media On-Demand Producer, a component of the Windows Media Tools, simplifies the creation of streaming media content. Once your streaming media content is created, you can publish it on a media server using Windows Media On-Demand Producer. Similarly, RealProducer, an integral part of the RealNetworks RealSystem 8, creates streaming media from audio and video. The media clips can be published on a RealServer using RealProducer.

Previously Published in *Managing Information Technology in a Global Economy* edited by Mehdi Khosrow-Pour, Copyright © 2001, Idea Group Publishing.

ACCESSING MEDIA FILES USING HTTP AND USING REAL TIME TRANSPORT PROTOCOL

Web browsers and Web servers form a client/server architecture that uses packet-switched messaging via the Internet. They use HTTP to transport Web documents composed of hypermedia across the Internet. Figure 1(a) and Figure 1(b) show the setup of a Web system for accessing video/sound files via HTTP and via Real Time streaming protocol respectively.

The protocol steps required for retrieving a sound file called *sample.au,* using HTTP and a streaming protocol, is listed below:

i) Click on the hyperlink that points to sample.au on the webpage.

ii) The Web browser translates this into a GET request containing the name of the file   to be retrieved and sends this request off to the server.

iii) The Webserver will respond to this request by sending a response message. In the first case the server sends the sound file within a HTTP response message. In the case of Real Time Streaming Protocol the HTTP response message does

Figure 1(a). Set up of a Web system for accessing video/sound files via HTTP

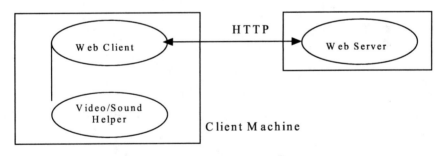

Figure 1(b). Introducing a streaming protocol by adding a new client/server pair

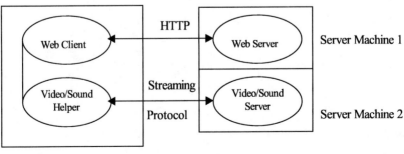

not send the sound file, but it contains the call parameters such as the IP address required by the helper client for contacting the server and retrieving the sound file.

iv) The Web client uses the information in the *content-type* field of the response message to start a sound player as a helper and passes the parameters it has received from the Web server. In the first case the player downloads the complete sound file and simply plays it. In the case of Real Time Streaming Protocol the sound player helper contacts the sound server specified by the IP address, independently of the Web client, and the file is transferred using a streaming protocol. The goal of such a streaming protocol is to start the output of the file as soon as enough data of the file has arrived.

CREATING STREAMING MEDIA FILES

To achieve streaming of media files, the streaming client/server network application uses the following technologies:
• Server Side – digitize, compress and packetize
• Client Side – depacketize, decompress and playset

A live feed is normally converted using a digitizer board with a specific sampling frequency. The sampled digitized data is then compressed using a software or hardware codec such as the following:
• Audio - GSM, PCM, ADPCM, DVI, LPC, CELP
• Video - H.261, H.323, MPEG, M-JPEG, NV

Once compressed, the data is then packetized and encapsulated inside an application transport protocol such as RTP before delivery on the network. After the streaming data reaches the destination, the client software processes the data. The client parses the packet and buffers the data into memory. The buffered data is then subjected to the appropriate decoder software or hardware followed by playout to the output device. The playout device can be a speaker or video display, or the data can be archived to a file on the file system.

Controlling Packet Loss

Most real time audio and video applications used on the Internet today do not retransmit lost packets. Instead, the applications only play the packets that they receive and simply leave out lost packets. In other words, the streaming protocol must be designed in such a way that the information transmitted is useful even in the presence of packet loss. To control packet loss, a technique called *rate-adaption* can be used. Using the information contained in the *receiver report* part of the RTP packet, the sender will automatically adjust the encoding method to vary the bandwidth.

Controlling Delay

Another issue, which is as serious as the packet loss, is the problem due to uneven time gap between packets arriving at the destination. Imagine two audio packets that are stored in the queue of a router. One is stored before and the other is stored behind a big packet from another data stream (e.g., an ftp) going through the router. The router sends packets with constant throughput. Consequently, the two audio packets that arrived with correct 20ms interspacing at the router leave the router with a different packet interspacing. This effect, also called *jitter*, is usually handled by introducing a *playout-buffer* at the receiver and by adding a timestamp to each packet.

REAL TIME PROTOCOLS (RTP & RTCP)

The Real Time Transport Protocol is an IETF Standard described in RFC:1889, which provides end-to-end network transport functions for transmitting real-time data, such as audio, video, or simulation data, over multicast or unicast network services. It generally runs on top of UDP, though it is designed to be able to run with other underlying protocols as well. While streaming real-time data via RTP, information is packetized and encapsulated inside an IP packet as shown in Figure 2.

Figure 2. RTP information is packetized and encapsulated inside an IP packet

IP Header	UDP Header	RTP Header	RTP Data Specific Header	RTP Data

Figure 3. (a) RTP Client/Server, (b) Web Client/Server

RTP	HTTP
UDP	TCP
IP	IP
ETHERNET	ETHERNET

The RTP stack can be compared to the Web stack as shown in Figure 3. RTP carries only 28 bytes of header information, as compared to several thousand bytes of header information each HTTP request is bundled with. That's why RTP is a highly efficient protocol for real time media delivery. The data transported by RTP in a packet, for example, audio samples or compressed video data, is called the RTP payload.

The audio conferencing application used by each conference participant sends audio data in small chunks of, say, 20 ms duration. An RTP header followed by

Figure 4. Multicast system supported by RTP

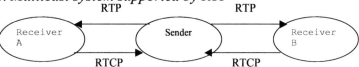

one chunk of data is embedded in a UDP packet. The RTP header indicates what type of audio encoding (PCM, ADPCM or LPC) is contained in each packet so that senders can change the encoding during a conference, for example, to accommodate a new participant that is connected through a low-bandwidth link or to react to indications of network congestion. RTP packet sequencing and time-stamping services allow RTP-based clients and servers to deliver real time services such as synchronized presentations on end-systems even under badly congested network conditions. The sequence numbers included in RTP allow the receiver to reconstruct the sender's packet sequence. The sequence number also allows the receiver to estimate how many packets are being lost.

The RTP data transport is augmented by Real Time Control Protocol (RTCP) to allow monitoring of the data delivery in a manner scalable to large multicast networks and to provide minimal control and identification functionality. As the name suggests, this protocol only carries control information, not the actual data. Figure 4 shows the basic structure of the system supported by RTP.

RTP Level Relay – Mixers and Translators

Mixer is an intermediate system that receives RTP packets from one or more sources, possibly changes the data format, combines the packets in some manner, and then forwards a new RTP packet. For example, consider the case where the conference participants in one area are connected through a low-speed link, whereas the majority of participants from other areas enjoy high-speed network access. Instead of forcing everyone to use a lower-bandwidth, reduced quality audio encoding, a *mixer* may be placed near the low-bandwidth area. This mixer resynchronizes incoming audio packets to reconstruct the constant 20 ms spacing generated by the sender, mixes these reconstructed audio streams into a single stream, translates the audio encoding to a lower-bandwidth one, and forwards the lower-bandwidth packet stream across the low-speed link.

Translator is an intermediate system that forwards RTP packets with their synchronization source identifier intact. For example, some of the intended participants in the audio conference may be behind an application-level firewall that will not let any IP packets pass. For these sites, two translators may be installed, one on either side of the firewall, with the outside one receiving all multicast packets through a secure connection and sending them to the translator inside the firewall.

Figure 5. The format of the RTP header

```
0                   1                   2                   3
0 1 2 3 4 5 6 7 8 9 0 1 2 3 4 5 6 7 8 9 0 1 2 3 4 5 6 7 8 9 0 1
┌─────┬─┬─┬─────┬─┬─────────────┬───────────────────────────────┐
│V=2  │P│X│ CC  │M│PAYLOAD TYPE │        SEQUENCE NUMBER        │
├─────┴─┴─┴─────┴─┴─────────────┴───────────────────────────────┤
│                          Time stamp                           │
├───────────────────────────────────────────────────────────────┤
│          Synchronization Source (SSRC) Identifier             │
├───────────────────────────────────────────────────────────────┤
│            Contributing Source (CSRC) Identifiers             │
└───────────────────────────────────────────────────────────────┘
```

The translator inside the firewall sends them again as multicast packets to a multicast group restricted to the site's internal network.

RTP Data Transfer Protocol

Figure 5 shows the format of the RTP header. The numbers on top of this figure give the bit numbering for the different fields. One row corresponds to 32 bits, or four bytes. This header is followed by the actual data, containing for example sound and video. The first twelve octets are present in every RTP packet, while the list of CSRC identifiers is present only when inserted by a mixer.

The fields in the header have the following meaning:

- Version (V): 2 bits - Identifies the version of RTP.
- Padding (P): 1 bit - If this bit is set, the packet contains one or more additional padding octets at the end, which are not part of the payload.
- Extension (X): 1 bit - If this bit is set, the fixed header is followed by exactly one header extension.
- CSRC count (CC): 4 bits – Contains the number of Contributing Source Identifiers that follow the fixed header.
- Marker (M): 1 bit – The interpretation of the marker for a particular application or format is defined by a profile.
- Payload type (PT): 7 bits – Identifies the format of the RTP payload and determines its interpretation by the application.
- Sequence number: 16 bits – Increments by one for each RTP data packet sent.
- Timestamp: 32 bits – Rrepresents the instant at which the data was sampled.
- Synchronization Source Identifier (SSRC): 32 bits – A number assigned randomly when a new stream is started.
- CSRC list: 0 to 15 items, 32 bits each – Identifies the contributing sources for the payload contained in this packet.

RTCP Packet

An RTCP packet looks much the same way as an RTP packet except that there is no data part (figure 6).

Figure 6. An RTCP Packet

IP Header	UDP Header	RTCP Header

RTCP Header consists of the following parts:

- Receiver Report (RR) contains information of the quality of reception of different RTP streams at a particular receiver.
- Sender Report (SR) contains information about the status of the RTP stream sent out.
- Source Description (SDES) contains information about a source.
- BYE is the last packet sent for an RTP stream.
- APP refers to application of specific functions.

MEDIA FORMATS

While the intent of this paper is not to give a complete course in digital signal processing, this section gives an overview of the media formats.

Digital Audio Concepts

The basic steps involved in transmitting analog audio data over a digital are: sampling, quantization, and packetization. These processing steps are used in sound formats such as PCM, which directly encode the analog signal generated by the microphone. Low bandwidth sound formats such as GSM and LPC use a different approach based on speech synthesis techniques. Their bit stream can thus be conceived as a set of commands to a speech synthesizer.

Table 1: Common sound sampling rates

Samples / sec	Description
8000	A telephony standard that goes together with u-law
11025	A quarter of the CD sampling rate, or half the Mac sampling rate
16000	Used by G.722 compression standard (telephony), or half of 32000
16384	csound/BICSF (= 16 * 1024)
16726.8	NTSC television rate
18.9 k	CD-ROM/XA standard
22050	Half the CD sampling rate
22255	22254.545454545454 –Mac rate - Horiz. Scan rate of the 128k Mac
32000	Used in digital radio, long play DAT, and Japanese HDTV
32768	csound/BICSF (= 32 * 1024)
37.8 k	CD-ROM/XA standard for higher quality
44056	Used by professional audio equipment
44100	Sampling rate of CD and Digital Audio Tape (DAT) players
48000	The DAT sampling rate for domestic use
49152	csound/BICSF (= 48 * 1024)
50000	Used in software DSP

Sampling Rates. The common sample rates are listed in Table 1 along with the devices with which they are most frequently used.

Sound Compression Schemes. The three requirements of a good compression technique are: maintaining the quality of the original sound, fast processing, and achieving a good compression factor. There are several well-standardized schemes for sound data compression that are based on three basic methods:

- using a compact numerical representation for the sample values,
- using standard data compression techniques one can compact blocks of samples,
- performing some kind of analysis (e.g., spectral) of the sound data to get a more compact representation (as in FFT-based or LPC vocoders).

One of the most popular methods of the first kind is called μlaw or ulaw encoding. Because the compression uses a simple mathematical function of each data value, one can easily expand μlaw samples in real time. Using this technique to compress 16 bit samples is clearly audible, though, as a decrease of approximately 24 dB in the dynamic range of the signal.

Another encoding similar to μlaw is called A-law and is used as a European telephony standard. CCITT defined public standards for compressing voice data in CCITT G.721 (ADPCM at 32 kBaud) and G.723 (ADPCM at 24 and 40 kBaud). IMA's DVI ADPCM is a standard that compresses 16 bit sound data into only 4 bits. Microsoft created their own variant of ADPCM for use in their WAV file format.

LPC-10E is defined by US DOD Federal Standard 1015 and stands for Linear Prediction Coder (Enhanced) and has a 2400 bits/sec rate. The LPC coder fits speech to a simple, analytic model of the vocal tract, then throws away the speech and ships the parameters of the best-fit model. An LPC decoder uses those parameters to generate synthetic speech that is usually more or less similar to the original.

GSM 06.10, which stands for Global System for Mobile Communications, is a European standard originally for use in encoding speech for satellite distribution to mobile phones. It compresses 160 13 bit samples into 260 bits (or 33 bytes), i.e. 1650 bytes/sec (at 8000 samples/sec). It results in very good compression with good quality output, but is very costly in terms of performance.

MPEG is an audio/video compression standard that has gained wide acceptance across industries. It has become popular to use the audio portion of the standard to store audio files since it provides near CD quality output at relatively low bit rates. It is very computational intensive, especially during the encoding phase. There are three layers supported, with the third layer the most popular. Players that can decode higher layers can also decode lower layers. Layer I MPEG audio files usually have the extension .mpg, layer II usually have the extension .mp2, and layer III usually have the extension .mp3. The audio compression is pretty good.

Table 2: Sound file formats

Format Name	File Extension	Hardware platforms or software tools on which used
NeXT/Sun	.snd, .au	NeXT, Sun, DEC
AVR	none	Atari/Apple
SPHERE	none	NIST/ARPA
IFF	.iff	Amiga
AIFF	.aif(f)	Apple, SGI, etc.
AIFC	.aif(c)	Apple, SGI
WAV	.wav	Microsoft/IBM
(E)BICSF	.sf, .snd	CARL / UNIX / IRCAM
VOC	.voc	PC Soundblaster
MOD	.mod, .nst	Amiga
MIME	none	
MIDI SDS	none	MIDI

Table 3: Sound payload types currently defined in RTP

Payload Type Number	Sound Format	Sampling Rate	Troughput
0	PCM μlaw	8 KHz	64 Kbit/s
1	1016	8 KHz	4.8 Kbit/s
2	G.721	8 KHz	32 Kbit/s
3	GSM	8 KHz	13 Kbit/s
4	unassigned		
5	DVI4	8 KHz	32 Kbit/s
6	DVI	16 KHz	64 Kbit/s
7	LPC	8 KHz	2.4 Kbit/s
8	PCM A-law	8 KHz	64 Kbit/s
9	G.722	8 KHz	48-64 Kbit/s
10	L16, two channels	44.1 KHz	
11	L16, one channel	44.1 KHz	
12	unassigned		
13	unassigned		
14	MPEG Audio	90 KHz	
15	G.728	8 KHz	16 Kbit/s

Sound Formats. Table 2 presents an overview of some of the most widely used sound file formats.

Table 3 shows the sound payload types currently defined in the RTP Audio/Video profile and the bandwidth they require. The main goal for a speech encoder is intelligibility, whereas that of an audio encoder is to include transmission of music. Therefore, bandwidth requirements for speech coders are usually lower than the requirements for general, high quality audio coders.

Making Sound Robust Against Packet Loss. In a sound transmission, a packet loss will result in a silence period. The impact of packet loss can be kept low by reducing the packet length and thereby reducing the length of silence period. Many encoders use a length of 20 milliseconds. RealAudio software uses the *sample interleaving* technique for reducing the impact of audio packet loss. The disadvantage of this technique is that it increases the delay between sender and receiver. This is because the receiver must wait until all interleaved packets have arrived before he can start playing the audio. This is not a problem for audio-on-demand applications. However, it creates difficulties in two-way conversations, such as in an Internet telephone.

A standard alternative technique to packet retransmission is to handle packet losses by forward error correction. In this scheme, each packet contains information about previously transmitted packets in addition to its own data. However, forward error correction is only useful if exactly one packet was lost. If several packets in a row are lost, only the last packet can be recovered by the receiver, and the user will hear the effect of packet losses for all other packets. Forward error correction also increases the minimal end-to-end delay and it also increases bandwidth requirement for the transmission due to additional data added.

Video

There are many file formats for still images, video, and audio that you will constantly encounter while using the Internet.

JPEG Format. Before JPEG compression, each pixel is represented in 24 bits. This size is reduced both by converting the original information into a more compact encoding, and by leaving out information that cannot be perceived by the human eye. The JPEG compression process is a three-step procedure, the first step being a *lossless* DCT Transformation followed by a *lossy* second stage called *quantization.* The final step in the JPEG process is a lossless encoding step.

Motion JPEG (MJPEG). M-JPEG uses a sequence of JPEG compressed still pictures to provide moving images without accompanying sound. Because pictures do not rely on information stored in other frames, they are easier to decode than an MPEG audiovisual presentation, but are not so highly compressed.

Video Compression. MPEG and H.261 are two video compression schemes based on temporal redundancy. In the block-oriented system of image compression, temporal redundancy corresponds to blocks whose values do not differ considerably from image i to image i+1 and blocks that have changed their position from image i to image i+1. For a given block in image i+1, *motion detection* determines which blocks in image i+1 are "sufficiently different" from the blocks in image i. This decision depends on a threshold value for the minimal difference that is required between two blocks for them to be considered as different. Only the sufficiently different blocks are candidates for transmission. We refer to these blocks as *target blocks.*

With *differential coding*, a target block is not compressed directly. Instead, the difference between the values of a target block and a reference block contained in the previous picture are computed. Only this delta block is compressed, using the conventional steps of image compression described above. This will considerably reduce the data volume that must be transmitted for image i+1. In order to identify the best reference block for a given target block, an additional step can be inserted between motion detection and differential encoding. This optional step is called *motion compensation* and is also known as *predictive coding*.

H.261 uses the preceding block for motion compensation (*forward prediction*). In MPEG, two additional prediction modes are possible. *Backward prediction* determines a motion vector for a target block using a reference block from the image following the current image. Interpolation gives motion vectors for both the preceding and the following image. This results in a higher compression ratio for MPEG when compared to H.261.

The MPEG1 specification is defined in three parts: system, video and audio. It describes the basic format of the video or audio stream. These formats define the Elementary Streams (ES)–compressed video and audio data are referred to in MPEG documentation as "Elementary Streams." The MPEG1 system specification defines an encapsulation of the Elementary Streams that contains Presentation Time Stamps (PTS), Decoding Time Stamps, and System Clock references and performs multiplexing of MPEG1 compressed video and audio Elementary Streams with user data. The MPEG2 system specification defines two system stream formats: the MPEG2 Transport Stream (MTS) and the MPEG2 Program Stream (MPS). The MTS is tailored for communicating or storing one or more programs of MPEG2 compressed data and also other data in relatively error-prone environments. The MPS is tailored for relatively error-free environments.

Encapsulation of MPEG Elementary Streams with RTP. The ES types belonging to MPEG1/MPEG2 video and MPEG1/MPEG2 audio are directly encapsulated with RTP and a distinct RTP payload type is assigned to each of them. Presentation Time Stamps (PTS) of 32 bits with an accuracy of 90 kHz shall be carried in the fixed RTP header. All packets that make up an audio or video frame shall have the same time stamp.

Table 4 shows the video payload types currently defined in the RTP audio/video profile.

Making Video Robust against Packet Losses. The motion-predicted blocks are an example of inter-packet dependencies. If the reference block of a motion predicted block is lost, displaying this block will not have a very positive effect on the video display. Another example of inter-packet dependency is inter-encoded blocks in H.261. Therefore, the following thumb rules can be applied to make video robust against packet losses on the Internet:

Table 4: Video Payload Types Currently Assigned in RTP

Payload Type Number	Video Format
24	unassigned
25	CelB
26	Motion JPEG
27	unassigned
28	nv
29	unassigned
30	unassigned
31	H.261
32	MPEG Video
33	MPEG2 Transport

- Avoid all motion prediction.
- Do not use differential coding and use only intracoded blocks.
- Use a relatively high value for the motion detection threshold to find the differential blocks between two images (conditional replenishment).
- Use wavelet encodings for video.

Of course, applying the first three rules becomes difficult when the encoder does not know that the video will be transmitted over the Internet. This is typically the case for hardware codecs. For instance, using commonly available MPEG coders for preparing videos that will be transmitted over the Net usually has unsatisfactory results.

INTERNET MULTICASTING – MBONE

The MBONE is an outgrowth of the first two IETF *audiocast* experiments in which live audio and video were multicast from the IETF meeting site to destinations around the world. This is a virtual network. It is layered on top of portions of the physical Internet to support routing of IP multicast packets, since that function has not yet been integrated into many production routers. The network is composed of islands that can directly support IP multicast, such as multicast LANs like Ethernet, linked by virtual point-to-point links called *tunnels*. The tunnel endpoints are typically workstation-class machines having operating system support for IP-multicast and running the *mrouted* multicast routing daemon. Some of the ISPs already support the handling of multicast IP packets. Internet multicasting is a standard developed and tested by the IETF (RFC 1112).

Internet Group Management Protocol (IGMP) enables Internet multicasting or IP class-D addressing. Currently all operating systems support the IGMP layer in their IP stack. The IP stack and the header fields in an IGMP are shown in Figures 7(a) and 7(b) respectively.

Figure 7(a). The IP Stack

Mbone Client/Server
UDP
IGMP
IP
Ethernet

Figure 7(b). The header fields in an IGMP message

IGMP Version (4 bit)	IGMP Type (4 bit)	Unused (4 bit)	16 Bit Checksum
Class D Multicast Group Address			

An MBone-compliant audio/video streaming application stamps the multi-media data packets with RTP and IGMP before releasing the data onto the network. The IP routers are intelligent enough to realize that these packets are the class-D IP multicast packets.

CONCLUSION

The media content can be classified into two: broadcast and on-demand. The media server uses two types of connections for delivering these contents to the clients: unicast and multicast. With unicast, a separate connection is maintained between each client and the server. Both broadcast and on-demand contents can be delivered to clients with a unicast connection. Broadcast content can also be delivered with a multicast connection.

Chapter 17

Relevant Aspects for Test Delivery Systems Evaluation

Salvatore Valenti, Alessandro Cucchiarelli, and Maurizio Panti
University of Ancona, Italy

INTRODUCTION

The number of educational institutions seeking solutions to the problems associated with the burden of expanded student numbers is increasing every day. Most solutions to the problems of delivering course content, supporting student learning, and assessment may be found through the use of computers, thanks to the continuous advances of information technology. According to Bull (1999), using computers to perform assessment is more contentious than using them both to deliver content and to support student learning. In many papers, the terms Computer Assisted Assessment (CAA) and Computer Based Assessment (CBA) are often used interchangeably and somewhat inconsistently. The former usually covers all use of computers in assessment, including reporting and marking, such as in optical mark reading. The latter is often restricted to the use of computers for the entire process, including delivery of the assessment and provision of feedback (Charman and Elmes, 1998). In this paper we will adopt the term Computer Based Assessment and we will discuss some issues related to the online assessment of students.

The interest in developing CBA tools has increased in recent years, thanks to the potential market of their applications. Many commercial products, as well as freeware and shareware tools, are the result of studies and research in this field made by companies and public institutions.

For an updated survey of course and test delivery/management systems for distance learning, see Looms (2000). This site maintains a description of more than one hundred products and is constantly updated with new items.

Previously Published in *Challenges of Information Technology Management in the 21st Century* edited by Mehdi Khosrow-Pour, Copyright © 2000, Idea Group Publishing.

Such a large number of assessment systems available obviously raises the problem of identifying a set of criteria useful to an educational team wishing to select the most appropriate tool for their assessment needs. From a survey of all the material available on the Net, starting from the results returned by the most common search engines and then going to a number of sites maintaining links related to educational resources (CAA Centre, 2000; ERIC®, 2000; TECFA, 2000), it appears that only two papers have been devoted to such an important topic (Freemont and Jones, 1994; Gibson, Brewer, Dholakia, Vouk, and Bitzer, 1995). The major drawback shown by both papers is the unstated underlying axiom that a CBA system is a sort of monolith that must be evaluated as a single entity. This is false, since the structure of a CBA system is very complex, as shown in Figure 1.

According to Figure 1, a CBA system is composed by:

- A Test Management System (TMS), i.e., a tool providing the instructor with an easy to use interface, the ability to create questions and to assemble them into tests, and the possibility of grading the tests and to make some statistical evaluations of the results;
- A Test Delivery System (TDS), i.e., a tool for the delivery of tests to the students. The tool may be used to deliver tests through paper and pencil, locally, on a LAN, or over the Web;
- A Web Enabler that may be used to deliver the tests over the WWW. The Web Enabler may be implemented as a separate tool. In many other cases, producers distribute two different versions of the same TDS, one to deliver tests either on single computers or on LAN, and the other to deliver tests over the Web. This is the policy adopted for instance by Cogent Computing Co. (2000) with CQuest-Test and CQuest-Web;
- Some utilities for Test Building Support – a set of tools that may provide the teacher help to build up both well-formed questions and tests. An instance of a TBS utility is represented by "Better Testing," developed by Question Mark

Figure 1: The complete structure of a CBA tool

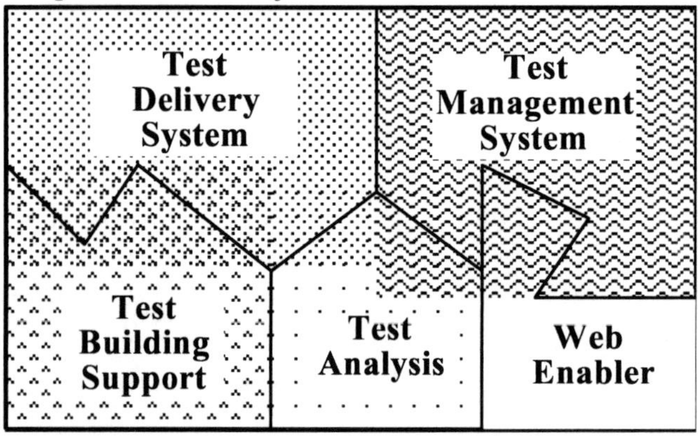

Computing Ltd. (2000) and sold separately with respect to the TDS/TMS application;

- Some utilities for Test Analysis – a set of tools that may be used to analyze the performances of the students individually and with respect to the class. As an example, Assessment System Co. delivers a large set of different programs both for item and test analysis. "These programs are based on classical test theory, on Rasch model analysis using the 1- 2- and 3-parameter logistic IRT model, on non-parametric IRT analysis, and on IRT analysis for attitude and preference data" (Assessment System Co., 2000).

Obviously the modules composing a CBA system may be integrated in a single application, as for instance InQsit (2000), developed by Ball State University, or may be delivered as separate applications. As an instance of this latter policy, we may cite ExaMaker & Examine developed by HitReturn (2000); in this case Examine (the TDS) is provided free of charge.

Therefore, it is very important to identify some metrics that can be used to evaluate all the modules that belong to this general structure of a CBA system.

The purpose of this paper is to present a proposal for a framework that may help to identify some guidelines for the selection of a Test Delivery System.

Three main functional modules roughly compose a Test Delivery System: a student interface, a question management unit, and a test delivery unit. Therefore, we have decided to organize our framework by identifying some metrics that may support the evaluation of the functional modules and other metrics that may support the evaluation of the system as a whole. Finally, we discovered the need of introducing some domain-specific metrics to evaluate the system with respect to the cheating issue.

We will present the metrics for the evaluation of a TDS at the component element; then we will discuss the metrics for the evaluation of a TDS at system level, and next we will introduce some remarks on cheating and on the possible countermeasures to be adopted. Some final remarks and hints for further research will follow.

METRICS FOR THE EVALUATION OF A TDS AT COMPONENT LEVEL
Interface
Although there is a lot of work in the literature on the criteria to be adopted for the evaluation of a Graphical User Interface (GUI) from the point of view of usability (see for instance Gilham, Kemp, and Buckner, 1995, and Nielsen and Molich, 1990), this issue seems to attain little importance when evaluating any commercial product.

We strongly believe that the evaluation of the interface is a qualifying aspect for the evaluation of a CBA system and obviously for a TDS. This becomes dramatically true if we take into account the fact that neither the teacher nor the students involved in the use of a TDS necessarily have degrees in computer science nor may be interested in acquiring skills in this field.

In the following, we will list some well-known guidelines that may be used to evaluate a GUI. As Nielsen & Molich (1990) simply proposed, the interface must be easy to learn, efficient to use, easy to remember, error-free, and subjectively pleasing.

Some of the criteria that may be adopted to evaluate the usability of a GUI are summarized in the following list:

- *Speak the user's language (multilinguality & multiculturality).*

With respect to this point, it is worth remembering that the European Union (EU) comprises eleven official languages plus a large number of national specific versions and regional languages. Additional language requirements are issued by the European Free Trade Association, involving four more countries, and by Eastern Europe.

It is obvious that the assessment process of users with different languages should be done according to a chosen language and in a familiar cultural environment (meaning, for instance, taking into consideration the cultural bias or acceptability of icons, key words, etc.).

The availability of features that allow switching among different languages, yet maintaining the same assessment capabilities, would be very valuable. This aspect may be very interesting for educational institutions providing cross-country's learning material (CEN/ISSS WS/LT, 2000).

- *Be accessible.*

Accessibility is used in this context as the usability of information systems by persons who cannot use the standard text and image-based computer interaction.

The United Nations estimates that approximately 10% of the population of a country has some sort of disability (impairment). These data vary considerably from country to country, rising up to 25% of the population whenever moderate forms of sight and hearing losses are taken into account. With respect to the accessibility issue, the EU promotes a cross-program theme in the fifth framework program for research.

Obviously, the availability of tools able to improve the accessibility of a TDS may be of great importance for any educational institution (CEN/ISSS WS/LT, 2000).

- *Provide feedback.*

This item is related to the ability to provide information to the student once the answer to a given question has been entered. Feedback will be discussed in some more detail in the next section.

- *Provide clearly marked exits.*

According to King (1998), who conducted an evaluation questionnaire on the CAA examination process at the University of Portsmouth – UK, about 6% of students providing adverse comments (7 out of 112) addressed the problem of obtaining an end screen to be sure of having answered all questions.

Question Management

Among the issues to be taken into account to evaluate the Question Management unit of a TDS are: the ability to provide multiple attempts at solving a question, the ability to provide feedback and tutorials on the topic covered by the questions, and the capability of including multimedia in questions that have been selected.

Retries

This item is related to the ability to allow multiple attempts in answering a question. Obviously, this ability may be of great importance for self-assessment, since it may be useful to improve the knowledge of the student while reducing the need of providing feedback and/or tutoring.

On the other hand, the impossibility to change the answer to a question during an examination is often perceived as unfair by the students. According to a study conducted by King (1998) on the evaluation of a CAA protocol, about 34% of the students providing adverse comments needed the ability of repeating/retrying responses. It is worth outlining that allowing multiple attempts at question answering may affect the use of adaptive systems whenever item presentation depends on previous responses.

On the other side, retries may represent a vehicle for cheating, as will be shown later in this paper.

Feedback and Tutorials

This item is related to the ability to provide information to the student once the answer to a given question has been entered. The feedback may be provided after each question (this solution being preferable for self-assessment), after a set of questions covering a given topic, or at the end of the test, and can be based on the overall performance. Furthermore, the feedback may be used to indicate the correctness of the answer, to correct misconceptions, or to deliver additional material for deepening and/or broadening the coverage of the topic assessed by the question. Tutorials represent an extended approach to provide additional information to the students. The existence of some facility for ease inclusion of tutorials in the TDS represents an important feedback aid. As an example, Perception provides explanation-type questions that may be used for "information screens, title pages, or to display large bodies of text" (Question Mark Computing Ltd., 2000).

Multimedia

The use of questions incorporating multimedia, such as sound and video clips or images, may improve the level of knowledge evaluation. This aspect may be of great importance, for example, in language assessment, where the comprehension of a talk or a movie can be assessed by recurring to multimedia only.

The use of multimedia can raise issues related to portability and interoperability, since it may require special hardware and software, both for the server delivering the questions and for the client used by the students. Furthermore, it may raise the costs for the adopted solution. These issues may not represent a problem whenever a Web Enabled TDS is selected, since the nature of the WWW is inherently multimedial. In this case, the choice of standard plug-ins for the most common browsers may reduce risks of portability and of interoperability. Since most plug-ins used to grant access to multimedia sources are usually free of charge, their use may not interfere with cost problems.

Test Management

Among the issues taken into account to evaluate the Test Management unit of a TDS, we have identified the ability to provide help and hints, the ability to make tests available at a given time, and the capability of grading the tests.

Help and Hints

This item concerns the capability of the system to provide directions about the completion of the test and hints that usually are related to the contents of the questions. This item represents a further measure of the ease of use of the application from the student's point of view.

Restricted Availability

Tests can be made available at a specified date and time. They can also be made unavailable at a different date and time. This allows test designers to specify exactly when people can access a test.

It should be possible to leave out either or both of the restrictions to provide maximum flexibility. This lends itself nicely to the computer lab setting where students are required to complete an online test during a specified time frame on a specified day.

Restricted availability may raise some concerns with respect to the policies for handling borderline situations, this will be discussed later in this paper.

Grading

Obviously, any software for assessment should be able to compute student grades. Furthermore, grades must be delivered as feedback to the course coordinator, to the instructor, and to the students. Each of these categories of users needs to obtain a different kind of feedback on the grades associated with a test. For instance, a student needs to know where she stands with respect to other students and to the class average, besides her own individual and cumulative grades. This need raises obvious concerns about privacy, which may be faced through the security facilities provided with the assessment tool.

METRICS FOR THE EVALUATION OF A TDS AT SYSTEM LEVEL

Among the issues taken into account to evaluate a TDS from a systemic point of view, we have identified security, survivability, and communication with other software.

Security

There is a wide range of security issues related to the use of TDSs. Among these issues, it should be outlined that there are a lot of concerns on the security of the availability of the test material, of the HTML code that implements testing, of the identification of the user (both instructors and students), and so on. In the next paragraphs we will discuss some issues related to security.

With respect to security concerns about the test material and its HTML code, it must be outlined that while commercial programs usually implement encrypting approaches, a lot of issues should be taken into account for freewares. In fact, most freeware applications rely either on Perl/CGI or on JavaScript. From the point of view of security, the use of a CGI-based application may raise an important problem: since a CGI program is executable, it is basically the equivalent of letting the world run a program on the server side, which is not the safest thing to do. Therefore, there are some security precautions that need to be implemented when it comes to using CGI-based applications. The one that will probably affect the typical web user is the fact that CGI programs need to reside in a special directory, so that the server knows to execute the program rather than just display it to the browser. This directory is usually under direct control of the webmaster, prohibiting the average user from creating CGI programs.

On the other hand, since the JavaScript code runs on the client side of the application, the obvious drawback of this approach is that the assessment program cannot be completely hidden, and a "smart" student can access the source discovering the right answer associated to each question. In any case, some sophisticated techniques can be used to partially overcome the problem, which can be reduced to a minimum (Cucchiarelli, 2000).

Survivability

The complexity of an information system is determined partly by its functionality (what the system does) and partly by global (non-functional) requirements on its development costs, performance, reliability, robustness, and the like. According to the current literature on Software Engineering a formal definition or a complete list of non-functional requirements do not exist. Among the non-functional requirements identified in a report by the Rome Air Development Center (Bowen, Wigle and Tsay, 1985), survivability, i.e., the ability of a system to perform under adverse conditions, may be of great importance for a Test Delivery System. In particular, it is self-evident that no termination procedures should result in any loss of data. To ensure this, both student and system files should be updated after each transaction, so that no data is lost if the test is terminated because of machine or power failure (Ring, 1994). With respect to this aspect of survivability, a TDS should collect the following data for each test: student identifier, question identifier, and the student's response, at minimum.

The possibility of providing examination printouts may further enforce the survivability of the system.

Finally, after a crash the system should be able to restart from the point of termination with all aspects of the original status unchanged, including the answers already given and the clock still displaying the time remaining.

Heard, Chapman and Heath (1997) have provided a very useful protocol for the implementation of summative computer-assisted assessment examinations. Recommendations are made that when booking examinations, spare capacity should be allowed both in numbers of PCs and time allocation and that a server should be dedicated for examination use. Tasks are identified for staff from both the academic department and the service provider and these need to work closely together before, during, and after examinations. Any institution should draw up similar procedures and then seek agreement from its authoritative bodies before adopting TDSs.

Communication

Communication with other existing software may be very useful both for exporting answers and for calling external applications. Exporting answers is usually performed through test files and data conversion utilities. This may be useful to customize the reports generated by the application or whenever an analysis more detailed than that allowed by the assessment tool is needed to evaluate the results obtained.

Furthermore, many available tools enable the calling of a program as a block within a question. The called program returns a score in points that may be added to the test score. This may be useful for assessing abilities that cannot be evaluated through the basic question-answer paradigm of most assessment tools.

> Some tools allow external applications to be called at the very end of the test phase for printing certificates for all users who pass the test; for the electronic submission of the answer file to a central location for analysis and evaluation; for the storage of the results in a file to be accessed by a user program (Question Mark Co., 2000).

Finally, communication with other software is required in order to allow the integration with TMSs distributed by different commercial producers.

CHEATING

The term "cheating" is used to address dishonest practices that students may pursue in order to gain better grades. Copying from books and assignments set in previous years, collusion amongst students in preparing assignments, getting help from relatives, using illegal notes in tests, sending colleagues to take one's place in assessment, and copying during classroom tests are just some examples of school assessment dishonesty.

According to literature on academic dishonesty, it appears that cheating is practiced by students at all levels of schooling, ranging from "approximately 40% in the upper primary year to nearly 80% in the latter years of secondary school falling to approximately 40% again in tertiary institutions" (Godfrey and Waugh, 1998). This old problem has new life with the widespread use of computer and Web-based assessment. Many researchers suggest that this phenomenon can be discouraged, although not entirely prevented, by using certain simple practices, such as informing students of the penalties for cheating and enforcing those penalties, ensuring that seating arrangements in examination and testing centers are adequate to prevent cheating, and being aware that cheating seems more likely to occur in larger classes than in smaller classes. Teachers can also assist in the discouragement of cheating by being aware of the high frequency of the phenomenon and acknowledging the pressures under which many of these students are working. They must be patient and caring in their approach and make certain that students know that they can come to them for help or assistance and that some students may require more attention at times than others. Parents, of course, can assist in discouraging cheating by ensuring that their children are not overly pressured in their academic endeavours (Godfrey and Waugh, 1998).

In this section we will discuss cheating control from the technical point of view, presenting some requirements that should be satisfied either at component or at system level of a TDS. More in detail, we will discuss how an attempt at controlling cheating may affect the interface, the question management, and the test management functional blocks of a TDS. Then we shall discuss some remarks of the effects of cheating control on the security of a TDS.

Cheating Countermeasures at Component Level

Any system should attempt to ensure that any given student takes the right test at the right time and that the right student takes the test. The latter task may be solved only through organizational countermeasures and will be discussed at the end of this section. The former task is not difficult and is usually handled by asking students for their name and/or an identification number.

The previous remark implies that the interface of a TDS should be designed so that access control could be enforced. This implication becomes less trivial than how it may appear at a first glance if we take into account the fact that access control should be enforced by the teacher, too, in order to avoid unauthorized access to tests before they are administered. Most systems actually on the market allow three classes of users to access the system: student, teachers, and administrators, each with different privileges and allowed functions.

Another issue affecting the interface of a TDS is linked to the possibility of copying tests from the workstations. Printing and saving browser information on a disk is done through their caching feature. By disabling the cache system, it is possible to prevent students from making unauthorized copies of tests they are taking. Implementing the «kiosk» mode available for most major browsers prevents copying the text from the browser, using email, or accessing any other applications.

Some TDSs are designed to hand the test in for marking via email. This raises "the concern that students may catch on to the format of the results email and attempt to create a fake one (naturally with very good overall results). It is possible to detect such email messages by paying close attention to things such as the user-id, when, and where it was emailed from, etc., however, that requires a lot of awareness from those administering the test. To prevent this situation, the test designer can specify a verification code, or secret code, to be used with each test. The code is only included in the email message that is sent to the administrator. It is impossible for students to find out what this code is as long as the problem files are not accessible to the general public" (WebTest, 1996).

From the point of view of question management, some TDSs provide the ability of scrambling the answers, so that the same question is never submitted in the same examination with the answers in the same position. In order to obtain well-formed questions, answers like "None of the above" or "All of the above" should be avoided in multiple choice questions, as suggested in the literature (Gronlund, 1985). Obviously, the previous considerations are valid for multiple choice and for multiple answer questions only, while they do not make sense for short answers, essays, or hot-spot questions.

Another aspect that may affect cheating from the point of view of question management is the possibility of attempting multiple responses to the same question that we addressed as the "retries issue" in the previous section of this paper.

In fact, students may try to access all the hints provided to questions and then backtrack through the pages only to proceed again as if they have never seen them (and thus not losing any marks for seeing them). In order to avoid this drawback, the test designers of WebTest (1996) were provided with the ability to disable backtracking. This solution raised a number of problems (as, for instance, the need of appropriate warning messages to be issued to inform the user not to click Back or Reload), including the fact that clicking the Reload button has the same effect as moving backward and forward, thus corrupting the test again.

From the point of view of test management, most TDSs provide the ability of scrambling the position of questions inside a test. This obviously may raise the concern that questions related to the same topic may be spanned around, thus implicitly increasing the level of difficulty of the test, and therefore representing a sort of unfairness to students. Furthermore, it must be taken into account the fact that question scrambling may interfere with adaptive testing where the set of items that constitute the exam is not predefined and depends on the students' performance level.

As discussed earlier in this paper, restricted availability of the tests may prove useful to ensure that a given student takes the right test at the right time. Obviously, constraining the time limits for the execution of tests imposes both functional and non-functional requirements on the architecture of the TDS. As an instance of the former class of requirements, we may cite both the possibility of displaying a clock with the residual time available and the existence of appropriate warning messages as the time limit approaches. As an instance of the latter class of requirements, we may mention the existence of policies for handling "border-line" situations such as: What should happen to the student who does not complete the test on time? Should a student's test terminate and be handed in automatically? Or should the student be allowed to finish the test and hand it in himself under the assumption that the test-administrator will eventually make her leave?

Cheating Countermeasures at System Level

The existence of features for locking out the access to the operating system may be very useful to prevent cheating if the Test Delivery System is running locally or over a LAN. Obviously, this becomes impossible and/or useless whenever the test is taken over the Internet. With relatively common technical knowledge and tools the students may intercept IP packets and read them. Tests transmitted by the TDS could thus be stolen. A possible solution to avoid this problem may require adding data encryption-decryption features to the TDS.

Ensuring that the right student takes the test cannot be handled in a cost-effective way without human intervention. Therefore, the following discussion is independent from the software adopted, but is related to the organizational aspects of Computer Based Assessment. For students doing the test on site and

Table 1: Metrics for the evaluation of a TDS

Issue		Metrics
Component level	Interface	❋ Friendly GUI
	Question Management	❋ Types of questions ❋ Question Structure: (retries, tutorial building)
	Test Management	❋ Help & Hints ❋ Restricted Availability ❋ Grading
System Level		❋ Security ❋ Survivability ❋ Communication
Cheating		

under supervision, the procedures are the same as for a conventional test. If students are taking the tests at remote locations, some form of human supervision is normally required. Most educational organizations address this issue by asking students to arrange for their tests to be proctored by an approved education agency and thus paying any proctoring fees. Approved agencies include a college testing center or the office of a public or private school administrator. Working with small classes is referenced in the literature as a good starting point for reducing cheating (Davis, Grover, Becker and McGregor, 1992).

Using alternative assessment methods that do not rely on multiple choice questions can further discourage cheating. For example, short answers or fill-in-the-blank question types seem to be less subject to cheating. Furthermore, assigning each assessment worth only a few points can be a good countermeasure for controlling the pressure to cheat.

Godfrey and Waughn (1998) discuss a list of other issues that should be taken in account to reduce or prevent cheating.

FINAL REMARKS

In this paper we have discussed a framework that may be useful in assisting an educational team in the selection of a Test Delivery System. The framework has been obtained by modifying and extending existing work on the field (Freemont and Jones, 1994; Gibson et al. 1995). Three main functional modules roughly compose a Test Delivery System: a student interface, a question management unit, and a test delivery unit. Therefore, we have decided to organize our framework by identifying some metrics to support the evaluation of the functional modules and other metrics to support the evaluation of the system as a whole. Finally, we have discovered the need of introducing some domain-specific metrics to help evaluate the system with respect to the cheating issue.

The next step in our research will be the integration of this framework with the one devised by Valenti, Cucchiarelli and Panti (2000) for Test Management Systems, in order to identify a general framework for the evaluation of a Computer Based Assessment System.

At the same time, our research effort is aimed at reviewing the commercial and freeware applications referenced in Looms (2000) using the metrics identified. The resulting framework has been summarized in Table 1.

REFERENCES

Bloom, B. (1956). *Taxonomy of educational objectives.* Handbook I, cognitive Domain. New York: David McKay Co. Inc.

Bowen, T. P., Wigle, G. B., and Tsay, J. T. (1985). *Specification of software quality attributes.* Rep. RADC-TR-85-37. Griffits Air Force Base, NY: Rome Air Development Center.

Bull, J. (1999). Computer-assisted assessment: Impact on higher education institutions. *Educational Technology & Society, 2,* (3).

CEN/ISSS WS/LT (2000). *Learning technologies workshop: A standardization work programme for learning and training technologies & educational multimedia software.* CWA. Retrieved from http://www.cenorm.be/isss/Workshop/LT/draft-final-report/cwa4-5.pdf.

Charman, D. and Elmes, A. (1998). *Computer-based assessment (Volume I): A guide to good practice.* University of Plymouth: SEED Publications.

Cogent Computing Co. (2000). http://cqtest.com/.

Crabbe, J., Grainger, J., and Steward, R. (1997). Quality assessment of computer based learning. *Educational Computing, 8,* (3), 17-19.

Cucchiarelli, A., Panti, M., and Valenti, S. (2000). Web-based assessment of student learning. In A.K. Aaggarwal ed., *Web-based learning and teaching technologies: Opportunities and challenges.* Hershey, PA: Idea Group Publishing, pp. 175-97.

Davis, S. F., Grover, C. A., Becker, A. H., and McGregor, L. N. (1992). Academic dishonesty: prevalence, determinants, techniques and punishments. *Teaching of Psychology, 19,* (1), 16-20.

Freemont, D. J., and Jones, B. (1994). Testing software: a review. *New Currents 1.1.* Retrieved from http://www.ucalcary.ca/Newsletters/Currents/Vol1.1/TestingSoftware.html.

Ebel, R. L. (1979). *Essentials of Educational Measurement.* Englewood Cliffs, NJ: Prentice Hall.

ERIC®. (2000). Clearinghouse on assessment and evaluation. http://ericae.net/.

Gagné, R. M., and Briggs, L. J. (1979). *Principles of instructional design,* (2nd ed.). New York: Holt, Rinehart and Winston.

Gibson, E. J., Brewer, P. W., Dholakia, A., Vouk, M. A., and Bitzer, D. L. (1995). *A comparative analysis of Web-based testing and evaluation systems*. Proceedings of the 4th WWW conference, Boston.

Gillham, M., Kemp, B., and Buckner, K. (1995). Evaluating interactive multimedia products for the home. *New Review of Hypermedia and Multimedia*, pp. 199-212.

Godfrey, J. R. and Waugh, R. F. (1998). The perception of students from religious schools about academic dishonesty. *Issues in Educational Research, 8* (2), 95-116.

Grondlund, N. E. (1985). Measurement and evaluation in teaching. New York: Macmillan Pub. Co.

Hazari, S. I. (1998). Evaluation and selection of web course management tools. Retrieved 10, 01, 1999 from the World Wide Web: http://sunil.umd.edu/webct.

Heard, S., Chapman, K., and Heath, S. (1997). Protocol for the implementation of summative computer-assisted assessment examinations. UK: University of Aberdeen, CLUES.

HitReturn. (2000). http://www.hitreturn.com/index.htm.

InQsit. (2000). http://www.bsu.edu/inqsit/.

King, T., Billinge, D., Callear, D., Wilson, S., Wilson, A., and Briggs, J. (1998). *Developing and evaluating a CAA protocol for University Students*. Proceedings of the 2nd Annual Computer Assisted Assessment Conference, Loughborough.

Looms, T. (2000). *Survey of course and test delivery / management systems for distance learning*. Retrieved at http://tangle.seas.gwu.edu/~tlooms/assess.html.

Nielsen, J., and Molich, R. (1990). *Heuristic evaluation of user interfaces*. Proceedings of CHI 90, 249-56. New York, NY: ACM.

Question Mark Computing Ltd. (2000). http://www.questionmark.com/home.htm.

Ring, G. (1994). Computer administered testing in an IMM environment: Research and development. In McBeath, C. and Atkinson, R. (eds.), *Proceedings of the second international interactive multimedia symposium*, (478-84). Perth, Western Australia: 23-28 January, Promaco Conventions. Retrieved at http://cleo.murdoch.edu.au/gen/aset/confs/iims/94/qz/ring1.html.

TECFA. (2000). http://agora.unige.ch/tecfa/edutech/welcome_frame.html.

Valenti, S., Cucchiarelli, A., and Panti, M. (2000. Some guidelines to support tool selection for computer assisted assessment. In M. Khoswor-pour (ed.), *Challenges of Information Technology Management in the 21st Century*. Hershey, PA: Idea Group Publishing, 609-13.

WebTest. (1996). Retrieved at http://fpg.uwaterloo.ca/WEBTEST/WEBTEST_intro.html.

Chapter 18

An Overview of Agent Technology and Its Application to Subject Management

Paul Darbyshire and Glenn Lowry
Victoria University of Technology, Australia

Agent software is an emerging technology that has its roots firmly in AI research. With the recent proliferation of 'agent' applications in areas such as e-commerce and Internet marketing, much of the application of agents can now said to be in the domain of Information Systems. One of the possible applications of agent technology is that of web-based courseware, and in particular, subject management software. However, there is much confusion over just exactly what an agent is. This paper provides an overview of agent software and in particular that of autonomous agents. The application of autonomous agents to educational courseware and its benefits are discussed, and a project is described which is using autonomous agents to aid in web-based subject management tasks.

INTRODUCTION

The term "*agent*" is being increasingly used by computer researchers, software developers and even the average computer user, yet when pressed, many would be unable to give a satisfactory explanation of just what an agent really is. This can be readily forgiven, as even the "experts" cannot agree on a definition for an agent (Nwana, 1996; Wooldridge, and Jennings, 1995). Agent software is an emerging technology which promises to be many things to many people; however, the technology is still in an embryonic stage. Despite this, the range of organizations and disciplines researching and pursuing agent technology is broad.

Previously Published in *Challenges of Information Technology Management in the 21st Century* edited by Mehdi Khosrow-Pour, Copyright © 2000, Idea Group Publishing.

The more recent notable applications for agents include e-commerce, Web marketing and Internet search agents. What these applications have in common of course is the Web. It seems that with the many types of Web-based software being developed, the Web is providing a good architectural framework for the development of agents. This is because the Web facilitates many of the characteristics of agent software, such as mobility and communication. With the development of web-based courseware, the way now lies open for the application of agent technology towards educational software development.

In the following sections the essence of *"agency"* is explored and a classification is provided. The notion of autonomous agents somewhat expands on the base idea of agency and is covered in the following section. Finally, the application of agent technology to educational software or courseware is discussed, and in particular, a current project is briefly described. This project is making use of autonomous agents by utilizing them in conjunction with web-based subject management courseware that has been previously developed.

WHAT IS AN AGENT

Agent technology emerged from the field of AI research, so often the term *"Intelligent Agent"* is heard being used. However, agents need not be intelligent; in fact, most people do not need *"smart agents"* (Nwana, 1996). Other adjectives often used with agents are: interface, autonomous, mobile, Internet, information, and reactive. The term 'agent' can be thought of as an umbrella under which many software applications may fall, but it is in danger of becoming a *noise* term due to overuse (Wooldridge, and Jennings, 1995).

What makes agents different from standard software are the characteristics that agents must possess in order to be termed agents. There are a number of classification schemes that can be used to typecast existing agents, for example, *mobile* or *static*, *deliberative* or *reactive*, but Nwana (1996) classifies agents according to primary attributes which agents should exhibit (see Figure 1). The

Figure 1: Nwana's classification

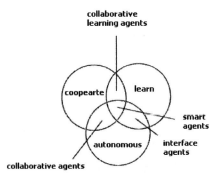

three primary attributes are *cooperation, learning* and *autonomy.* These attributes are laid out as intersecting circles in Figure 1, and to be classified as an agent, software must exhibit characteristics from any of the intersecting areas.

Nwana uses the diagram in Figure 1 to to derive four types of agents: *Collaborative, Interface, Collaborative Learning,* and *Smart* agents. However, Nwana recognizes that the categories in the diagram are not definitive and agents can also be classified by their roles, and so adds to that list *Mobile, Information/Internet, Reactive,* and *Hybrid* agents.

Wooldridge (Wooldridge and Jennings, 1995) takes a more formal approach to the definition of agent, falling back to the more specific meanings from AI researchers. However, he notes that as the AI community cannot agree on the question of *What is Intelligence?*, a less formal definition may be needed to include many software applications being developed by researchers in related fields. To this end, Wooldridge introduces the notions of *weak* and *strong* agency.

Strong agency takes on the specific meaning from AI research, implying that agents must exhibit mental notions such as knowledge, belief, intention, and obligation, with some researchers considering emotional characteristics as a requirement. If this definition of agent is strictly adhered to, many software applications claiming to use agent technology would be rejected as such.

In the weak notion of agency, the term agent can be applied to software that exhibits the following characteristics:

- Autonomy: agents operate without direct human intervention and have some control over their actions and internal state.
- Social Ability: agents interact with other agents and humans through some defined protocol.
- Reactivity: agents can perceive their environment and can respond to it in a timely fashion.
- Proactiveness: agents do not just respond to the environment, but can take a proactive role and exhibit some goal-oriented behavior.

The definitions of Nwana and Wooldridge above are not wholly incompatible. They do identify common characteristics which agents should exhibit, but most of the agent types identified by Nwana would come under Wooldridge's weak-agent classification. The characteristics of *autonomy, cooperation, intelligence, reactivity* and *proactivity* have also been identified by other researchers. Gilbert et al. (1995) provides a model where the degree of agency can be crudely measured by an agent's position in a three-dimensional space relative to a 3-D axis. This model has been refined (Agent Technology, 1999) with the refined version, using the three dimensions of *Intelligence, Autonomy*, and *Social Ability* defined from the list above. This model is shown in Figure 2.

Figure 2: 3-D space Model of Agency

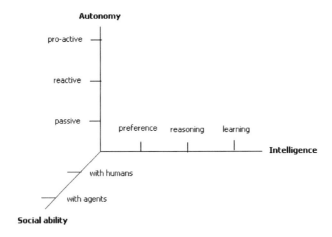

In order to qualify as an agent in this model, software must exhibit at least the minimal characteristics in each dimension. That is, it must be able to communicate with the user, allow users to specify preferences, and be able to work out for itself how to accomplish tasks assigned to it. While this model may not be ideal, it does provide for a more simplistic definition based on the common agent characteristics identified by a number of researchers.

AUTONOMOUS AGENTS

One of the important characteristics of agents, just identified, is that of *autonomy*. Agents do not have to be intelligent; indeed, after forty years of trying to build knowledge-based agents, researchers have still not been able to build a base of common sense information that intelligent agents may need to operate within their environment (Maes, 1995). Until truly smart agents are feasible and commercially viable, it is the degree of autonomy that agents exhibit that will determine their usefulness to many users.

The current dominant metaphor of user interaction with a computer is direct manipulation (Maes, 1994). In this metaphor, the user is required to initiate all tasks directly and monitor all events. This metaphor will have to change in order for users to make more efficient use of computer systems. One particular technique from AI research, namely the use of autonomous agents, can be used to build a complimentary interaction metaphor called indirect manipulation (Maes, 1994). With indirect manipulation, the user works together with a software agent, where both may initiate tasks and monitor events.

These types of agents will take on the role of personal assistants to help users perform tasks and in time may learn to become more effective. We can see this type of software already in existence. For example, the subroutines in word processors automatically check for spelling as you type and sometimes offer suggestions for the completion of words based on what was previously typed. Some of these also automatically capitalize words at the beginning of sentences. While some of these software examples may not exactly fall under our previous definitions of agent, they are small examples of the types of autonomy and cooperation that agents, and particularly autonomous agents, will play in future. Autonomous agents have the potential to radically alter the way we work, but this will begin to appear in commercially available products as an evolutionary process rather than a revolutionary one (Nwana, 1996).

A further definition of an autonomous agent can be found in Franklin and Graesser:

> An **autonomous agent** is a system situated within and part of an environment that senses that environment and acts on it, over time, in pursuit of its own agenda and so as to effect what it senses in the future (1996).

As well as the emphasis on autonomy, autonomous agents have a sense of temporal continuity in that they persist over time. Most software programs are invoked, they run their course, and then finish. For example, a payroll program may be invoked once a week to perform its payroll run but would fail the test of agency, as its output would not normally affect what the payroll program would sense the following week. The payroll program does not persist beyond the completion of its task. An autonomous agent, on the other hand, would continue to persist and monitor/affect a portion of its environment according to its specific task.

Franklin and Graesser also propose an initial taxonomy of autonomous agents based on biological models (Franklin and Graesser, 1996), and this is shown in Figure 3. Further classifications of agents may be obtained by adding a list of features of the agent. For example, mobile, information, planning, and learning can be used.

AGENTS AND THE WEB

Many agents (or software masquerading as agents) have been developed for use on the Web in recent years. Some examples of these are Weiss (1999) and Nwana (1996):

- BarginFinder: compares prices and shops from Internet stores for CDs.
- Jasper: works on behalf of a user or community to store and retrieve useful information on the WWW.
- Internet Softbot: infers which Internet facilities to use and when from high-level search requests.
- Webwatcher: An Internet spider that searches and indexes the Web (according to our definitions, this is not an agent yet).

Figure 3: An initial taxonomy of autonomous agents

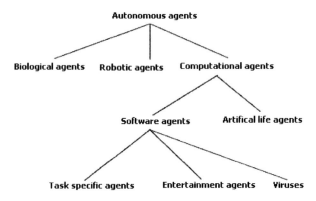

These examples are typical of the types of tasks assigned to agents operating on the Web; however, there have been so many developed in the last few years that they have been termed *Information/Internet agents*. The reason for the term Information is that these agents have access to at least one, and usually many, more sources of information. Most of these agents have come about because of the demand for tools to help manage the enormous growth of information available on the Web. The majority of the Internet agents to date are static and not mobile (Nwana, 1996), but there has been much interest generated in mobile agents in the last two years.

Another reason that we can expect to see the growth of Internet agents in future is that the Web provides an almost perfect architectural framework in which to place such agents. Recall that in order to be an agent, software must exhibit minimal characteristics, e.g., Figure 3. Some of these characteristics are mobility, social ability, and intelligence. The infrastructure of the Web provides a mechanism for most of an agent's required characteristics to be realized. Agents can implement mobility and communication requirements by using standard Internet protocols. Also, the infrastructure is mostly in place with world wide connectivity.

Given the number of applications being either currently built for or being ported to the Web, the conditions are right for a dramatic increase in the number agents designed to operate in the Web environment.

AGENTS AND SUBJECT MANAGEMENT

There have been many courseware products developed over the years since the advent of Computer Aided Learning (CAL) and Computer Managed Learning (CML). Since the development of the Web in the early 1990s, the development of such systems on the Web gained momentum as the new paradigm became available for CAL and CML developers. There are now some very good com-

Figure 4: Representation of first and second tier software development

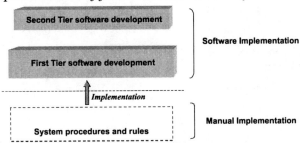

mercial and non-commercial courseware products that allow delivery of educational material and performance of administrative functions via the Web. This includes products such as *TopClass*, *Learning Space*, *Virtual-U*, *WebCT*, *Web Course in a Box*, *CourseInfo*, and *First Class*.

The development of courseware products such as those just mentioned represents the first stage (or *first tier*) in the development of educational courseware. The first tier of development represents the codification into software of those system procedures and rules that originally constituted the *manual* system. As with many other Information Management systems developed from previous manual systems, once implemented, the users and developers find that they are then in a position to think about doing things that could not be previously done.

If the current web based courseware products represent the development of the first tier of such systems, then we must now ask ourselves the following question: *What can we now do that could not be performed (or not easily performed) previously?* If from this we can identify further areas for refinement and gain, then this development would represent the transition to a second tier of software. We can think of this development as the second stage or *evolutionary step* of courseware products. A representation of the first and second tier development is shown in Figure 4.

A number of second tier improvements can be envisioned for web-based courseware. For example:

• Monitoring of student study patterns;
• Monitoring and investigation of student learning processes;
• Presenting tailored study material to students based on performance history; and
• Personalized helpful online hints based on the current session and Web navigation.

Web-based autonomous agents (or autonomous Internet agents) are a method whereby second tier improvements may be delivered. The recent agent technology makes many of the above enhancements feasible, whereas without agents, the delivery of some of the above enhancements would be difficult at best. For instance, the presentation of tailored study material to a student could be accomplished with the use of a mobile agent. This agent could search the Web for material relevant to the difficulty a student is having with a particular topic. The monitoring of a student's learning process could be accomplished previously; however, the time and effort involved for a subject coordinator made this impractical. This could now be accomplished with the use of a personalized autonomous agent that could monitor what a student does on a computer during a subject session.

The above examples target the student as the stakeholder to benefit from these possible second tier improvements. While the improvements are technically feasible, the implementation would not be trivial by any means. All the previous examples are also involved in the subject delivery aspect of courseware. If we consider possible second tier improvements for the *subject management* component of courseware, some worthwhile but more modest improvements can be achieved with the use of suitable autonomous agents.

We can define subject management as *"those tasks of subject delivery which do not play a part in the instructional role and whose functions are directed towards the control, administration, and testing of the learning process."* This is a slight variation of the definition for Computer Managed Learning (CML) offered by Stanford and Cook (1987). Some possible second tier improvements for the subject management component of courseware include:

- Monitoring of assignment submission patterns by individual students;
- Notification to the subject lecturer of late assignment submission;
- Notification to students of assignment due dates based on past late submission patterns; and
- Arrangement of personalized meeting times for individual students based on performance.

Over the past three years we have implemented a web-based subject management system to provide functionality for both staff and students. This includes bulletin and notice boards, web-based assignment submission, provision of student marks via secure web-based lookup, and provision of web-based subject configuration for subject coordinators. This system is documented in Darbyshire and Wenn (1998) and Darbyshire (1999). A research project is currently implementing second tier improvements to the web-based subject management system developed using autonomous agents. The project will also quantify any improvements observed.

Benefits from the implementation of the first tier stage included:

- More timely dissemination of important notices for students and staff;
- Flexibility in assignment submission for students;
- Flexibility in access to submitted assignments for staff;
- Reduction of paper handling and transfer (e.g., assignments, assignment sheets etc.); and
- Flexibility in dissemination of results to students.

Second tier development includes the use of autonomous agents to facilitate some of the subject management improvements noted above. By targeting the subject management component, benefits can be gained by both students and staff, but it is anticipated that there will be more tangible benefits for academic staff. In the current climate of education commercialization and economic pressure, any measurable benefits would be welcome. A more detailed project description is provided in the following section.

PROJECT DESCRIPTION

The proposed structure of the second tier subject management system is shown in Figure 5. Currently, the Central Point system (Darbyshire, and Wenn, 1977) consists of a number of Microsoft Access databases that contain information submitted by both staff and students (Darbyshire, and Wenn, 1998). A number of HTML and Cold Fusion scripts are provided for access to the system. The student gains access by one set of scripts, and a second, secure, password protected set of scripts is provided for staff. This second set of scripts facilitates the subject management functions.

Three autonomous agents are being implemented initially to perform some of the more simple improvements identified as second tier subject management functions. One autonomous agent will monitor assignment submissions by students as well as the due date for assignments. This information is stored in the assignment box database, and the assignments are submitted to the appropriate assignment

Figure 5: Structure of second tier system

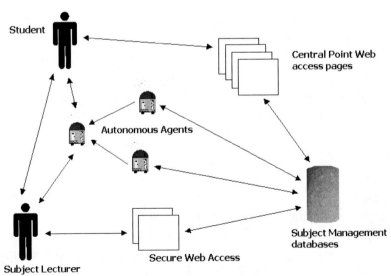

box. The role of this agent is monitor the submissions and, as the due date approaches, will warn the students that have not submitted assignments of the impending deadline. Once the deadline passes for each assignment, it will close the assignment box and notify the subject coordinator of this, and any students that have not submitted work, will be notified that it is now outstanding and must be submitted in person. Another autonomous agent will have access to both assignment submissions and grade information. This second agent will monitor the grades received by students as they are entered and notify the poorer performing students early for each assignment to start early and seek help at the beginning.

In the diagram in Figure 5, there is a third autonomous agent shown that communicates directly with both the students and the subject lecturers. This will be an *interface* agent that is responsible for both human-agent and agent-agent communication. These have not been discussed as yet, but, simply put, an interface agent facilitates communication between humans and agent, or between different agents. This alleviates the problem of all agents having to possess this ability. Interface agents are an area of intense study among agent researchers, with the role of believable emotions considered by some necessary for such agents.

The tasks for the agents described above are modest, but some of the issues involved in their implementation are detailed and non-trivial. For instance, how will the agents remember things, how will they learn over time the poorer performing student's habits, how will the agents communicate with each other, and how will the interface agent communicate with staff and students? To aid in the ease of implementation, the interface agent will initially communicate with both students and staff via email. Other associated difficulties are being solved over time. None of the agents described here are designed to be mobile during these initial development stages.

While the actual agent functions themselves are small, their successful implementation should result in some measurable improvement. Even if it is only something else the subject coordinator does not have to do, it indicates a step in a forward direction. The successful implementation will also result in expertise gained in order to implement further, more complex and rewarding second tier tasks via the use of autonomous agents.

CONCLUSION

There is a current proliferation of research on agent technology. Many experts agree that agents will change the way we work with computers, but that this change will be a slower evolution, rather than a revolution. It is important that we understand the basic concepts of agents and exactly what agents are. There is also much attention at the moment on the use of web-based agents (Internet agents), and this is as much a result of the need to manage the information explosion as it is the excellent environment that the Web provides for agent development.

With the development of web-based courseware, the development of autonomous agents to aid in managing the educational process could lead to significant improvements. The research project briefly described in this paper is implementing simple autonomous agents to aid in the web-based subject management software described in previous papers. It is anticipated that some measurable benefit will be observed, thereby paving the way for more complex agent development as part of second tier development or courseware evolution.

REFERENCES

Agent technology: An overview (1999). In *Proceedings of 10th Australasian Conference on Information Systems*. ACIS'99. Wellington, New Zealand.

Darbyshire, P. (1999). Distributed web-based assignment submission and access. *International Resource Management Association*. IRMA'99. Hershey, PA.

Darbyshire, P., and Wenn, A. (1977). Central point: Cyber classroom. http://busfa.vut.edu.au/cpoint/cp.cfm.

Darbyshire, P., and Wenn, A. (1998). Cross campus subject management using the Internet. *International Resource Management Association*. IRMA'98. Boston, MA.

Franklin, S., and Graesser, A. (1996). Is it an agent, or just a program?: A taxonomy for autonomous agents. In *Proceedings of the 3rd International Workshop on Agent Theories and Architectures*. Springer-Verlag.

Genesereth, M., and Ketchpel, S. (?). *Software agents*. Stanford Univeristy: Computer Science Department.

Gilbert, D., et al. (1995). *The role of intelligent agents in the information infrastructure*. USA: IBM.

Maes, P. (1994, July). Agents that reduce work and information overload. *Communications of the ACM, 37*, (7).

Maes, P. (1995, September). Intelligent software. *Scientific American, 273*, (3), 84-86.

Nwana, H. (1996). Software agents: An overview. *Knowledge Engineering Review, 11*, (3).

Stanford, J.D., and Cook, H.P. (1987). Computer managed learning: Its application to increase student achievement using formative self-assessment. *CALITE 87*. Sydney, Australia: University of New South Wales.

Weiss, M. (1999). *A gentle introduction to agents and their applications*. Mitel Corp. Retrieved from http://www.magma.ca/~mrw/agents/, January 10, 1999.

Wooldridge, M., and Jennings, N. (1995, June). Intelligent agents: Theory and practice. *Knowledge Engineering Review, 10*, (2).

Chapter 19

A Comprehensive Approach to Teaching Visual Basic Programming

Yun Wang
Mercy College, USA

Visual Basic (VB), a graphical user interface (GUI) application and object-oriented program, has been adopted as an entry-level programming course in computer information science curricula at many colleges. Compared with "C," Pascal, or other traditional teaching programs, VB is rather a new subject in the field. Correspondingly, studying effective approaches to teaching VB has brought tremendous interest in academic communities. The author has primarily taught VB as a college course for several terms, and he began his new comprehensive VB teaching approach described by this article in 1998. After a three-semester trial period, the VB course outcome is encouraging. This article is dedicated to documenting the comprehensive VB teaching approach and serves as a summary report for future improvement. This article first introduces the background of the VB course taught in the author's institution. Secondly, it briefly outlines previous teaching approaches and describes the newly implemented one in detail. Then it examines existing course questions and proposes future revisions by studying the results of this new teaching approach. Finally, a summary is given to call for more research.

Previously Published in *Challenges of Information Technology Management in the 21st Century* edited by Mehdi Khosrow-Pour, Copyright © 2000, Idea Group Publishing.

INTRODUCTION

VB was chosen to be taught for course CS238 titled "Graphical User Interface Application Development" because of its popularity in industry and its excellent presentation in object-oriented programming and GUI applications. CS238 is a required foundation course for computer information systems students.

The CS238 class usually has thirty students with a diverse computing background. Many students have full-time non-IT jobs and return to make career changes. A portion of students work for the college IT division and are familiar with school computer systems. Only 3 to 5 students currently are programmers. None or very few students learned VB before. The prerequisite of CS238 is CS220, "Introduction to Programming Using Application Software," or CS231, "Foundations of Computing II." CS220 teaches Access and CS231 studies Java. The prerequisite ensures that students possess either basic programming concepts or familiarity with the GUI operating environment. The textbook for CS238 is *An Introduction to Programming Using Visual Basic 6.0,* by David I. Schneider, published by Prentice Hall. It's well-written and straightforward for both instructors and students to follow. Each chapter is accompanied with one case study, and a learning version of VB compiler CD-ROM is included in the book.

PREVIOUS TEACHING APPROACH

Prior to 1998, CS238 was a lecture-dominated course. A wide range of content in each chapter was covered by the lecture, and many textbook examples were reiterated. Programming projects were assigned after class and students did projects in non-class time. There were neither writing nor group assignments. Students' grades depended heavily on three written tests. Most students had proposed the following questions after their taking CS238: Can we practice more real world VB programming projects? Can we have labs within the class time? Can we give more weight to projects for final evaluation? Can we have a more instructor-student interactive teaching learning style?

NEW TEACHING APPROACH

This comprehensive approach was initially implemented in Fall, 1998 and continued through Summer, 1999. The work incorporated students' evaluation, department curricular updates, and faculty member input.

Lecture

The class is divided into lecture and lab evenly. At the first class, students hand in their own information sheets, including what specific topics they are interested in learning, previous programming skills, computing background, job natures, etc. They introduce themselves to the class following my own introduction. Twenty

Table 1: CS238 anonymous survey

Survey Questions	Strongly Agree	Agree	Disagree	Don't Know
Recommend this course to other students	84%	10%	3%	3%
If a second and advanced VB course is offered, will take it	94%	0	6%	0
Learn a great deal of GUI and OOP basics from this course	87%	13%	0	0
Generally it's a good and practical course.	91%	3%	6%	0

(Approximately 92 students participated in the survey through Fall of 1998, Spring of 1999, and Summer of 1999. There are no similar survey data existing prior to Fall of 1998.)

minutes spent on such discussion is worthwhile. The firsthand information is critical to me to understand my students' learning profiles and it helps students begin to know each other and provides a basis for a later group project.

At the beginning of each class, I let students ask questions about their readings and homework. If there are no questions, then I ask them a few. I try to get students involved in class as early as possible. Some studies indicate that students who do not participate at the beginning of class are more likely to get lost through the course (Buckland, 1997). Usually lecture time is often, ironically, too precious to waste on deep understanding, given the large volume of content that must be taught in the lecture (Buckland, 1997). Assisting students to "deeply understand" teaching content is the ultimate goal of lectures. I restructured teaching content to cope with lecture time restraints. I firmly believe that lectures should not only transfer the instructor's knowledge to students but also, most importantly, teach students a mechanism to learn further skills. I teach VB special featured concepts/syntax followed by examples typically ranging from easy to difficult. Assuming my students already have basic programming concepts, I rarely cover VB's features that are similar to other languages, for example, the syntax of loops. I require my students to read chapters before attending class and self-study for content not covered in lecture but required within the course scope. I always design one comprehensive example to illustrate multiple concepts/syntaxes. I make it very clear to my students that the lecture is only a guide to how to study, and they have an obligation to self-study materials required by the course. Often, quite few students miss on self-study questions in the first test, and they do quickly learn the lesson.

I sometimes use teaching by error in my class. I write codes with syntax/logical error on the board. I wait for students to point out mistakes and, if no one does, I remind students to take a second look. I praise those who catch mistakes and extra points are rewarded. I try to remember students' names after the first three classes. As a student myself several years ago, I would be upset if my professor would not remember my name after several mid-sized classes. In summary, lecture has been reshaped as a highly interactive process in which students assume more responsibility for content mastery.

Lab

Lab is the added class component as the result of the new approach. Students like lab because they use lab to work on projects previously done in after-class time. They get more hands-on programming experience, and they can consult with the instructor to solve "mysterious" programming errors. In the first three labs, I demonstrate problems on the computer very gradually, and students practice simulated examples. I walk around to see if they have questions. I will help them as much as I can. I want to ensure that every student has a solid beginning with VB.

My role as a "lab assistant' changes to an "advisor" after three labs. I expect students to possess the necessary skills/knowledge to do projects independently. When students ask questions, first I evaluate how difficult the problems are. I won't answer anything if they are easy, and I provide only guidelines instead of full solutions for difficult ones. I want students to work hard and sweat to accomplish projects. In most cases, one project is due within two labs lasting two and half-hours. I run the student's projects on the computer and do the grading on the spot to demonstrate how I grade them. Some students are not used to this style of project work. After they make more effort and understand the real world deadline programming practice, they begin to enjoy it. Lab is the most dynamic part of class. For me, student lab performance is a reflection of how well I teach. On the other hand, for students, working on projects in lab indicates how much they have learned from the lecture and how well they translate it into practice.

Grading Method

The new grading method reflects the importance of projects. Forty percent of the course grade is now based on performance on projects, up from twenty percent. Although the number of written tests has not changed, the percentage has decreased from eighty to sixty. Additionally, I have the option to add an extra credit project and/or curve test scores. The details are following: projects, 40% (7 programming projects and 1 group case study, 5 points each); written tests, 60% (tests are formatted as multiple choice and short answers; Test I=15%, Test II=20%, Final=25%).

Course Assignments

Course assignments include homework, reading chapters, and projects. Homework and reading chapters are voluntary assignments and bear no grades. They have a direct connection with the written test and are designed to reflect the scope of the test. Students who skip those assignments will barely pass tests. There are seven programming projects and one case study. These are drawn from a bank of projects combined with textbook exercises, real world problems, and case studies. I spend a great deal of time collecting suitable real world problems. My industry friends provide assistance, and I select problems suitable for students in terms of implementation feasibility and application of concepts/syntax taught at class. Students love real world problems, and they consider the problems more challenging and practical. They are also highly motivated.

In business education, case studies have played an important role in training student's analytical and problem solving skills by placing them in the position of real decision-making and requiring them to analyze the situation and make recommendations for actions (Christensen, (1987). Current IT education seems to ignore managerial skill training required by most employers. I decided to use a group case study project as part of the class assignments (worth five percent of the course grade). Students get a sense of what it is like to work on a real project. Since "case studies attempt to simulate many of the complexities of real managerial decision-making situations by only providing limited or inaccurate information from which conclusions are required to be drawn and devise action plans," the students will gain valuable experience for their future employment (Whiddett, Handy and Pastor, 1997). The group case study project involves writing, speaking, and no VB programming. Five to six students form one group and choose a case study project. They study, analyze, summarize, and present the case to the class. All case studies are related to IT system topics. The student group discusses what the problems are, who the stakeholders are, provides feasible solutions, and finally presents this case to the class. This group case study project may seem irrelevant to VB programming, but I require it for two main reasons: (1) sharpen student's writing, reading, communication, and presentation skills as required in a regular IT position. Students get a chance to work with peers in a cooperative environment similar to the real job setting. Students realize a tech person will not advance without strong writing, reading, communication, and presentation skills; and, (2) prepare students for higher level courses such as system analysis.

Results of the New Teaching Approach

Positive outcomes are suggested by the following evidence, student's anonymous survey results, and test score statistics. At the end of each semester, in addition to college student evaluation forms, a special CS238 four-question anonymous survey is conducted.

Table 2 compares academic year '96-97's CS238 written test scores with academic year '98-99's. The student number in academic year '96-97 is 83, and 95 for academic year '98-99. Overall, there is a higher percentage of students getting test scores above 79 in '98-99 and a close comparison at the range of '70-79.

Table 2: CS238 test score

Test Score	90-100	90-100	80-89	80-89	70-79	70-79	60-69	60-69	< 60	< 60
YR.	96-97	98-99	96-97	98-99	96-97	98-99	96-97	98-99	96-97	98-99
Test										
I	15%	12%	25%	26%	40%	39%	10%	8%	10%	15%
Test II	10%	20%	20%	23%	25%	30%	40%	20%	5%	7%
Final	18%	19%	14%	25%	40%	39%	23%	7%	5%	10%

(All tests have a 100 scale. The two year's test scope and formatting are same. Testing questions are similar.)

In my opinion, the positive results rely on two main factors: (1) students are highly motivated to study hard by this interactive teaching approach; and (2) more emphasis and practices on projects produce a better written test score.

Discussions and Implications

Though the new approach promises a good overall picture, there are still problems and issues the new approach has not solved. First, as indicated in Table 2, the test failure rate has increased under the new approach. Many educational studies have suggested that a highly motivated and interactive teaching approach adversely affects poor students. How to help "troubled" students and keep them up with the class pace is a question requiring ongoing effort. Second, VB as a client application in a standard client-server model has much functionality for students to study and practice, and a comprehensive system is needed in the learning process. Limited by the educational institution's resources, many educators share a common dilemma that a broad range of worthwhile topics can not be covered. For example, while I am teaching the chapter about VB database management, I encounter difficulties in demonstrating the concept of the interaction of server database and client VB interface because of the non-compiled lab system with VB. A feasible solution is to team up with the industry to get system support. In the next phase of the new approach, I will design a field trip to company systems to help students better understand VB as a client in the client-server framework. Third, all tests so far are traditional paper-pencil exams. I am considering replacing one test with a lab exam to promote the importance of projects.

SUMMARY

This paper reports a comprehensive approach to teaching VB in my institution. It introduces the course background and describes details of new teaching implementations. The result of the new approach is documented. A discussion of issues in the new approach follows. This paper is aimed at exchanging VB teaching ideas and improving entry-level programming course teaching.

ACKNOWLEDGEMENTS

I would like to thank Dr. Rao, Dr. Paris, Professor DiElsi, Dr. Marx, Dr. Somolinos, and Professor Scott for their generous help and advice to my teaching career and the writing of this article. I also thank all my CS238 students for their support to make VB programming courses more interesting, challenging, and successful.

REFERENCES

Buckland, R. (1997, July 2-4). Can we improve teaching in computer science by looking at how English is taught? In *Australasian Conference on Computer Science Education*. The University of Melbourne, Australia.

Christensen, C.R. (1987). *Teaching and the Case Method*. Boston, MA: Harvard Business School.

Whiddett, R., Handy, J., and Pastor J. (1997, July 2-4). Cross-sectional case studies: Integrating case studies and projects in I.S. management education. In *Australasian Conference on Computer Science Education*. The University of Melbourne, Australia.

Chapter 20

What Do Good Designers Know That We Don't?

Morgan Jennings
Metropolitan State College of Denver, USA

The research reported in this paper was an investigation of the engaging and immersive properties of game and learning environments. The qualitative study was done in cooperation with six elite designers and two team members of recognized and/or award-winning products. From the findings, a prescriptive aesthetic framework was developed based on (a) data and (b) aesthetic experience literature. Aesthetics were reviewed because popular multimedia environments appear to arouse the same characteristics as aesthetic experience. Results indicate that this may indeed be the case.

INTRODUCTION

In a rich learner-centered environment, the learner is more actively engaged in the process of learning and not merely an observer (Duffy and Jonassen, 1992; Hannafin, 1992; Jennings, 1996; Rieber, 1996). While the Web has the elements (e.g., audio, video, graphics, asynchronous and synchronous communication, group participation) for providing authentic and meaningful experiences for the learner (Relan and Gillani, 1997), current models do not provide this kind of a design context (Tessmer and Richey, 1997). Identifying a model or framework for creating engaging and immersive environments that can be applied to web-based learning was the focus of this study.

Engaging and Immersive Learning Environments

The idea of engaging and immersive environments is certainly not new, but research into their creation and use is currently receiving a high degree of attention (cf. Balmouth,

Previously Published in *Challenges of Information Technology Management in the 21st Century* edited by Mehdi Khosrow-Pour, Copyright © 2000, Idea Group Publishing.

1996; Geirland, 1996; Khaslavsky and Shedroff, 1999; Laurel, 1993; Luskin, 1996; Winograd, 1996) from diverse fields. Laurel (1993) writes: "Think of a computer, not as a tool, but as a medium" (p. 126). This medium can be used to create engaging and immersive experiences that she compares to theater productions where the users are not merely observers, but actors in the play.

An engaging and immersive framework may be based on a perspective that has its roots in certain hedonic unifying concepts, such as our delight in well-ordered universe. These concepts, common to much of human experience, are generally referred to as aesthetics. It is important to understand that in this context the term aesthetics is used more broadly than the usual notion of *visual beauty* or *theory of the beautiful*. Aesthetics in this extended sense encompasses more than sensory experience and includes the concepts that allow mathematicians to speak of a *beautiful* equation or engineers of an *elegant* design solution. This extended concept of aesthetics includes perceptual, cognitive, and affective components.

Aesthetic experience, comprised of the characteristics of unity, focused attention, active discovery, affect, and intrinsic gratification (Beardsley, 1970, 1982) may be a means to produce engaging and immersive environments.

PURPOSE OF THE STUDY

Successful games and learning products seem to utilize a holistic and multi-modal approach to engagement and immersion. In other words, popular multimedia environments appear to contain many of the criteria necessary for an aesthetic experience. The study had two purposes. First, to determine if aesthetic characteristics were part of the design process of successful developers of game and educational environments, and second, to develop a framework based on their techniques. It was done in cooperation with six elite designers and two team members of recognized and/or award-winning game and educational products.

This research study is one of the steps toward support for *cognitive aesthetics* (Jennings, 1996) which has been proposed by this author and is defined as the merging of learning and aesthetic principles to create natural and pleasing learning environments.

LITERATURE REVIEW

The important aspects of aesthetic literature for this research were (a) the viewpoint of both philosophers and researchers that contribute to the understanding of aesthetics as an affective and cognitive experience, and (b) the characteristics of such experiences. Aesthetic experience is a sensory and thought-provoking event, often intense in nature which is distinguished by a particular set of characteristics.

Aesthetic Characteristics

Aesthetic literature clearly identifies some common characteristics of an aesthetic experience (Beardsley, 1958, 1969, 1970, 1982; Berleant, 1970; Dewey, 1934). Those provided by Beardsley (1970, 1982) are often considered a compilation of philosophical discussion on characteristics of aesthetic experience (Csikszentmihalyi and Robinson, 1990).

- Unity/Wholeness: Unity comes from the feeling of a high level of integration and coherence of all components related to the experience.
- Focused Attention or Object Directedness: Effortless direction of thoughts, feelings, and actions toward an activity results in a feeling of increased or magnified energy and feelings.
- Active Discovery: "The excitement of meeting a cognitive challenge" (Beardsley, 1982, p. 292).
- Affect: "Emotion carries the experience forward, binding parts and moments together" (Kupfer, 1983, p. 72). Affect is the spice that flavors experience and keeps us coming back for more.
- Intrinsic Gratification or Felt Freedom: An activity without regard to monetary, moral, practical goals or external rewards. The focus is on the process, not on the ultimate arrival.

When these characteristics occur in combination, the result is sagacious engagement and immersion in an activity, or in other words, an aesthetic experience. This kind of experience is perceived as sensuous and singularly unique. It is different from any other kind of experience because of a combination of characteristics (Csikszentmihalyi and Robinson, 1990; Beardsley, 1958, 1982).

Support for Aesthetic Experience

Two empirical research studies have particular significance in support of aesthetic experience and the findings from my study. Csikszentmihalyi and Robinson (1990) identified features of aesthetic experience based on expert knowledge of museum curators that could be used to enhance the art experience for non-experts. High percentages of participants spoke of attention, discovery, and emotional and intellectual involvement which correlate with Beardsley's aesthetic characteristics. Worth noting is that eighty percent of the participants "described the experience of art as something very different, very special, compared to the rest of their experiences" (p. 136).

Further support comes from Jones (1997) who interviewed computer game players for the purpose of applying the elements to learning environments. Similar results were found between Jones's study and the one being reported in this article. He found that:

- High-quality graphics, sound and animation are important;
- A mix of strategies such as higher order thinking and problem-solving skills and

twitch (reacting quickly to circumstances) helps users remain engaged;
- Games provide a means to build new information or schema;
- Games provide room for failure;
- Believable and accurate context (real or imaginary) is important; and
- User interest in the problem is important.

The results from Csikszentmihalyi and Robinson (1990) and Jones (1997) seem to add credibility to characteristics of engaging and immersive environments and to the aesthetic framework derived from this study.

METHOD AND RESULT

Qualitative research methods (Strauss and Corbin, 1990) were used. The eight participants were leaders in the industry. They were selected because they have designed recognized and/or award-winning educational or game environments that appear to be engaging and immersive. The findings indicate that the developers, in large part, employ structure and content that is consistent with the characteristics of aesthetic experience.

PRESCRIPTIVE AESTHETIC FRAMEWORK

Table 1 presents the aesthetic framework derived from the data. Major headings (e.g., UNITY) are the characteristics from aesthetic experience which relate to ideas expressed by the developers. For each characteristic, specific techniques are listed along with justification for their uses based on aesthetic literature. A subcategory was established when at least four of the developers spoke of similar phenomena.

CONCLUSION

A person who is attentive, emotionally involved, and engaged in discovery within a learning environment is more likely to learn and to enjoy the experience. An aesthetic framework such as the one proposed may be a design instrument used to accomplish this. Supplying holistic and relevant educational experiences that provide opportunities for learners to be engaged and immersed may encourage a love of learning.

The connection between aesthetic experience and learning is compelling. "Aesthetic activity involves a *transformation* of everyday perceptual, cognitive and affective processes giving rise to a uniquely structured aesthetic object" (Cupchik and Winston, 1996, p. 72), or more broadly, an experience. This kind of activity seems to be what we want to create in any learning environment.

It is worth noting that the techniques used by the participants were similar, but the users, media, and applications were quite diverse. The delivery media included computers (WWW and CD-ROMs), workshops, and television. Such diversity may indi-

Table 1: Prescriptive aesthetic framework

UNITY: The coherence and completeness of objects or ideas. Unity is the wholeness of an experience.

TECHNIQUES

Context	Story	Metaphor	Mini Gestalt	Media
Provides richness and depth to content by creating an experience	Sets a scene that creates empathetic connection.	Assembles all parts into a whole.	Provides complete content for the particular context.	Engages all of the senses with high-quality media, particularly sound. All pieces of the environment must be harmonious – they must fit the theme.

JUSTIFICATION

Helps create cognitive continuity and memorable experiences.	Personalizes the content.	Links information for recall.	Provides a holistic and realistic portion of content.	Provides a visceral, holistic environment. The harmony and fittedness of the theme is the essence of unity.

FOCUSED ATTENTION OR OBJECT DIRECTEDNESS: Elements that bring about focus or a desire to proceed with an activity.

TECHNIQUES

Familiarity	Props	Overview	Media
Go from the known to the unknown.	Use props and interactive processes.	Provide users with the big picture.	Provide interactive processes. Use eye-catching graphics and high-quality audio.

JUSTIFICATION

Users pay more attention to what they know and understand.	Props help users become and remain actively involved.	A overview provides the users with a focus for concentration.	Interactivity helps keep users motivated. Color and sound direct the user's attention.

ACTIVE DISCOVERY: The process of actively seeking answers or resolutions to cognitive challenges.

TECHNIQUES

Problem-solving	Play	Replay	Fill-in-the-blanks	Media
Provide contextually accurate, meaningful, and purposeful guided activities.	Provide an environment that allows users to explore and experiment.	Provide users with many alternatives and options to pursue. Allow them to try different things. If they fail, provide useful feedback.	Allow users the opportunity to make connections and inferences.	When appropriate, use animation to portray concepts.

JUSTIFICATION

Solving problems is a natural way to learn.	Play is a natural and active means of learning.	Success breeds boredom. Provide feedback to users to understand where they went wrong, which provides info on how to be successful.	This helps users to feel active and involved. It helps them to feel 'smart.'	Animation can often graphically depict a procedure or concept better than words or still images.

AFFECT: An emotional investment that helps create a personal link to an experience or activity.

TECHNIQUES

Shared Experience	First Person	Intrigue	Media
Provide a means for users to interact with others.	Set up the environment so that users have some control over or are part of the environment.	Let the plot thicken, the story unfold, the picture evolve.	Use contextually accurate media for continuity and accuracy. Use enticing graphics.

JUSTIFICATION

We, as a species, are a "small group animal" and feel a need to communicate.	The user has more of an emotional investment when the outcome is dependent upon their input.	Surprise and mystery entices users to stay tuned-in and to remain motivated.	Users notice inappropriate media use. It breaks their concentration and involvement. Enticing graphics create a desire to explore.

INTRINSIC MOTIVATION: A feeling of pleasure, reward and satisfaction from an activity

Personal Motivation	Ownership/Invest	Satisfaction
Include innovative techniques to sustain motivation.	Give guided control to the user. Provide users with meaningful activities and opportunities.	Provide a means for the user to be successful.

JUSTIFICATION

A user's initial desire to interact with an environment is important for motivation. Some newness, such as challenges, is refreshing.	Guidance helps users understand the environment and the content. Users want their actions to have value.	Success feels good and helps motivate users to continue.

cate the general applicability of these techniques across a broad range of applications and through different media. The similarity of design techniques extended to both educational and game environments, which is particularly interesting in light of the recent interest in looking at what games may provide educational environments (e.g., Jones, 1997; Rieber, 1992, 1996). Further exploration seems warranted.

While recognition of the connections between aesthetics and learning is not a new concept, it seems to be a particularly relevant one now because of technological advancements of multimedia technology. Ongoing empirical aesthetic research based on information processing is continuing to establish common ground between perceptual and cognitive theorists and aestheticians (e.g., Neuprend, 1988; Cupchik & Winston, 1996). The path of aesthetics seems to be merging with the road to learning.

REFERENCES

Balmuth, M. (1996, September). M & A pulse column. *Upside, VIII*, 104-105.

Beardsley, M. C. (1958). *Aesthetics: Problems in the philosophy of criticism.* New York: Harcourt Brace.

Beardsley, M. C. (1969, Fall). Aesthetic experience regained. *The Journal of Art Criticism, 28,* 2-12.

Beardsley, M. C. (1970). *Aesthetic theory and educational theory.* In R. Smith, (Ed.), *Aesthetic concepts and education* (pp. 3-20). Chicago: University of Illinois Press.

Beardsley, M. C. (1982). *Some persistent issues in aesthetics.* In M. J. Wreen & D. M. Callen (Eds.), *The aesthetic point of view: Selected essays* (pp. 285-87). Ithaca, NY: Cornell University Press.

Berleant, A. (1970). *The aesthetic field: A phenomenology of aesthetic experience.* Springfield, IL: Charles C. Thomas.

Csikszentmihalyi, M. (1990). *Flow: The psychology of optimal experience.* New York: Harper & Row.

Csikszentmihalyi, M., and Robinson, R. E. (1990). *The art of seeing: An interpretation of the aesthetic encounter.* Malibu, CA: J. Paul Getty Trust.

Cupchik, G. C., and Winston, A. S. (1996). *Confluence and divergence in empirical aesthetics, philosophy, and mainstream psychology.* In C. G. Cupchik & A. S. Winston (Eds.), *Cognitive ecology* (2nd ed., pp. 61-85). San Diego: Academic Press.

Dewey, J. (1934). *Art as experience.* New York: Minton, Balch & Company.

Duffy, T. M., & Jonassen, D. H. (1992). *Constructivism: New implications for instructional technology.* In T. M. Duffy & D. H. Jonassen (Eds.), *Constructivism and the technology of instruction: A conversation* (pp. 1-16). Hillsdale, NJ: Lawrence Erlbaum Associates, Inc.

Geirland, J. (1996, September). Go with the flow. *Wired*, pp. 160-61.

Hannafin, M. J. (1992). Emerging technologies, ISD, and learning environments: Critical perspectives. *Educational Technology Research and Development, 40*, (1), 49-63.

Jennings, M. M. (1996). *Aesthetics and learning: Toward a synthesis*. Retrieved from: http://www.edtech/unco.edu/coe/edtech/gradstudents/jennings/jennings.html.

Jennings, M. M. (1998). *An aesthetic framework derived from the creative and conceptual design process of master designers of educational and game environments: A qualitative research perspective.* Doctoral dissertation, University of Northern Colorado, Greeley, 1998). UMI Dissertation Services, 9839536.

Jones, M. G. (1997, February). *Learning to play; playing to learn: Lessons learned from computer games.* Paper presented at the annual convention of the Association for Educational Communications and Technology, Albuquerque, NM.

Khaslavsky, J., and Shedroff, N. (1999) Understanding the seductive experience. *Communications of the ACM, 425*, pp. 45-49.

Kupfer, J. H. (1983). *Experience as art: Aesthetics in everyday life.* Albany, NY: State University of New York Press.

Laurel, B. (1993). *Computers as theater.* Reading, MA: Addison-Wesley.

Luskin, B. (1996). Toward an understanding of media psychology. *T.H.E. Journal: Technological Horizons in Education, 23*, (7), 82-84.

Neuprend, R. W. (1988). *A propositional view of aesthetic experiencing for research and teaching in art education.* In F. H. Farley & R. W. Neuprend (Eds.), *The foundations of aesthetics, art and art education* (pp. 273-319). New York: Praeger.

Relan, A., and Gillani, B B. (1997). *Web-based instruction and the traditional classroom: Similarities and differences.* In B. H. Khan (Ed.), *Web-based instruction* (pp. 41-58). Englewood Cliffs, NJ: Educational Technology Publications.

Rieber, L. (1992). Computer-based microworlds: A bridge between constructivism and direct instruction. *Educational Technology, Research and Development, 40*, (1), 93-106.

Rieber, L. (1996). Seriously considering play: Designing interactive learning environments based on the blending of microworlds, simulation, and games. *Educational Technology, Research and Development, 44*, (2), 43-58.

Strauss, A., and Corbin, J. (1990). *Basics of qualitative research: Grounded theory procedures and techniques.* Newbury Park, CA: Sage.

Tessmer, M., and Richey, R. C. (1997). The role of context in learning and instructional design. *Educational Technology, Research and Development, 45*, (2), 85-115.

Winograd, T. (1996). In T. Winograd (Ed.), *Bringing design to software* (pp. v-ix). New York: ACM Press.

Chapter 21

Learning with Multimedia Cases in the Information Systems Area

Rikke Orngreen
Copenhagen Business School, Denmark

Paola Bielli
SDA Bocconi, Italy

The entrance of interactive multimedia systems into the arena of education and training has meant that in only a couple of years, a number of multimedia case studies for educational and training purposes in the Management of Information Systems area have emerged, and the tendency seems to be increasing. Use of such Information and Communication Technologies (ICT) is often claimed to be both valuable and effective for conveying the intended learning. However, because of the novelty of this area, very little is written about the role that a multimedia case study can play and how to apply such cases in a learning environment. Through the BUSINES-LINC project, sponsored by the European Commission, eighteen multimedia cases have been developed, with the objective to support innovative business solutions, especially in the e-commerce area.[1] The research study presented in this paper is currently rigorously investigating possible learning scenarios for three Italian and three Danish cases through the collection of qualitative and quantitative empirical data. Our objective is to gain experience in and knowledge about how the chosen learning objectives from a multimedia case are best transferred to the users. The results of the research study will guide instructors and developers of different types of multimedia cases to better contemplate their learning objectives and course structure according to their target group. The paper first presents a short introduction to the field and the theoretical foundation

Previously Published in *Managing Information Technology in a Global Economy* edited by Mehdi Khosrow-Pour, Copyright © 2001, Idea Group Publishing.

of the research study. Then the methodological aspects are described, and finally, our current experiences and preliminary results are conveyed, together with a short overview of the issues, which we are currently investigating further by means of our empirical material.

INTRODUCTION

The method of teaching with cases has existed for much more than a century in law and medical schools, but it was not used in the business area until 1910, when Dr. Copeland from the Harvard Business School was encouraged to do so by his dean. In 1921, Dr. Copeland wrote the first book containing written cases (Leenders and Erskine, 1989). A traditional, paper-based case, it describes a company, its strategies, objectives, and often a current problem which a decision-maker is facing. The case enables the student to get a feeling of the organization, its problems and opportunities, and in class the student discusses the possible solutions to the presented problem. In the case-based learning model, a traditional paper case is thus defined to be a description of real events, which contains interesting decisions that have been structured in a way that stimulates the students to reflect and discuss them (Mauffette-Leenders, Erskine, and Leenders, 1997).

The method of case-based learning has won a widespread use in business schools for executive and MBA training programs from all over the world. The model of learning by cases consists of much more than the actual case itself. In general, the North American/Canadian approach, when teaching with cases, is to let the students prepare the case individually and in groups, then they discuss the case in a plenary session, and maybe they also write an assignment over the subject (Erskine, Leenders and Mauffette-Leenders, 1998). This implies that a case cannot be evaluated in itself, but has to be assessed in the learning process it is being used, while considering the learning objectives and target group for that session.

Interactive[2] multimedia allow the user to navigate and interact with the system and can support the creation of new meanings (reflections) and enhance communication. The change in media usage from the traditional paper-based cases to multimedia cases poses some very interesting challenges, from the perspective of learning and pedagogical strategies as well as considerations on which techniques to use when evaluating the use of such cases (Orngreen, Christiansen, Nielsen, and Siggaard Jensen, 1999).

The underlying pedagogical theories of case-based learning are action learning and experiential learning (see, for example, Hazard, 2000 and Dewey, 1994). In David Kolb's experiential learning cycle, people reflect over their experiences, which founds the basis for their internal subjective interpretation and individual formulation of concepts that explains the world as they have experienced it; this again leads to a set of actions in the external world, providing new experiences for that individual (Kolb, 1984). According to Leidner and Jarvenpaa's classification of learning approaches in the I.S. field, the form of action and experiential learning present in case-based learning corresponds with the constructivistic and the sociocultural model of learning (see Bielli and Basaglia, 2000).[3]

When setting up learning objectives for cases, which are related to those two learning models, it is the ability to analyse, diagnose and make good argumentations for plausible recommendations about the case situations that are considered vital (Heath, 1998). The features (to analyze, diagnose, and argument) can be compared with the much-used "Bloom's learning taxonomy." Bloom and Krathwohl (1984) suggested classifying learning objectives with reference to the complexity of information processing needed in the learning process (Figure 1). According to this model, case-based learning objectives aim at learning at the higher levels.

The objective of a case-based learning process is also to "engage the imagination of the participants, and it [the case] must contain many possible directions and solutions so as to generate strong debate from which everyone can learn" (Hazard, 2000). This means that cases with only one solution are not optimal, as they often mislead the students into thinking that they have now learned a series of methods or templates, which they can use in similar situations (a sort of recipe).

RESEARCH QUESTIONS AND METHOD

Using the described general outline of case structure and pedagogical use of cases, the research study aims to investigate how the learning objectives of a multimedia case-based learning scenario are best transferred to the case users. Through the use of multimedia case studies[4], the project investigates the impact of both design and use issues. In particular, the research project focuses on the following questions:

- Which elements of the case and the applied learning process motivate the users to lead a discussion and to reflect on the content of the case?
- Are there changes in the effectiveness and efficiency of the learning process based on multimedia cases compared to a traditional learning process?
- Do the multimedia case content, structure, and user interface meet the expectations of the students?
- What are pros and cons of working with multimedia cases?

The research project uses triangulation between different qualitative and quantitative techniques to ensure that the findings in the qualitative data material have a somewhat general character. A questionnaire, with both open and closed questions (see Appendix A), has been used in all classes, which enables a comparison

Figure 1: Bloom's learning taxonomy for cognitive learning objectives (BUSINES-LINC D6, 2000)

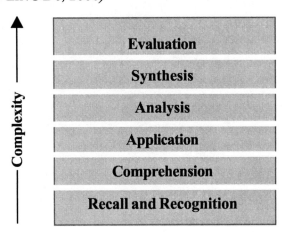

Table 1: Overview of the six cases used in the research study

Cases / Variables	Sogema (Italian)	e-ticket (Italian)	Iris (Italian)	LEGO (Danish)	ALKA (Danish)	Rockwool (Danish)
Main topic	Selection process and feasibility studies of I.S. projects	Assessment process and alternative evaluation in the e-commerce (B2C) area	Decision drivers in B2B e-commerce projects	Alternative evaluation and decision on future in the e-commerce (B2C) area	Assessment process of e-business project and business plan for e-commerce (B2B) project.	Evaluation of Business Process Re-engineering Project
Learning objective and Expected output	Simulate the decision process. Output: Feasibility studies	Simulate the decision process. Output: Identifying decision drivers, deciding the preferred alternative and justifying the decision.	Simulate the assessment process. Output: Identifying decision drivers, designing alternative paths, comparing alternatives	Simulate the decision process. Output: Identifying decision drivers, deciding the preferred alternative and justifying the decision.	Simulate the assessment process. Output: Business Plan	Assessment process. Output: Identifying decision drivers, and compare alternatives
Organisation in focus	Sogema, small service company in the logistics field	Chartanet and its main customers (theatres as La Scala, Il Piccolo, Carlo Felice)	Iris, service company in the information technology industry	The LEGO company (the dep. dealing with branding and selling on the Internet)	The insulation company Rockwool Denmark A/S	The insurance company ALKA
User's expected role / Characteristic of case structure	Newly appointed I.S. Director in the Virtual organisation: Amegos.	Potential entrepreneur in Virtual organisation: The new firm the user might found	Consultant Virtual organisation: Antos, service company for B2B projects	Consultant for the LEGO Company Management	New project member of the E-business project at Rockwool A/S	Assessment of BPR project, (not a role-playing case).
Media usage	Short interviews with the real company persons, then actors	Short interviews with the real company persons, then actors	Short interviews with the real company persons, then actors	Video, sound and text Interviews with the managers of the LEGO Company. The use of a narrator /speaker.	Actors (sound and text) staging employees of Rockwool (a project member and sales consultant)	Video interviews and the use of a narrator /speaker

of the collected data from the six cases (Table 1).[5] Different qualitative evaluation methods and techniques have been and are being applied, particularly observation and video analysis, as well as focus group and interviews (of both students and instructors). (See Appendix B.)

Figure2: Learning scenarios, which the research study investigates

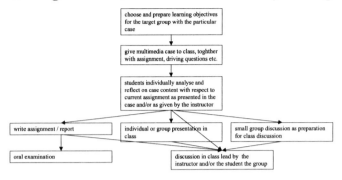

Given Bloom's taxonomy of learning objectives, both the Italian and the Danish cases used in this study aim at pursuing a combined objective portfolio. That is to say, each case has more than one learning objective. They include the analysis mode by letting the student contemplate the available information and relate them to their knowledge about information systems and management theories and experiences. By allowing the users to undertake a decision-making role, risk assessment and project selection will support the evaluation mode. Besides, some of the multimedia cases include templates and theoretical chapters (typical of the recall/recognition and Application steps), enabling the user to review his/her own know-whow and to implement a standard format.

Figure 2 illustrates the paths of learning scenarios used in this research study in varied educational environments, from undergraduate to MBA programs and executive training.

PRELIMINARY RESULTS

Traditional paper-based cases provide an excellent means to get students to play the role of the decision-makers and let them deduct some possible answers to the questions extracted from the case. These answers should rely on their previous theoretical knowledge and practical experiences. Multimedia cases can further enhance this experience by providing a feeling of submergence into the situation depicted by letting the students be subjected to the emotional aspects (like pressure from the board of the company, etc.) in an intense and visual manner. The multimedia case can be designed so that it reassembles the culture of a particular sector or industry, which is one of the reasons why ITC material is being given a lot of attention for in-house business and management competence development.

All the cases in this study have a design that exploits the possibility of surrounding the user with a more naturalistic set of material than what a paper-based case can provide. The two Danish cases, Rockwool and LEGO, let the user play a role in the organization in focus. Since both companies, at the time of the development of the case, were just at the point of major decisions regarding their Internet strategies, this gives the user the possibility to assess their current solutions and come up with future strategies and decisions. Another example is the Italian Sogema case, which brings the students "into play" by first giving the students an introduction to the real Sogema company and then letting them play the role of an IS director in its virtual counterpart organization, named Amegos.

Unlike full-time students, managers and executives have limited time for competence development, and often they prefer to use this valuable time to discuss the hardcore facts of other companies instead of practicing finding information, which they have already learned from their everyday work. This means managers have a need for addressing the top levels of Bloom's hierarchy, where full-time students (undergraduate and graduates) often also need to train the lower levels, like recognition, comprehension, and application skills.

As a consequence, the Danish cases, like a traditional paper-based case, contains less unprocessed or raw data, than, for example, other large simulation-like games do, in order to apply for the needs of the managers/executives.[6] Observation in classes showed that discussion went smoother with the MBA and executive course than with the graduate students. This indicates that because of their work experience and general up-to-date knowledge about the IS sector, the MBA students where able to relate the case to their own world a lot better than the graduates were. Adopting a more theory-based approach with undergraduates and graduate students, where the students should assess the solution in the cases according to the theory addressed in the course, seemed more successful.

To be able to combine different learning objectives in one case study, the Italian research team identified another approach: they moved from a real company with real projects and problems to a virtual organization. In other words, the real organizations provided the environment - the projects with their real data, etc. - but then the user plays in an invented reality. This shift is necessary because some simplifications are needed, some positions must be exaggerated, and some figures must be changed to be able to *transfer* the real company into a multimedia reality. Besides, the user is usually expected to make decisions and to assess the effects of his/her decisions in the company, and it was not appealing to imagine alternatives, which had not taken place in the real organization.

It is our experience with the Italian cases that beginners follow a more sequential approach, accessing first the theoretical documents and then trying to solve the business problems; whereas experienced learners immediately play the suggested roles and use theories as eventual support material.

The authors found that time devoted to prepare and use the case is two to three times more than for traditional cases, and thus the focus moves from only in-class activities to individual preparation. However, for multimedia cases the instructor's influence on the case-based learning process is still significant. The personal character of the teacher, his/her experiences, etc., can bring a very poor case "home," so to speak, or drive a rather interesting and high quality multimedia case off the track (Napell, 1994).

Even though the multimedia cases in this research study were originally designed to be used in an offline environment, they support the transition to remote/distant on-line teaching. One online teaching event has been tried with the Danish LEGO case and showed that if such an approach should succeed, technical issues have to be well-planned in advance. Little things such as getting the right plug-ins seem still to be a problem. Thus, it is still important to investigate the use of multimedia cases in class and in some online programs.

In order to further validate and verify the experiences mentioned here, the research will continue to analyze the collected data. The authors will be able to present a large part of these results in Spring, 2001. At present, impacts on effectiveness are difficult to assess, but some facts could be stated:
- The students perceived the case preparation as less boring than traditional cases;
- The students have built a *real* feasibility study, business plan, or a decision process in an environment, which is close to a real organization; and
- After a while the students still remember the case title and issues dealt with.
    With reference to efficiency, some considerations must be pointed out:
- Time needed to solve the case is much higher than for traditional cases;
- The obsolescence of the case is relatively rapid;
- The presence of templates and standard outputs speeds up the solution of the case;
- The use of a CD-ROM offers a single interface or environment where the user can find all the needed information; and
- The Internet links in the browser environment, in which the six cases are developed, provide access to additional material, such as other companies in the same sector or with similar solutions, the press, etc. However, this is at the risk of the user getting information, which jeopardizes the intended learning structure/idea or that the user gets "lost in hyperspace."

These considerations are partly contradictory: some of them envision an increase of efficiency, while others suggest negative impact on time necessary for the learning process. At present, we have not yet analyzed all our available data, constraining us to draw final conclusions on this issue. We are thus currently investigating which multimedia elements influence the efficiency in which student groups. The findings will be rigorously compared with our quantitative and qualitative data material, enabling us to describe the implications a chosen multimedia case design may have in specific learning scenarios and with specific user groups.

APPENDIX A

A total of 102 questionnaires have been collected until now. Also, nine substantive process questionnaires have been collected (those are large questionnaires, which cover the preparation and use process thoroughly).

Appendix A Table: The questionnaire used for the analysis of the Danish cases

	Fully Agree	Agree	Rather Agree	Rather Disagree	Disagree	Fully Disagree
• I had a computer available to work on the case outside the university or I had enough possibility to work on the case in the school's computer rooms.						
• I had a satisfying amount of information available to work on the case on my own.						
• The information provided in the case gave me a realistic insight into the subject (The process of Rockwool A/S company's entrance into the e-business world by use of digital technical manuals and software).						
• I got a clear understanding of what the purpose of the site Rockwool.dk is?						
• The text and graphics were understandable and well organised.						
• The multimedia elements (mix actors speak and more objective text) were a good way of getting a deeper and more varied understanding of the Rockwool case						
• The business plan was clear and usable.						
• I had to search outside the case to write the business plan						
• The Internet links were up to date and useful.						
• The case has intensified my interest in the subject.						
• The case was easy to use and navigate in.						
• The case was well structured.						
• The case had an overall professional appearance.						
• It was fun to work with the case.						
• I recommend you to use the case in future courses.						

1. Please, describe your overall reaction to the case and the case discussions today:

2. What did you like best?

3. What did you like least?

4. Do you believe you could use the learnings from the case or the discussions today in your future study or work situation? (if yes, which learnings, if no, why not?)

5. If you could change one thing to improve the case, what would you change?

6. How much time did you spend working on the LEGO case (total)?

7. With whom did you work with the Case, Individually, in a group, during class discussion?

8. How did you work with it (Did you solve the assignment, the questions provided by the instructor, did you take notes...)?

9. Do you have any other comments (also use the back of this page)?

APPENDIX B

The table illustrates the different evaluation methods, which have been used in this research study. Indeed, the project group believed that one important research step might have been experts' and students' assessment. An evaluation framework was developed, including several actors and tools, as shown in the table below.

The classification of whether a person is "external" versus "internal" to the project bases on the knowledge or involvement of the instructor. BUSINES-

LINC project members and colleagues at least partially working in developing the cases are classified as internal reviewers. This means that in a class taught by a person from the BUSINES-LINC project, the users/students of this class are also identified as internal students. The number written in parenthesis after each case indicates the number of times this case has been evaluated using this particular method.

Appendix B Table: Empirical data collected/method used

Students & Reviewers	Questionnaire	Focus groups	Methods / tools used			
			Template	Written statement	Observation	Video Analysis
INTERNAL						
Peer Expert	Sogema (1) e-ticket (1) Iris (1)	ALKA (2) LEGO (1) Rockwool (1)	LEGO (1) Rockwool (1)	ALKA (1) LEGO (1) Rockwool (1)		
User	LEGO (2) Rockwool (1) Sogema (3) e-ticket (2)	ALKA (1)			LEGO (2) Rockwood (1)	LEGO (2) Rockwood (1)
Teacher		Sogema (1) e-ticket (1) Iris (1)		Sogema (1) e-ticket (1) Iris (1)		
EXTERNAL						
Expert				ALKA (2) LEGO (1)		
User	ALKA (3) LEGO (2) Sogema (1)	ALKA (1) LEGO (2) Sogema (4)			ALKA (2) LEGO (6)	ALKA (1) LEGO (5)
Teacher				ALKA (2) LEGO (2) Rockwool (1)		

REFERENCES

Bielli, P., and Basaglia, S. (2000, July). Multimedia case studies: development and use in management education. In *Proceedings of the 8th European Conference on Information Systems (ECIS)*. Vienna, Austria.

Bloom, B. S., and Krathwohl, D.R. (1984). *Taxonomy of educational objectives, Handbook I: Cognitive Domain*. New York.

BUSINES-LINC consortium *D6 – Part II: Updated BUSINES-LINC Learning Concept,* report, which was part of a deliverable to the European Commission. Originator: University of Cologne, March 2000

BUSINES-LINC consortium "Procedures for Quality Assurance", Workpackage input paper. Originator: Copenhagen Business School, October 1999

Dewey, J. (1994). *Teaching in Education*. In L. Barnes, C. R. Christensen, and A. Hansen (Eds.), *Teaching and the case method*, (3rd ed., pp. 9-14). Boston, MA: Harvard Business School Press.

Erskine, J.A., Leenders, M.R., and Mauffette-Leenders, L. A.(1998). *Teaching with cases*. Canada: Richard Ivey School of Business, the University of Western Ontario.

Hazard, H.(2000, Spring). Action learning carried beyond case teaching. *ECCHO, The Newsletter of the European Case Clearing House*, pp. 5-6. Bedford, UK: The European Case Clearing House, Cranfield University.

Heath, J. (1998). *Teaching and writing case studies: a practical guide.* Bedford, UK: The European Case Clearing House, Cranfield University.

Kolb, D. (1984). *Experiential Learning: Experience as the source of learning and development.* New Jersey: Prentice Hall.

Leenders, M. R. and Erskine, J. A. (1989). *Case research: The case writing process,* (3rd ed.). Canada: Richard Ivey School of Business, the University of Western Ontario.

Leidner, D. and Jarvenpaa, S.L. (1995, September). The use of information technology to enhance management school education: A theoretical view. *MIS Quarterly*, pp. 265-91.

Mauffette-Leenders, L. A., Erskine, J. A., and Leenders, M. R. (1997). *Learning with cases.* Canada: Richard Ivey School of Business, the University of Western Ontario.

Napell, M. (1994). *Six common non-facilitating teaching behaviors.* In L. Barnes, C. R. Christensen, and A. Hansen (Eds.), *Teaching and the Case Method,* (3rd Ed., pp. 199-202). Boston, MA: Harvard Business School Press.

Orngreen, R., Christiansen, E., Nielsen, J., and Siggaard Jensen, S. (1999). Artefacts, body and space. Accepted paper for workshop to the Computer-Supported Cooperative Learning Conference in Stanford, California.

ENDNOTES

[1] Project BUSINES-LINC - Business Innovation Networks – Learning with Interactive Cases has six business schools from Europe as participants: University of Cologne (Coordinator), Copenhagen Business School, Norwegian School of Economics and Business Administration (Bergen), Rotterdam School of Management, SDA, the business school of Bocconi University (Milan), and Stockholm School of Economics.

[2] Interaction is here intended as the ability of the system to give feedback to the user or to react to any decision or course of action he/she follows.

[3] For an overview of the classification according to training objectives and learning approaches in the I.S. field, see Leidner and Jarvenpaa (1995).

[4] For a detailed description of the project and the list of cases, see http://www.wi-im.uni.koeln.de/blinc/.

[5] The questionnaire was developed by Rikke Orngreen in the BUSINES-LINC project as part of the Quality Assurance Framework (BUSINES-LINC, 1999).

[6] Simulation games often contain a lot of financial information, full balance sheets, documents from meetings, full transcriptions of interviews, etc.

Chapter 22

Who Benefits from WWW Presentations in the Basics of Informatics?

Pekka Makkonen
University of Jyväskylä

This paper describes the use of WWW-based guided tours as a complementary addition to conventional lectures in the basics of informatics. Learning can be promoted in the spirit of constructivism, situated action, and cognitive flexibility when organizing a WWW coursework. We analyze the benefit of an optional coursework, including the use of guided tours and the use of search engines and directories on the WWW. This paper presents who benefits and who does not benefit from our optional coursework. The analysis is based on the background information and prior computer experience of the students, as well as pre and post tests. The study found that our WWW-based coursework suits best for females and all students except the students of economics. The students who are not familiar with computers and the Internet benefit more from WWW-based learning. Age and the number of years studied at a university do not affect the effectiveness of the WWW coursework. The results show that our WWW coursework suits for basic course level students in informatics, regardless of age. However, in the continuing courses of informatics, the coursework is probably less effective.

INTRODUCTION

For example, Isaacs (1994) and Rosenthal (1995) have reported problems in regard to traditional lecture-based teaching, including ineffectiveness, an increase in passivity, and isolation of students. In the context of technology, revisions have been suggested to improve lecturing as a teaching method by activating students in different conventional ways (Jacobson, Maouri, Mishra and Kolar, 1996). From this perspective, lecturing is not without potential if the previously mentioned problems can be corrected, but other learning methods must also be considered.

Hypertext and the WWW (the World Wide Web) enable learning as knowledge construction, allowing information and concepts to be represented as a learner adopts them. This helps meaningful learning. One alternative to conventional lectures is a presentation on the WWW. This presentation can be supported by coursework emphasizing learning as knowledge construction.

Hypertext and hypermedia have some problems. They do not typically offer an explicit mechanism to help learners better interpret and assimilate information, the context surrounding their creation and use, or the perspectives on the information of the author or other learners (Wan and Johnson, 1994). Improving information access without supporting learning leads directly to the problems of "information overload" and being "lost in hyperspace." Thus, students need some degree of guidance. Additionally, the form and structure of hypermedia presentations must be discussed. This is more important in the era of the WWW.

The WWW provides both the possibility to organize information in a strict form and opportunities for free "surfing" with its advantages and disadvantages. To realize the benefits of the WWW, we suggest a solution of three layers: (a) the support of guided tours as a slideshow on the WWW, (b) the support of appropriate links, and (c) the support of search engines and directories. This approach may provide a basis for a successful WWW coursework.

This paper introduces our WWW-based coursework as a way to apply the WWW in the learning of basic concepts in informatics. Additionally, it presents who benefits from the WWW coursework in education. This study defines the concept "benefit" related to the quality of learning concepts. The analysis is based on the psychology of knowledge and a pre-questionnaire.

LEARNING CONCEPTS

This study understands learning as knowledge construction in the spirit of constructivist theory (constructivism). An individual learns new concepts in relation to his/her prior knowledge.

This psychological perspective of our research can be divided into the perspective of cognitive psychology and the perspective of developmental psychology. They both emphasize learning as knowledge construction.

Perspective of Cognitive Psychology

Cognitive psychology distinguishes declarative and procedural forms of knowledge. Declarative knowledge represents cognizance or awareness of some object, event, or idea (Ryle, 1949). Procedural knowledge describes how learners use or apply their declarative knowledge. Structural knowledge mediates the translation of declarative into procedural knowledge and facilitates the application of procedural knowledge. It is the knowledge of how concepts within a domain (e.g., in informatics) are interrelated (Diekhoff, 1983). We comprehend learning as a knowledge construction process of both declarative and structural knowledge where a learner's goal is to approach an expert's knowledge structure or the requirements of a course.

Perspective of Developmental Psychology

In developmental psychology, conceptual knowledge can be approached using Collis's (1975) modification of Piaget's stages of development. This approach creates a basis for evaluating learning outcomes, emphasizing the quality of learning concerning a single concept and interrelatedness between the concepts.

Based on Piaget's stages of development, a SOLO (Structure of the Observed Learning Outcome) taxonomy divides learning outcomes into five classes. These classes reflect the quality of a learning outcome. Learning outcomes (i.e., definitions of concepts) can be classified as follows using the SOLO taxonomy (Biggs and Collis, 1982):

1. Prestructural,
2. Unistructural,
3. Multistructural,
4. Relational, and
5. Extended Abstract.

A student's response can be classified according to the capacity, relating operation, and consistency and closure of his/her response. Pre-structural responses are based on irrelevant or inappropriate data (level 1). Unistructural responses are based on conclusions on one aspect (level 2). Multistructural responses are based on isolated relevant data (level 3). Relational responses are based on relevant data and an understanding of the interrelations of different data in responses (level 4). Extended abstract responses are based on an understanding of data and interrelations both in the context of a question and in unexpected situations (level 5).

CONSTRUCTIVISM

Widely discussed views associated with (computer-supported) learning include behaviorism and its opposite, constructivism. Behaviorism focuses on a student's behavior in relation to teaching, while constructivism is interested in the mental processes, which affect behavior. A traditional lecture is mainly based on the behaviorist approach, while coursework and projects are constructivist learning.

Constructivism asserts that learners construct knowledge (Brandt, 1997). Learning is comprehended as the development of a learner's mental models (or declarative and structural knowledge). Brandt (1997) emphasizes that constructivism is a basis when applying the WWW for learning. While the goal of constructivism is to recognize and help to facilitate a learner's ability to construct knowledge when applied to teaching information retrieval on the Internet, it also provides the teacher with a structure for teaching. By focusing on concepts and connecting them to mental models, teachers can gain both confidence and control over the amount of material they cover in the small blocks of time usually allotted to teaching. Integrated with experiences that learners use to alter and strengthen mental models, the constructivist approach to teaching information retrieval also gives users the structure needed to get the most out of the Internet. However, traditional instruction is needed to support the constructivist environment (Silverman, 1995).

THE WWW IN LEARNING

The problems inherent in hypermedia, such as disorientation, navigation inefficiency, and cognitive overload, are multiplied on the Internet (Brandt, 1997). These problems can be overcome using the constructivist approach, but it is useful to discuss the use of the WWW from other perspectives. One alternative is trails and guided tours as a way of improving the usefulness of the WWW. Additionally, the concepts of situated action and cognitive flexibility can be discussed from the perspective of the WWW-based education.

One way to organize a WWW presentation is trails and guided tours. Trails connect a chain of links through information spaces (Bieber, Vitali, Ashman, Balasubramanian and Oinas-Kukkonen, 1997). These can include "recommended" trails through a network. Guided tours restrict users to the trail, prohibiting detours. While trails lower the cognitive overload by recommending the next logical link to take, guided tours reduce the overload further by removing all other choices.

The success of a computer-supported learning environment depends on the context in which that software is used (Koschmann, 1996). The term "situated action" emphasizes the interrelationship between an action and its context of performance (Chen and Rada, 1996). It stresses a person's responsiveness to the environment and focuses on the improvisory nature of human activity (Nardi, 1996) and the local management of activity as mediated by relevant environmental cues (Agre and Chapman, 1987; Suchman, 1987). The implications for learning are that appropriate actions are generated from recognition of opportunities given by the context.

Additionally, Jacobson et al. (1996) emphasize the meaning of cognitive flexibility theory affecting hypertext-based learning. This theory proposes that complex knowledge may be better learned for flexible application in new contexts by employing case-based learning environments.

Based on the above material, we must discuss what the right amount of behaviorist teaching is and we must analyze what the right way to use the WWW is. Active learning must be promoted, and the pitfalls of the WWW must be avoided. Additionally, support for students is needed in learning based on the WWW.

COURSE AND ITS WWW COURSEWORK
Experiment

At our university an introductory course in informatics lasts 10 weeks including lectures (eight hours), compulsory exercises in basic skills with personal computers and the Internet (eighteen hours), and a final examination.

In 1998 our approach to using the WWW for education was to combine
* trails and guided tours,
* both behaviorist teaching and constructivist learning,
* situated action, and
* cognitive flexibility theory.

In the WWW-based learning, the basic point is situated action. The constructivist approach is the commonly accepted principle for learning. Since the structural form of knowledge is typical for the basic concepts of informatics (Makkonen, 1999), it is natural to approach the course from the perspective of constructivism. However, in our context, students may need guidance at the beginning, and traditional educational methods based on behaviorism are partly appropriate.

The students were introduced to our approach. The pre-questionnaire, which was administered at the beginning of the course, supported our approach.

Based on the above-mentioned, the lectures consisted of
* printed lecture notes,
* conventional lectures,
* lecture notes on the WWW, including links to supporting sites, and
* optional WWW coursework concerning lecture notes on the WWW.

As mentioned earlier, conventional lectures and printed lecture notes are needed as a behaviorist part of the course, but WWW material provides an opportunity for the constructivist approach. The lecture notes were organized in the form of a guided tour as a slideshow using Microsoft Powerpoint '97 and its Internet assistant providing support for a student who is at the beginning of learning in informatics. Each slide may include a set of links to interesting WWW sites, and the slideshow can also be comprehended as a trail. Our slides included links concerning the critical concepts to the link pages, which were evaluated as supporting learning. The form of a lecture is flexible and it can be seen as a trail or a guided tour depending on the situation. Based on our approach, a student can also support his or her learning using search engines and directories. This allows different views and brings a real constructivist way to learning.

To realize the benefit of our WWW approach, we organized a coursework in which students were expected to enter their findings in their diaries, including their opinion about (a) the form of presentation, (b) the links provided by the teacher, and (c) the links found by the students themselves using search engines and directories (i.e., Altavista and Yahoo). The students were expected to give examples of what they had learned during the coursework. To promote the students' participation in the optional coursework, the students got credits by completing the coursework for the examination. The students had six-and-a-half weeks for the coursework before the examination. The work was conducted as an individual task or in groups of two or three students.

Sample

One hundred and three minor students, 77 females and 26 males, whose mean age was 23 years (range 19-42 years) entered the course and completed both pre- and post-treatments. They all participated in the computer exercises (18 hours), and all the students had the same exercises. Participating in the lectures (8 hours) and the coursework was optional.

Forty-six of the students, 38 females and 8 males, whose mean age was 22 years (range 19-40 years), participated in the optional coursework. Seventeen of them completed the coursework individually, 23 in groups of two students and 6 in groups of three students. The students spent 13 hours (range 5-30 hours) on the coursework on average. They attended 6.5 hours of lectures and spent 43 hours on the course on average. We call this group the WWW group in this paper.

Fifty-seven students, 39 females and 18 males, whose mean age was 23 years (range 19-42 years) did not complete the optional coursework. These students attended 4.9 hours of lectures and spent 31 hours on the course on average. We call this group the non-WWW group in this paper.

Collecting Data

We utilized a SOLO taxonomy-based measure to analyze learning (Makkonen, 1999). Both the pre-treatment and the post-treatment contained fifteen separately selected items. These items were chosen randomly from eighty-eight critical concepts to learn of the whole learning area. Those concepts were selected by the group of the teachers (n=12) of informatics in our university. In each test, respondents produced fifteen definitions of randomly selected concepts. In the responses the students were expected to define concepts using certain sentences clarifying the basic properties of each concept and connections between these properties. The responses of the students were ranked from 1 to 5 based on the quality of learning. The basis for the rankings was the contemporary definitions of these concepts that were included in our material.

To study who benefits and who does not from the WWW coursework, data were collected by administering a pre-questionnaire to the students, including general information like gender, age, number of years studied at the university, and faculty. Additionally, we gathered information about the experience with computers and the Internet. The respondents ranked their skills or knowledge or the amount of use/training on a 5-point Likert scale (where 1=very poor/little and 5=very good/much).

Results

Since the data based on the responses of the students disagreed with the normal distribution, the Mann-Whitney test was appropriate to compare means. We found based on the SOLO taxonomy that the WWW coursework improves learning outcomes significantly in our context (Makkonen, 1999). Cronbach's alpha to show the reliability was 0.72 in the pre-treatment and 0.77 in the post-treatment. In this paper we report the results based on those previous results (Makkonen, 1999) and the general background and the prior experiences with computers.

Table 1: Analyzing responses based on gender

	Mean of WWW Group	Mean of Non-WWW Group	p
Females (n)	38	39	
Beginning of Course	1.56	1.59	313
End of Course	2.65	2.45	<001
Males (n)	8	18	
Beginning of Course	1.75	1.84	.222
End of Course	2.48	2.48	.834

Table 2: Analyzing responses based on faculty

Faculty	Mean of WWW Group	Mean of Non-WWW Group	p
Social Sciences (n)	9	15	
Beginning of Course	1.54	1.60	.540
End of Course	2.64	2.30	<001
Humanities (n)	28	28	
Beginning of Course	1.55	1.54	.018
End of Course	2.62	2.48	.030
Economics (n)	9	10	
Beginning of Course	1.75	1.67	.324
End of Course	2.61	2.54	.478
Other (n)	-	4	
Beginning of Course	-	2.05	-
End of Course	-	2.70	-

Results Based on Background

Analyzing data based on the gender showed that females benefit significantly more from the WWW coursework. Table 1 shows the details of analysis.

To clarify if the age affects learning, the Pearson correlation coefficients were calculated for both the WWW group and the non-WWW group. The correlation was not significant in either case. Thus, the age does not affect the benefit of the coursework significantly.

To clarify if the number of years studied at the university affects learning, the Pearson correlation coefficients were calculated for both the WWW group and non-WWW group. The correlation was not significant in both cases. Thus, the number of years studied at the university does not affect the benefit of the coursework significantly.

Analyzing data based on the faculty showed that both the students of social sciences and humanities benefit from the WWW coursework. Regarding the students of economics, no significant difference has been found. Table 2 shows the details of analysis.

Results Based on Prior Computer Experience

Analyzing data based on the prior training (before the course) of computers shows that the WWW coursework is beneficial for students who have had less prior training. First, we compared the students who have had prior training to the students who have not had it. Second, to clarify if the amount of prior training affects learning, the Pearson correlation coefficients were calculated for both the WWW group and the non-WWW group. The correlation was not significant in either case. Table 3 shows the details of comparing means.

Table 3: Analyzing responses based on prior computer training

Prior Training	Mean of WWW Group	Mean of Non-WWW Group	p
Yes (n)	33	42	
Beginning of Course	1.65	1.65	.935
End of Course	2.67	2.45	<.001
No (n)	13	15	
Begingining of Course	1.44	1.71	<.001
End of Course	2.49	2.49	.868

Table 4: Analyzing responses based on prior work experience with computers

	Correlation Coefficient of WWW Group	P (WWW group)	Correlation Coefficient of Group	p (Non-www. Group)
Beginning of Course	.144	.002	.141	<.001
End of Course	.079	.084	.008	.824

To clarify if the amount of prior work experience with computers affects learning, the Pearson correlation coefficients were calculated. Based on the analysis the WWW coursework is beneficial for the students who have less work experience with computers. Table 4 shows the details of analysis.

To clarify if prior general experience with personal computers affects learning, the Pearson correlation coefficients were calculated. For these analyses the students were expected to evaluate their experience based on a 5-point Likert scale. We analyzed if prior experience with personal computers affects learning. The positive correlation was significant at the level 0.01 at the beginning in both groups. At the end, the positive correlation was significant at the level 0.05 in the WWW group and at the level 0.01 in the non-WWW group. The result shows that the students who are not very experienced with personal computers can benefit slightly more from the WWW coursework. Table 5 shows the details of analysis.

We analyzed if prior experience with the Internet affects learning. The positive correlation was significant at the level 0.01 at the beginning in both groups. At the end the positive correlation was not significant in the WWW group and the

Table 5: Analyzing responses based on prior experience with personal computers

	Correlation Coefficient of WWW Group	P (WWW group)	Correlation Coefficient of Non WWW Group	p (Non-www. Group)
Beginning of Course	.224	<001	.194	<.001
End of Course	.083	.029	.147	<.001

Table 6: Analyzing responses based on prior use of Internet

	Correlation Coefficient of WWW Group	P (WWW group)	Correlation Coefficient of Non WWW Group	p (Non-www. Group)
Beginning of Course	.190	<.001	.141	<.001
End of Course	.006	.879	.122	<.001

Table 7: Analyzing responses based on knowledge of basic concepts of information technology

	Correlation Coefficient of WWW Group	P (WWW group)	Correlation Coefficient of Non WWW Group	p (Non-www. Group)
Beginning of Course	.235	<.001	.236	<.001
End of Course	.091	.017	.158	<.001

positive correlation was significant at the level 0.01 in the non-WWW group. The result shows that the students who are not very experienced with the Internet can benefit more from the WWW coursework. Table 6 shows the details of analysis.

We analyzed if prior knowledge of basic concepts of information technology affects learning. The positive correlation was significant at the level 0.01 at the beginning in both groups. At the end the positive correlation was significant at the level 0.05 in the WWW group and at the level 0.01 in the non-WWW group. The result shows that the students who are not very experienced with basic concepts of information technology can benefit slightly more from the WWW coursework. Table 7 shows the details of analysis.

Finally, we analyzed data based on owning a PC and the Internet connection. The analysis showed that the WWW coursework is beneficial especially for the students who do not own them. Table 8 shows the details of analysis.

DISCUSSION

Our results show who wins and loses by participating in the WWW coursework. Regarding the general background, the WWW coursework suits best for females and all faculty except the students of economics. The age and the years studied in the university are not important factors concerning WWW-based learning. Regarding the previous computer related background of the students, it appears that the students who are not familiar with the computers and the Internet benefit more from the WWW coursework. The result reflects the importance of

Table 8: Analyzing responses based on possessing personal PC and Internet connection

Owning a PC (or another Microcomputer	Mean of WWW Group	Mean of Non WWW Group	P
Yes (n)	25	34	
Beginning of Course	1.63	1.77	.002
End of Course	2.58	1.77	.002
No (n)	21	23	
Beginning of Course	1.55	1.51	.655
End of Course	2.68	2.34	<.001
Owning Internet Connection			
Yes (n)	9	13	
Beginning of Course	1.75	1.96	.009
End of Course 2.44	2.66	.051	
No (n)	37	44	
Beginning of Course	1.56	1.58	.304
End of Course	2.67	2.40	<.001

computer facilities in the campus area, since the students who do not own a PC or the Internet connection benefited most from the WWW coursework. On the other hand, these students were in the worst situation related to the knowledge of basic concepts at the beginning of the course. Generally, the results provide more evidence that the WWW coursework is one effective way for WWW-based education. Outside informatics, we can recommend it to any subject in which knowledge consists of concepts forming knowledge structures. In the continuing courses of informatics, the WWW coursework may be less powerful, because in our study the students who were familiar with computers benefit less from the WWW coursework.

REFERENCES

Agre, P. E., and Chapman, D. (1987). Pengi: An implementation of a theory of activity. *Proceedings of AAAI-87*. Los Altos, CA.

Bieber, M., Vitali, F., Ashman, H., Balasubramanian, V., and Oinas-Kukkonen, H. (1997). Some hypermedia ideas for the WWW. *Proceedings of the 30th Hawaii International Conference of Systems Science*. IEEE Computer Society Press.

Biggs, J. B., and Collis, K. F. (1982). *Evaluating the quality of learning. The SOLO taxonomy (structure of the observed learning outcome)*. New York: Academic Press.

Brandt, D. A. (1997). Constructivism: Teaching for understanding of the Internet. *Communications of ACM, 40* (10), 112-17.

Chen, C., and Rada, R. (1996). Modelling situated actions in collaborative hypertext databases. *Journal of Computer Mediated-Communication, 2*, (3), http://www.ascusc.org/jcmc/vol2/issue3/chen.html.

Collis, K. F. (1975). *A study of concrete and formal operations in school mathematics: A piagetian viewpoint*. Melbourne: Australian Council for Educational Research.

Diekhoff, G. M. (1983). Relationship judgment in the evaluation of structural understanding. *Journal of Educational Psychology, 71*, 64-73.

Isaacs, G. (1994). Lecturing practices and note-taking purposes. *Studies in Higher Education, 19* (2), 203-16.

Jacobson, M. J., Maouri, C., Mishra, P., and Kolar, C. (1996). Learning with hypertext learning environments: Theory, design, and research. *Journal of Educational Multimedia and Hypermedia, 5*, (3/4), 239-81.

Koschmann, T. (1996). *Paradigm shifts and instructional technology: An introduction*. In T. Koschmann (Ed.), *CSCL: Theory and Practice of an Emerging Paradigm* (pp. 1-23). Mahwah, NJ: Lawrence Erlbaum.

Makkonen, P. (1999). The WWW-based presentations as a complementary part of conventional lectures in the basics of informatics: Is it worth it? *Proceedings of the IRMA Conference*. Hershey, PA: Idea Group Publishing.

Nardi, B. (1996). *Studying context: A comparison of activity theory, situated action models, and distributed cognition*. In B. Nardi (Ed.), *Context and consciousness* (pp. 69-102). Cambridge, MA: MIT Press.

Rosenthal, J. (1995). Active learning strategies in advanced mathematics classes. *Studies in Higher Education, 19* (2), 223-28.

Ryle, G. (1949). *Collected papers, Vol II. Critical essays*. London: Hutchinson.

Silverman, B. G. (1995). Computer supported collaborative learning (CSCL). *Computers in Education, 25* (3), 81-91.

Suchman, L. (1987). *Plans and situated action: The problem of human-machine communication*. Cambridge, UK: Cambridge University Press.

Wan, D., and Johnson, P. M. (1994). Computer supported collaborative learning using CLARE: The approach and experimental findings. *Proceedings of the ACM Conference of CSCW*.

Chapter 23

Towards an Automatic Massive Course Generation System

Ahmed H. Kandil, Ahmed El-Bialy, and Khaled Wahba
Cairo University, Egypt

This paper considers a system for massive course generation. The output of this system is a course arranged in a hierarchical structure of chapters and pages. Each page consists of multimedia components such as text, sound, music, image, video, animation, and graphics. The system has a hypermedia capability that is built on top of open Internet standards such as HTML. This enables the generated hypermedia courses to be broadcast on the Web and be navigated using any web browser. Students can evaluate their study and get a quantitative measure score for their study. Furthermore, the system is equipped with an automatic system for final exams generation. Finally, six courses of the senior year in the biomedical engineering department, Faculty of Engineering, Cairo University, were implemented using this generation system.

INTRODUCTION

In this paper, a course generation system has been developed. This system requires as input a prepared script of the course and its organization. This script is built as a hierarchical structure of chapters that includes pages. On each page, the instructor(s) should describe its contents in terms of multimedia components, such as text, sound, music, image, video, animation and graphics or even VRML (Virtual Reality Modeling Language) (Vince, 1998). The system has a hypermedia capability: It is built on top of open Internet standards such as HTML. This enables the generated hypermedia courses to be broadcast on the Web. The HTML enables the placing of the other multimedia components within the courses. The

Previously Published in *Challenges of Information Technology Management in the 21st Century* edited by Mehdi Khosrow-Pour, Copyright © 2000, Idea Group Publishing.

developed system interacts with the course instructor(s) through an easy interface. It provides the instructor with more than twenty different formats of HTML pages. Moreover, new formats may be designed and implemented if needed. Each chapter is followed by a set of questions. Once a student registers in the course, he can browse through the course using any web browser. Then he can evaluate his study by getting to the questions, answering them, and getting his score. This property will enable the student with a quantitative measure for his understanding of the course material. The questions can be updated and modified automatically every time. Moreover, different levels of help may be provided to the student to give him hints to solve the problem. If the student gets help, the score of the question will be decreased according to the level of help he has got. Six courses of the senior year in the biomedical engineering department, Faculty of Engineering, Cairo University, were implemented using this generation system.

In this paper, a system for automatic random generation of exams is provided. The system starts with a bank of questions. Each question is linked to a subject and a level of difficulty. Once it exists, the instructor can specify the number of questions in the exam and the subject of the questions, together with their level of difficulty. To facilitate the correction, each set of exams is generated with a model answer. The types of questions considered are multiple choice and true/false. Using this system, the students are divided into groups. Each group will have a different exam with the same degree of difficulty. So we can optimize the use of the same place by dividing the huge number of students into smaller groups, each having its own exam. Moreover, this system can be applied to perform remote testing on the Web. Each student in the lab will be able to answer a different exam with the same difficulty level at the same time. These exams are corrected automatically and the results are provided to the students. The system is interactive and easy to use.

SYSTEM DESCRIPTION

The proposed system is a systematic way for the generation of different courses with simple and easy steps for the instructors that requires no special or previous skills. The steps for the course generation are to fill some simple forms that contain all the information required for the course generation. This information is then stored in tables in a database. Finally, the instructor issues the command to convert all is information into HTML (Raggett, 1997; Lemay, 1995) pages, and the course will be available.

The produced HTML pages contain four basic components: paragraphs, images, sounds, and/or videos. A variety of pages can be obtained with different font, different colors, the use of tables in the pages, images, and their locations with respect to paragraphs, etc. A library of page styles is included to suffice the

instructor's need that contains up to about twenty different styles of webpages. These styles can be categorized into the following main types:
- Title page styles,
- Table of Contents styles,
- Normal page styles,
- Author Information page styles,
- Introductory page styles, and
- Cover page styles.

However, the program is equipped with the ability to generate extra new styles.

The Implementation of the HTML Pages

Three main functions are responsible for the implementation of the HTML pages:
- The first function is responsible to make the introductory page of the course.
- The second function is responsible to make the Table of Contents page. The resulting HTML is dynamic for any number of parts, chapters, and subjects.
- The third function is responsible to make all the other course pages.

These functions generate the HTML pages. It fills the different items of the chosen styles. However, if the user chooses a style and doesn't enter all the data required in that style - for example, a style contains three pictures and the user enters the name of only two - the function will delete the part of the page responsible for showing the third picture. The function does the same for empty paragraphs, sounds, and videos. The function is also responsible to link the hyperlinks in all the pages and to set the chosen general background to all pages.

Designing the Database

In order for any course to have a well-formed structure, a full database is designed that covers up all items related to the course. This database has to be fully described and fully linked. We have used Microsoft Access (Jennings, 1997) in designing and implementing the database.

The main table in this relation is the Books table. We have for any course a number of subjects, as the course can cover many subject titles. Each course has a certain style for the cover page and a certain style for the Contents page. Also, the course can be divided into more than one part, and each part can be further divided into more than one chapter. As we go deeper, the chapter is divided into different items, each containing some pages. We deduce that the Books table is linked with three tables, i.e., Subjects table, Contents table, and Styles table. These three tables are related to the Books table with the primary key BID (unique for each course).

Another table appears in this relation, the Instructor table. This table satisfies the security in preserving the rights to alter the course contents through a password to the instructor.

The following tables describe the fields of the tables in this database:

- *Instructor table fields*: Instructor ID, instructor password
- *Book table fields*: Name of the course, name of the author, name of the publisher, year of publication, volume number, name of the chosen style, primary key of the course, name of the cover of the course, name of the background, and ID of the instructor of the course
- *Styles table fields*: A unique number for the style, number of paragraphs in the style, number of images in the style, the name of the style, number of videos in the style, and number of sounds in the style
- *Content table fields*: Primary key for each chapter, name of the chapter, number of the chapter, name of the part that contains this chapter, number of the part, foreign key that give the primary key of the course in use, and name of the chosen style for the table of content
- *Item Names table fields*: Foreign key that gives the primary key of the chapter and name of the item
- *Subjects table fields*: Foreign key describing the primary key of Books table and name of the subjects

Course Pages

This part deals with pages of the course; we tried to simplify the user interface so that entering data of the course is done in a fast and efficient way.

Any page may contain text (number of paragraphs) that can be obtained through MS Word. Images to clarify and illustrate the written text can be used as background soft music that will not distract the student while navigating the course. AVI files, which are animated videos that can be inserted in the page, aid in the learning procedure for students.

A special editor is designed and implemented for the instructor to fill, modify, or preview each page. The instructor is requested to specify some information about the course (e.g., number of parts, chapters, and the items of that chapter). Without the previous step, the instructor can't get into this editor.

After filling the page, the instructor can preview this page in web form. The preview facility allows the user to make any changes in his, and if he is convinced he can save it. The user can change any of the data he entered at any time, except changing the style of the page.

The editor has the facility to allow the instructor to add hyperlink to any chosen word. The editor has also the following facilities:

- *PREVIOUS* and *NEXT*: to proceed to the previous page or to the next.

- *NEW CHAPTER*: to insert a new chapter.
- *NEW PAGE*: to insert new pages into the current chapter.
- *SAVE*: (from file menu) is enabled only if the instructor is entering new data or changing old ones.
- *GO TO CHAPTER*: to jump to a requested chapter (if the chapter exists).
- *GO TO PAGES*: to jump to a requested page number.
- *QUESTIONS:* to go to the question form.

Some other tables are added to accommodate the page contents of the courses. The main table used is the Pages table. This table is related to Table of Contents in a relation one to many with enforced referential integrity, (which means that if a course is deleted from the table of Books, all its components in other tables will be deleted immediately through the ChapterKey (Content) and ChapterID (Pages). Table of Images, Links, Paragraphs, Video, and Sounds are all related to the table of Pages in the same manner through IDP in the table of Pages and PageID in the other tables.

Details on Each Table

- *Pages table fields*: Unique number to describe the page, a style name used by this page, a number from the Table of Contents representing a key for this chapter to which this page is related, and the page number
- *Paragraphs table fields*: A number relating a paragraph to the page, the paragraph, a number representing the sequence of the paragraph within the page
- *Images table fields*: A number relating an image to the page, text representing the image name, the number of images within the page, a field specifying whether or not the image is a linking image, and the destination of the image if it is linked
- *Links table fields*: A number relating linking words to the page, texts representing the linking word, the destination of the linking word, and the number of that linking word in the page (maximum five)
- *Sounds table fields*: A number relating a sound to the page, a text representing the sound file name, the number of the sound within the page, no. 1 is the background sound
- *Videos table fields*: A number relating a video to the page, a text representing the video file name, the number of videos within the page

Saving the Course

When the instructor presses save, the program generates the cover page and a book ID page. It links them together and adds a link to the Table of Contents page. Then a procedure recalls one chapter after the other from the chapters saved in the database. For each chapter, pages are retrieved sequentially from the Pages table in the database. For each page the procedure calls all the paragraphs, the images, the sounds, the videos, and the links of the page, and HTML files are generated. All the addresses of the chapters are preserved. Accordingly, after generation of all pages, the program links all names of chapters in the Table of Contents page to the corresponding pages. Finally, all pages are linked to each other. As we can see, all the previous manipulations have been achieved by using file structure techniques.

DRILLING

In this section, we present how the instructor can add to each chapter drills and how exams are automatically produced through the fulfillment of specific criteria in degrees of difficulty in exams. After filling the contents of pages of a certain chapter in the course, the instructor is given the opportunity to go through steps of inserting some drilling exercises for this chapter. There are three different categories of questions. The instructor can choose any combination of them.

MCQ Type

For this type of question, the instructor is requested to fill in the following data:
- Question number,
- Wordings of the question, i.e., what the question says,
- The full mark to be given to this question while grading the exam,
- Answers 1-3, i.e., the different choices of answers, from which the student is to specify the right answer,
- The instructor specifies which of the three answers is the right one, and
- Difficulty of the question, i.e., each question is categorized under easy, medium, or difficult.

Problems type

Many similarities occur between this type and the one before. There is the question number, full grade, question wordings, and difficulty. But instead of just pointing out the right answer, one has to write the exact wordings of the answer. Givens and requirements are two new added items to this type. Images can also be added and previewed before saving the question in the database. This is done by browsing through already existing files in the existing drives in the PC.

Aided Problems (with Hints) type

The only added modification to the previous view is the hints part. The instructor gives a number of hints for solving the problem. The hints are arranged in a pre-specified order. The instructor gives the maximum number of hints to be given to the student while solving the question. Each hint is given an incremental number for ease of retrieval. After specifying the number of the hint for a given question, the wordings that appear to the student are inserted in the given area.

Database Design

Another six tables are added to the database to organize this process of the drilling questions.

The most important tables are:
- MCQs,
- Problems, and
- AidedProbs.

They are related to the course through its ID number. Any number of exams can be produced for each course. The extra three tables are introduced as follows:
- The Problems table: That is related to another two tables (table of Givens and table of Requirements).
- An AidedProbs table that is related to table of Hints, i.e., each aided problem may have several number of hints.
- MCQs require no further related tables.

Each one of these three tables has the chapter ID as a major field in the table, so that by specifying the chapter all questions for this chapter can be retrieved. Also, each of the Requirements and Givens tables has the question ID, so that for each problem the corresponding givens and requirements are retrieved. We deal with the table of Hints in the very same manner. Also, another important issue present in our case is that all the relationships are one-to-many relationships.

These relationships force us to deal with data in a specific manner. One is not able to delete an aided problem from a database without deleting its hints from the tables of Hints first. Also, a problem is not to be deleted before deleting its givens and requirements from their corresponding tables first. So deleting a problem record has to take place by first knowing its ID, deleting its corresponding givens and requirements if it is an ordinary problem, or deleting its hints if it is an aided problem. Finally, the corresponding record can be safely deleted. In the same manner of thinking, we have to first add a problem in the Problems table, know its ID, and then add its requirements and givens, or its hints.

Anatomical Structure of Tables

- *Problems fields*: Chapter ID, number of problems in the chapter, words of the question, mark given for this question, either easy, medium, or difficult, name and location of an image, right answer, and ID of problem
- *Givens fields*: Problem ID and wordings of the given
- *Requirements fields*: Problem ID and Wordings of the requirement
- *MCQs fields*: Words of the question, chapter ID, mark given for this question, either easy, medium, or difficult, wording of answer 1, wording of answer 2, wording of answer 3, right answer, number of MCQs in chapter, ID of MCQ

- *AidedProbs fields*: Chapter ID, number of aided problems in chapter, words of the question, mark given for this question, either easy, medium, or difficult, right answer, number of hints, and ID of aided problem
- *Hints fields*: Problem ID, number of hints for a question, and wording of the hint

GENERATION OF EXAMS

After specifying a course, the instructor can generate random exams using the predefined questions of the course. Every time the instructor chooses to generate a new exam, questions are picked randomly from the available bank of questions so there will never be two exams alike in their content. The instructor can pick from all types of questions, i.e., MCQs, problems, and aided problems. He is free to generate an exam that contains the same type of questions or a mixed exam.

As a start, the instructor has to type the title of the exam, then a window is enabled showing the three types of questions (MCQs, problems with givens and requirements, and problems with hints), with the MCQs first enabled. The instructor then chooses a chapter number and specifies the number of easy, medium, and difficult MCQ questions related to this chapter. According to the available bank, the instructor has to enter a number of questions that is less than or equal to the available ones.

When the instructor finishes these choices for one chapter, he presses on the *Next Chapter* button so the chapter will be incremented automatically, then the instructor can continue for the next chapter or choose another type of question. He can choose either problems or problems with hints and go through the same procedure of specifying the number of easy, medium, or difficult questions. On the other hand, he can choose to neglect the rest of the procedures and save the one type of questions exam. The grade of each question is calculated and an incremental total mark for each exam is finally produced. After finishing generating each exam, it is saved using Save in the File menu.

After filling the bank of questions, the instructor can generate exams randomly. This needs some modifications in the database. The relationship has to be extended as the following:

The exam is saved in four tables. In the Exams table, the exam title, its type, total number of questions, ID of the related course, full mark, and exam ID are saved.

According to the type of selected questions, they are saved in the corresponding table from the other three tables, where the exam ID is related to the table exams and question ID as well as the mark of it are saved.

- *Exams table fields*: Title of exam, number indicating type of exam, number of questions, ID of course, full mark of the exam, and exam ID

- *MCQ exam questions table fields*: Exam ID, question ID, and grade of question
- *Pexam questions table fields*: Exam ID, question ID, and grade of question
- *Exam questions table fields*: Exam ID, question ID, and grade of question

Random Generation of Exams

When the instructor specifies a certain number of easy MCQs, all MCQ questions with difficulty stated as easy are selected, and a search procedure selects the specified number randomly. This procedure is repeated for the other types of difficulties and the other types of questions. The last stage is the saving of the generated exams with question IDs.

Procedure

When the instructor searches his course and chooses to generate random exams, the course ID is received by the function load-form, which detects the last exam and increments the exam ID.

When the instructor starts to generate his exam, he types the exam title, specifies a question type, chooses a chapter, and types the number of easy, medium, and difficult questions.

When he presses on the *Next chapter* button, related to MCQs for example, the numbers in the text boxes are filled-in variables, which are used to declare dynamic arrays, which are filled with questions randomly using *Randomize statement.*

After pressing the *Next chapter* button, the instructor can specify a new type of questions or make the same procedure for a new chapter.

After finishing the exam, the instructor has to press *Save* from the file menu, where all the data in the arrays are saved in the tales of database shown above.

Printing of Exams

We have added an option to the instructor to print any of the exams he has generated. He can also print the model answers that could be used later for correcting the exam.

When the user chooses "Print Exam" from the File menu, he can choose a course from the list box. After that, all the generated exams of this course will be shown. The user can specify the exam type he wants by choosing one of four exam types. These types are multiple choice exams, problems requiring direct answers exams, aided problems exams, or combinations of all question types.

Finally, the instructor can choose if he wants to print the questions of the exam or its model answer. The printer window will be shown and the exam behind. The instructor can print exams of his course only according to the password of his course.

CONCLUSION

In this paper, we have described a package that is ready to generate courses in HTML pages in minimum time and effort.

This package is the result of project work in 1997. At that time no similar packages with the same extended facilities were available. The work is made around database tables that enable the instructor to go through and modify in very simple steps all the styles used in the course without any effort. This gives him the ability to generate new courses from the same material for higher student's levels. The package can produce stand alone courses to be distributed to the students, for examples, on CDs, where the Internet facilities may not be available. It can also generate client-server courses such as those widespread systems available in the market nowadays. It does not restrict certain operating systems rather than a browser.

Multimedia technology is expanding over time; therefore, the package can be extended to add any new media with no need for major changes. It has the capability to add on interactive modules for group discussion and video conferencing.

We used the program to generate some courses that are taught in the fourth year of Systems and Biomedical Engineering Department. An average course consisting of 100 A4 pages will require eight hours to be entered in the program and converted to HTML pages. So we succeeded in preparing six courses (Eckel, 1998; Gonzalez and Woods, 1992; Hill, 1990; Luger and Stubblefield, 1993; Ogata, 1995; Webster, 1978), which are ready as HTML pages and with different types of questions ready for processing.

These courses are:
- Discrete Time Control,
- Artificial Intelligence,
- Computer Graphics,
- JavaScript,
- Medical Imaging Systems, and
- Medical Instrumentation.

REFERENCES

Eckel, B. (1998). *Thinking in Java*. Prentice Hall Computer Books.

Gonzalez, R., and Woods, R. (1992). *Digital image processing*. Adison-Wesley Pub. Company.

Hill, F. S., Jr. (1990). *Computer graphics*. Maxwell MacMillan Int. Edition.

Jennings, R. (1997). *Special edition using Access 97*. Que.

Lemay, L. (1995). *Web publishing with HTML in a week*. Indiana: SAMS Publishing.

Luger, G. F., and Stubblefield, W. A. (1993). *Artificial Intelligence: Structures and strategies for complex problem solving,*(2nd ed.). Palo Alto, CA: Benjamin Cummings.

Ogata, K. (1995). *Discrete-time control systems,* (2nd ed.). Upper Saddle River, NJ: Prentice Hall.

Raggett, D. *HTML 3.2 reference specification W3C recommendation.* Retrieved on January 14, 1997 from http://www.w3.org/TR/REC-html32.html.

Vince, J. (1998). *Essential virtual reality.* Great Britain: Springer-Verlag.

Webster, J. G. (1978). *Medical instrumentation, application and design.* Houghton Miffilin Company.

Chapter 24

A Case Study of One-to-One Video-Conferencing Education over the Internet

Hock C. Chan, Bernard C. Y. Tan and Wei-Ping Tan
National University of Singapore

In a traditional classroom, students learn from the physical delivery of classes, which to a great extent depends on the teaching techniques employed by the instructor. In a virtual classroom, the physical delivery of classes depends not only on the teaching techniques chosen but also very much on the technologies used to deliver the teaching materials (Cyrs, 1994). With the increasing use of virtual classrooms, technologies have become a critical component affecting teaching and learning effectiveness (Alavi, 1994). Advances in information and communication technologies have significantly changed the ways students learn, the ways instructors teach and the means with which both parties access information (Leidner and Jarvenpaa, 1993).

Virtual classrooms have been investigated in the context of tele-learning (e.g., Alavi et al., 1995; Wheeler et al., 1995) and video-conferencing (e.g., Kydd and Ferry, 1994; Webster, 1998). While such technologies have allowed an instructor to deliver formal classes to students from another geographical location, these classes can be supplemented by informal computer-mediated interaction among the instructor and students through electronic mail or bulletin boards (Leidner and Jarvenpaa, 1995). Advances in internet technologies have opened up new ways for interaction among the instructor and students. For example, the instructor can now place the course materials on the World Wide Web for students to access.

Previously Published in *Web-Based Learning and Teaching Technologies: Opportunities and Challenges* edited by Anil Aggarwal, Copyright © 2000, Idea Group Publishing.

A more significant way with which the Internet has changed the dynamics of teaching and learning is to make possible direct personal tutoring over long distances. In this mode of learning, an instructor gives personal instruction and attention to a student at any point in time through the Internet. Although video-conferencing facilities can be used for this purpose of direct personal tutoring, the costs of doing so is prohibitive because instructors and students need to invest in the same set of specialized hardware and software. This situation has changed drastically with latest developments on Internet video-conferencing capabilities. With such capabilities, an instructor and a student located in different parts of the world can engage in a video-conferencing class using standard personal computers and very affordable off-the-shelf software (Alavi et al., 1995). Furthermore, instead of exorbitant international phone charges, the instructor and student will need to incur only minimal local phone charges.

Changes in the economics of direct personal tutoring over long distances (via Internet video-conferencing capabilities) can potentially lead to a proliferation of its use. Students are no longer subjected to the constraints of geographical barriers in their quest for knowledge. Instructors are no longer restricted by physical distances in their attempt to give personal attention to students. And since such technologies may fundamentally alter the mode of teaching and learning in the future, it is important that research be carried out to identify factors that may facilitate or hinder teaching and learning via Internet video-conferencing capabilities.

This chapter investigates the use of Internet video-conferencing for one-to-one distance education. Through in-depth observations of and interviews with two instructors and three students in Singapore, this chapter examines the impact of four critical factors (system characteristics, mode characteristics, social presence and media richness) on the effectiveness of teaching and learning in such a context. By focusing on one-to-one teaching and learning episodes involving the latest Internet technologies, this chapter has helped to fill a gap in knowledge that arises because current studies tend to concentrate on big virtual classroom settings (e.g., Alavi, 1994; Alavi et al., 1995).

BACKGROUND

Earlier studies on the use of information technology for education have focused almost exclusively on computer-aided instruction, where the students interact with educational software, either on personal computers or through the Internet (e.g., Schloss et al., 1988). For example, Leidner and Jarvenpaa (1993) examined the use of information technology in a traditional classroom setting where instructors had access to presentation software and students had access to spreadsheet and statistics packages. Alavi (1994) studied how a group decision support system could enhance group process gains and reduce group process losses (Nunamaker et al., 1991), thereby helping teams of students to learn from each other. Sanker et al. (1997) investigated two other instructional situations. In one situation, the instructor used a video-conferencing facility to deliver lectures from his office to students in a classroom. In the other session, students watched the instructor and a colleague solved a spreadsheet problem through a video-conferencing facility. In both cases, students did not get to interact with instructors. A common characteristic of these and other related studies is that information technology was not used to accomplish two-way communication between instructors and students.

Desktop video-conferencing facilities are a convergence of video-conferencing, audio-conferencing, software support tools and Internet tools, all packaged into the familiar and affordable personal computer (Alavi et al., 1995). Among many possible uses (Kydd and Ferry, 1994; Rosen, 1996), a useful application of desktop video-conferencing facilities is in education. With desktop video-conferencing facilities, an instructor and a student located at separate places can engage in a one-to-one instructional session on any subject matter. Unlike the settings studied in prior research, such a mode of instruction involves active on-line and real-time communication between the instructor and the student. Thus, factors affecting the communication process become very critical to the effectiveness of teaching and learning. As this mode of teaching and learning gain acceptance in the future, it is imperative that these factors be identified.

One-to-One Distance Education

There is a small body of literature on one-to-one distance education. Graesser and Person (1994) investigated the impact of questions asked on student achievements in one-to-one tutoring sessions on mathematics. They found that students self-regulated their learning by identifying knowledge deficits and asking questions to repair the deficits. As a result, the quality of questions asked was significantly correlated with student grades. In this case, the ability of students to ask quality questions would depend on the communication process between the instructor and the student. Graesser et al. (1995) carried out detailed analyses on the dialogue patterns of one-to-one tutoring sessions on mathematics. Among the components of contemporary pedagogical theories, they reported that collaborative problem solving, prompt question answering, and clarity of explanation using examples contributed significantly to learning effectiveness. Again, communication between the instructor and student would impact the extent to which these pedagogical components can be fulfilled.

Table 1: Factors Affecting Teaching and Learning Effectiveness

Factor	Key aspects of factor
System characteristics	Hardware, software, and bandwidth
Mode characteristics	Usefulness, challenge, attractiveness, and clarity
Social presence	Sociability, warmth, and personal focus
Media richness	Multiple cues and interactivity

Hume et al. (1996) examined the impact of hinting on one-to-one tutoring effectiveness. Hinting was a tactic employed by instructors to prompt students to recollect information already known or to make inferences to solve a problem. Hints were found to encourage students to engage in active cognitive processes that promoted long-term retention of information and deeper understanding. Since appropriate hints must be given depending on student responses, the communication process between the instructor and the student would play a key role in determining the success of this tactic. Chi (1996) studied the role of interaction between instructors and students on the effectiveness of one-to-one tutoring sessions. Detailed case studies of each instructor and each student revealed that instructor actions prompting for co-construction and student efforts leading to self-explanation could produce deep learning. Both these sets of activities would be facilitated by good communication between the instructor and the student.

The body of literature on one-to-one distance education motivates this research effort in two ways. First, like all the existing studies, this study seeks to identify factors that may enhance the effectiveness of teaching and learning in such an environment. In this study, effectiveness is measured by asking instructors to indicate their perceived ability to teach and asking students to indicate their perceived ability to learn via distance education, relative to traditional face-to-face education sessions. Second, while the results of all the existing studies alluded to the importance of communication between the tutor and the instructor, this issue has never been directly investigated. Therefore, this study focuses on identifying factors that may impact the communication process between the instructor and the student, thereby affecting distance learning effectiveness.

One-to-one distance education is examined in the context of desktop video-conferencing because the economy and prevalence of desktop video-conferencing facilities are likely to make it a dominant mode of distance education in the future. Table 1 presents four critical factors that can affect the success of using desktop video-conferencing facilities for one-to-one distance education. These factors are discussed in terms of their important characteristics and relevance in a one-to-one distance education context. In analyzing the cases included in this study, these four factors are used to evaluate the experience of each instructor and each student, and to relate that experience to their perceived effectiveness in teaching and learning respectively.

System Characteristics

Every desktop video-conferencing facility has both hardware and software components (Rosen, 1996). To support the required processing capacity, Pentium personal computers have been used for most such facilities. A digital camera and a video card are needed to capture images. A microphone, a sound card, and speakers are needed to capture and project voices. The software supporting instructional use of desktop video-conferencing facilities needs to be able to accommodate several windows on the monitor. A window is needed to display the captured images (of the instructor or the student) to the other party. Another window is needed for both the instructor and the student to chat with each other. A third window may serve as a whiteboard for both the instructor and the student to scribble information. In addition, the software should facilitate document sharing. For example, the instructor or the student can start a Word document and both can then take turns to edit the document. Because desktop video-conferencing hardware and software are relatively new and not totally stable (Halhed, 1996), hardware and software quality may impact the communication process between the instructor and the student, thereby affecting teaching and learning effectiveness (Webster and Hackley, 1997).

Desktop video-conferencing facilities may display degraded images due to the limitations in communication bandwidth and computing power. Gale (1994) reported that many affordable desktop video-conferencing facilities could not transmit high quality images because the communication bandwidth required for video signals is too high. Also, due to the processing time taken in compressing and decompressing video signals, there is usually a delay of at least a quarter of a second in video transmission. The results are grainy pictures and a lack of synchronization between video and audio signals (Tackett, 1995). With so many users on the Internet, communication bandwidth between any two desktop video-conferencing sites cannot be guaranteed. Therefore, limitations in communication bandwidth and computing power may influence the communication process between the instructor and the student, thereby affecting teaching and learning effectiveness.

In practice, one-to-one tutoring sessions commonly involve instructors and students with limited resources. These instructors and students may not want to commit more resources than is necessary for their distance education efforts. Therefore, research relating system characteristics to teaching and learning effectiveness can provide instructors and students of one-to-one tutoring sessions with some clues about the consequences arising from the limitations of their system resources.

Mode Characteristics

Four key perceptual characteristics of a mode of instruction determine its effectiveness: usefulness, challenge, attractiveness, and clarity (Champness and DeAlberdi, 1981; Sankar et al., 1995). Usefulness refers to the extent to which the mode of instruction is perceived to be appropriate for the learning task to be undertaken. Challenge is the extent to which the mode of instruction is perceived to be realistic and able to facilitate learning of difficult concepts. Attractiveness is the extent to which the mode of instruction is perceived to be lively, exciting, and interesting. Clarity refers to the extent with which the mode of instruction is perceived to allow comprehensible communication.

These characteristics have been used in other related studies. For example, Champness and DeAlberdi (1981) used the characteristics of clarity, usefulness, and attractiveness to study the effectiveness of teletext in improving the attention span of subjects. Sankar et al. (1995) assessed the effectiveness of modes of instruction using these characteristics. Sankar et al. (1997) also employed these characteristics to examine the effectiveness of video-conferencing in improving the attention span of subjects, by comparing traditional and video-conferencing modes of lectures for a large class in management information systems. In general, these four characteristics have been found to impact the teaching and learning effectiveness, both in traditional face-to-face setting and in technology-mediated settings.

One-to-one tutoring sessions, using desktop video-conferencing facilities, are a new and emerging mode of instruction. These four mode characteristics can potentially influence the way with which and extent to which instructors and students communicate during tutoring sessions as well as the consequences of that communication. Hence, these mode characteristics are potential determinants of teaching and learning effectiveness in the context of one-to-one tutoring sessions.

Social Presence

Social presence is defined as the extent to which a communication medium allows the actual physical presence of the communicating partners to be conveyed (Short et al., 1976). When people communicate, they exchange both task-oriented and interpersonal messages. The level of social presence is determined by the degree to which interpersonal information can be exchanged (Markus, 1994; Rice and Grant, 1990). Three variables typically used to gauge the level of social presence are sociability, warmth, and personal focus. A communication medium is considered to be high on social presence if it allows communicating parties to socialize with each other, feel the warmth of each other, and exchange messages that are personal in nature (Short et al., 1976). Rice (1984) suggests that social presence differences may be linked to restrictions that communicating media placed on nonverbal cues because these cues tend to be better for conveying emotions and subtleties.

Short et al. (1976) rank the following five communication media in order of decreasing social presence: face-to-face discussion, television, multi-speaker audio, telephone, and business letter. Evidence in the literature suggests that desktop video-conferencing may enable people to transmit more warmth and sociability than the telephone. Video images can help people, who have just met recently, to become more familiar with one another (Czeck, 1995). According to Czeck (1995), video images may be particularly important when communication is heavily geared toward the exchange of interpersonal messages, such as one-to-one communication between doctor and patient or between instructor and student. Thus, desktop video-conferencing allows for a more personal touch to electronic communication than electronic mails or discussion lists (Porter, 1997).

More evidence along this direction is provided by Wilbur et al. (1994), who showed that people tended to look at each other more frequently in the early stages of their work. As time progressed and people relaxed, conversations would take place with only occasional glances at each other. When asked, participants of that study reported that the initial ability to see each other helped them to get to know each other better, thereby facilitating subsequent communication. In addition to enabling familiarity, making eye contact and observing facial expressions are important for developing mutual trust and confidence (Ishii et al., 1992). Relationship between instructor and student can certainly benefit from eye contact and facial expressions because such signals allow the instructor to assess whether the student has understood the lesson.

As a critical aspect of electronic communication (Rice, 1993), social presence is likely to affect distance learning via desktop video-conferencing facilities. In the case of one-to-one tutoring sessions, the dyadic communication between the instructor and student can be effectively sustained through an intimate and open relationship between both parties (Panko and Kinney, 1992; Poole and Billingsley, 1989). Given that social presence may facilitate development of intimate and open relationships (Markus, 1994; Rice and Grant, 1990), this factor can be potentially important in shaping the communication process between the instructor and student, thereby affecting teaching and learning effectiveness of one-to-one tutoring sessions.

Media Richness

Media richness is defined as the extent to which a communication medium can facilitate shared understanding among the communicating partners (Daft and Lengel, 1986). Daft et al. (1987) note that equivocality, defined as the existence of multiple and conflicting interpretations for events and messages, is a central feature of human communication. To function together effectively, people must overcome equivocality and create common interpretations for events and messages. Rich communication media provide the capacity for people to accomplish this purpose. Variables typically used to gauge the level of media richness include multiple cues and interactivity. A communication medium is regarded as high on media richness if it allows communicating parties to exchange a large volume of information per unit time through rapid interaction and facilitates the use of a wide range of communication cues (Daft et al., 1987; Trevino et al., 1987). Examples of visual cues are body language and facial expression (Rutter and Stephenson, 1979). Examples of verbal cues include tone and loudness of voice (Cook and Lallijee, 1972). Examples of textual cues are printed figures and tables.

Trevino et al. (1987) rank communication media in order of decreasing media richness as follows: face-to-face meeting, telephone, and printed documents. Face-to-face meeting is the richest communication medium because there is interactivity or immediate feedback so that mutual understanding between communicating parties can be checked and differences in interpretations reconciled. This medium also carries visual, verbal, and textual cues. The telephone is a slightly less rich communication medium than face-to-face meetings. Although there is interactivity or immediate feedback, visual and textual cues are not available. Communicating parties have to rely solely on verbal cues to achieve mutual understanding. Printed documents are even less rich. There is neither interactivity nor immediate feedback. Only information that has been recorded in print is conveyed, limiting textual cues to information available in print. As a communication medium, desktop video-conferencing facilities are richer than telephone and electronic mail because such facilities carry visual, verbal, and textual cues. But such facilities may be less rich than face-to-face meetings because interactivity may be lower (Rice, 1992).

While many rational and social factors come into play when people select communication media for use (Webster and Trevino, 1995), interactivity between the instructor and the student is no doubt a critical success factor for distance education (Milhem, 1996). Rapid two-way communication between the instructor and the student ensure that materials can be effectively presented during an instructional session. It helps to establish connectivity between the students and the distance instructor. According to Garrison (1990), quality and integrity of instructional sessions depend upon sustained two-way communication. Without interactivity, distance learning degenerates into the old correspondence course model of independent study, where students become autonomous and isolated. Millbank (1994) studied the effectiveness of audio plus video communication in corporate training. After he introduced real-time interactivity, retention rate of the students was increased from about 20% (based on traditional classroom training) to about 75%. Borsook and Higginbotham (1991) list several key points for effective interactivity within computer-based instruction. These are immediacy of action where students can retrieve information without delay in a non-sequential manner, adaptability where communication is based on the needs of students, and two-way communication where students have freedom to clarify doubts anytime. Unlike traditional computer-mediated communication, students using desktop video-conferencing facilities have all these issues in their favor.

As a critical aspect of electronic communication (Rice, 1992), media richness is likely to affect distance learning via desktop video-conferencing facilities. In one-to-one tutoring situations, dyadic communication between the instructor and student must be sustained through interactivity and can be strengthened with the exchange of multiple cues (Panko and Kinney, 1992; Poole and Billingsley, 1989). Since these are important characteristics of media richness, this factor can certainly influence the communication process between the instructor and student, thereby impacting teaching and learning effectiveness of one-to-one tutoring sessions.

RESEARCH METHODOLOGY

A case study research approach is appropriate for examining a phenomenon in its natural setting (Benbasat et al., 1987; Yin, 1994). It is particularly useful for examining emerging phenomenon where the boundaries of investigation are not clear and the investigation effort must incorporate unexpected findings. This research approach provides researchers with in-depth answers to how and why questions, and allows initial versions of theories on an emerging phenomenon to be developed (Eisenhardt, 1989). More importantly, this research approach allows researchers to capture the context within which the emerging phenomenon occurs, thereby providing appropriate boundaries of applicability for the newly-developed theories (Miles and Huberman, 1994). Such theories can form the basis for survey research in the future, which in turn can help to refine the theories and their boundaries of applicability (Lee, 1991).

Prior to this study, a survey with undergraduates and high school students revealed that most of them had no experience with distance education via desktop-video-conferencing facilities (Tan and Chan, 1998). Since this mode of distance learning is relatively new and unfamiliar to many people in Singapore, the case study research methodology was employed for this study. When this mode of distance education becomes more common in the future, the findings of this study may be useful for guiding large-scale surveys (Fowler, 1988).

Research Context

Five subjects (two instructors and three students) volunteered for this study. All the one-to-one tutoring sessions involved two individuals interacting with each other. However, the primary research interest of this study was to identify factors that might influence the communication efforts of an individual (instructor or student) during the sessions, thereby impacting his or her ability to teach or learn. Therefore, each subject was examined as a separate case. Some prior studies on one-to-one tutoring sessions have also focused on the perceptions of an individual, rather than the interaction between two individuals, as a separate case (e.g., Chi, 1996). The two instructors were undergraduates from a large university. They each had about two years of experience with one-to-one tutoring in a traditional face-to-face context. The three students were attending high school. They had been receiving one-to-one tutoring from the two instructors for a year at their respective homes. All the instructors and students had no prior experience with distance education of any kind.

In this study, the topic of instruction was mathematics at a high school level. This topic was chosen for several reasons. First, it is quite complex and should stretch the desktop video-conferencing capabilities. Second, existing studies examining one-to-one distance education have used this topic (e.g., Graesser and Person, 1994; Graesser et al., 1995) and found it suitable for distance education research. Third, given that it is common for high school students to receive one-to-one tutoring in mathematics from undergraduates in Singapore, results of this study can potentially impact the way such instructional sessions are carried out in future (at least in Singapore).

All tutoring sessions were conducted using desktop video-conferencing tools and involved an instructor and a student. For each subject (instructor or student), data from five such desktop video-conferencing tutoring sessions were collected. To preserve the realism of the natural tutoring context, there was minimal control over the instructional process and materials (Eisenhardt, 1989; Yin, 1994). During each session, the instructor and student would proceed as they normally did, except that the session was conducted via desktop video-conferencing tools. To capture the context of these tutoring sessions, observations such as subject attitude, home environment, tutoring experience, and other demographic information were recorded.

All Pentium personal computers (266 MHz) used for desktop video-conferencing tutoring sessions in this study were connected to the Internet via either a local area network or a high-speed 56 kbps modem. Microsoft NetMeeting Version 2.1 was installed to facilitate communication. A digital camera and a video card were used to capture video signals. A microphone, a sound card, and two speakers were used to capture and project voice signals. This system created three windows on the monitor. One window allowed the instructor or student to see video images of the other party. The second window allowed the instructor and student to chat with each other. Information entered by one party was immediately visible to the other party. The third window served as a white board for the instructor and student to jointly type or scribble information. This system also provided for document sharing. For example, the instructor or student could start a Word document and both parties could then take turns to edit the document. Each party could follow every letter or stroke that had been added to the document by the other party.

Data Collection

To fully exploit the richness of data available in case studies, multiple methods for data collection (Miles and Huberman, 1994; Yin, 1994) were used to gather information on the five cases. One of the authors was present during each desktop video-conferencing tutoring session to observe the entire session. Detailed field notes were taken to record every incident that might affect teaching or learning effectiveness. Each session was also videotaped so that a more detailed analysis could be carried out and field observations could be confirmed. All screen movements during each session were captured with Lotus ScreenCam software. To elicit even more insight on each tutoring session, face-to-face interviews with the subjects were carried out at the end of the session. Each interview lasted about an hour. The open-ended questions asked during each interview were based on a case protocol developed prior to this study (using information obtained from the literature review). Having such a case protocol helped to ensure capture of all pertinent information and consistency across interviews, which in turn contributed to reliability of this study (Miles and Huberman, 1994; Yin, 1994). Where necessary, electronic mails and telephone calls were used to clarify interview responses with the subjects. The use of multiple methods for data collection allowed for triangulation of evidence and increased the credibility of the results of this study (Lee, 1991; Yin, 1994).

DATA ANALYSES

For each case, all the data collected through the multiple methods was pooled and then codified into key issues. These key issues were categorized under the four factors (system characteristics, mode characteristics, social presence and media richness) that could influence the communication efforts of the instructor or student, thereby affecting their effectiveness in teaching or learning respectively. The process of assigning key issues to factors was carried out by the authors. Disagreements, which occurred with less than 10% of all the key issues, were resolved through discussion and consensus. Results of data analyses were verified by the subjects, and some minor amendments (inclusion of new key issues or removal of existing key issues) were made based on the feedback from the subjects. The subjects also contributed additional insights on the reasons behind these results and highlighted the issues that were of particular concern to them.

Individual Cases

Tables 2 and 3 record the background information and key issues pertaining to Instructor A and Instructor B respectively. Tables 4, 5, and 6 record the background information and key issues pertaining to Student X, Student Y, and Student Z respectively. The key issues pertaining to system characteristics were obtained from field (denoted by [F]) and videotape observations (denoted by [V]). The key issues pertaining to the remaining three factors were elicited from both field observations and interviews (denoted by [I]) with the subjects. To avoid making this chapter exceedingly long, only the key issues that have been considered important by the subjects have been presented in Tables 2 to 6. In these tables, exact quotes from the subjects and exact sentences from the notes taken (that were representative of the key issues extracted) were shown.

Comparing Cases

Each subject was asked to sum up his or her overall perceived ability to teach or learn during the five sessions of one-to-one tutoring via desktop video-conferencing facilities. Two subjects (Instructor A and Student Z) gave favorable indication while three subjects (Instructor B, Student X, and Student Y) provided unfavorable feedback. Although only five cases had been examined in this study, a qualitative comparison between these two groups of subjects could yield preliminary but valuable insights on how the four critical factors might have affected communication between the instructor and student, thereby impacting teaching and learning effectiveness. Original quotes from subjects have been used to strengthen the discussion of the results of data analyses.

The evidence presented in Tables 2 to 6 suggests that subjects were affected by system characteristics. Those who experienced technical difficulties in starting up their systems and had more problems with visual and voice signals tend to form

Table 2: Experience and Opinions of Instructor A

Factor	Key aspects	Major issues
Background	Gender Age Education Experience	• Female • 21 • Final year computer science undergraduate • Given mathematics tutoring for 2 years
System characteristics	Hardware Software Bandwidth	• [F] System took a while (5-10 minutes) to establish connection • [F] System hung up 1-2 times during each session • [F] White board for chat could not display messages typed in by the student 30% of the time • [F,V] Visual signals were unclear 30% of the time • [F,V] Voice signals were inaudible 10% of the time
Mode characteristics	Usefulness Challenge Attractiveness Clarity	• [I] I could conduct mathematics tutoring from the comfort of my home • [I] I could electronically transmit my questions and answers to the student without having to print them • [I] I was able to use the system to explain difficult concepts to the student • [F,V] More efforts were undertaken by the instructor to explain mathematical concepts • [I] This way of tutoring was novel and interesting • [I] I preferred using the white board than writing on pieces of paper because it was neat • [I] This way of tutoring had improved my views on the use of computers • [F] The instructor traced the thinking process of the student clearly via the white board
Social presence	Sociability Warmth Personal focus	• [I] I engaged in less small talk with my student • [I] I shared fewer jokes with my student • [I] I did not feel any psychological distance with my student although we were physically separated • [F,V] The instructor monitored activities of the student consistently • [I] I had to miss out on some of the student actions
Media richness	Multiple cues Interactivity	• [I] It was really difficult to exchange non-verbal expressions • [I] It took me a long time to exchange ideas with the student • [F,V] The instructor provided prompt clarification to the student

poorer perceptions of their tutoring sessions. Hence, it seems worthwhile for instructors and students of such one-to-one tutoring sessions to invest in better capacity hardware resources. Subjects have attributed much of the system problems to "novelty of such applications of technologies" and "unpredictable traffic volume on the Internet". Although they were clearly frustrated when they encountered system problems, subjects were generally optimistic when asked to comment on the future of such applications. They believed that the "system problems could be alleviated with technological advancements" given the "rapid

Table 3: Experience and Opinions of Instructor B

Factor	Key aspects	Major issues
Background	Gender	• Female
	Age	• 21
	Education	• Final year computer science undergraduate
	Experience	• Given mathematics tutoring for 2 years
System characteristics	Hardware	• [F] System was slow (15-20 minutes) to establish connection due to technical difficulties
	Software	• [F] There were no software problems
	Bandwidth	• [F,V] Visual signals were unclear 50% of the time
		• [F,V] Voice signals were broken 30% of the time
Mode characteristics	Usefulness	• [I] I could conduct tutoring from my home without having to travel
		• [I] This would be the way to do tuition in the future but there was potential for improvement now
	Challenge	• [I] I was able to explain difficult mathematical concepts to the student via the system
		• [F,V] More efforts were undertaken by the instructor to explain mathematical concepts
	Attractiveness	• [I] I thought such tutoring sessions were amazing
		• [I] It was more convenient to write on the white board than on pieces of paper
		• [F] The instructor put in considerable effort to motivate the student to exploit learning tools
	Clarity	• [F] The instructor spent a lot of typing time trying to clarify her messages
Social presence	Sociability	• [I] I had difficulty relating to my student
	Warmth	• [I] I felt no psychological distance with my student even though we were not together
	Personal focus	• [I] I had a lot of difficulty trying to focus on my student
Media richness	Multiple cues	• [I] I had to convey my ideas slowly because of the restrictions in cues
	Interactivity	• [F,V] The instructor regularly checked whether the student could heard her
		• [F,V] The instructor provided prompt clarification to the student

advancements in processing speed of computers" and "increasing bandwidth of communication networks". Instructor B even suggested that, with technological advancements, "tutoring sessions via desktop video-conferencing facilities could one day become an alternative to face-to-face tutoring sessions". Similar optimistic projections have also been reported by other scholars (e.g., Jacobs and Rodgers, 1997; Wright and Cordeaux, 1996).

The results on mode characteristics suggest that subjects tend to have better perceptions of their tutoring sessions if they could see and exploit the benefits of such sessions, if they could understand complex concepts through this means, or if the ideas exchanged were clear enough to them. Ways to enhance exchange of

Table 4: Experience and Opinions of Student X

Factor	Key aspects	Major issues
Background	Gender Age Education Experience	• Female • 17 • Final year science student in high school • Received mathematics tutoring for 2 years
System characteristics	Hardware Software Bandwidth	• [F] System was slow (10-15 minutes) to establish connection due to technical difficulties • [F] System hung up 1-2 times during each session • [F] There were no software problems • [F,V] Visual signals were jerky and unclear 50% of the time • [F,V] Voice signals were inaudible 20% of the time
Mode characteristics	Usefulness Challenge Attractiveness Clarity	• [I] I thought the system was useful for mathematics tuition • [F] Less material was covered in each session compared to an average face-to-face tuition session • [I] I had great difficulty in understanding concepts • [I] The concepts taught by the instructor were confusing to me most of the time • [I] I felt the tutoring sessions were time consuming • [F] The student struggled with the limited working spaces available on the white board • [I] I found the system fun and interesting • [F,V] The student was sometimes annoyed by unclear diagrams and formulae • [I] The information conveyed was quite clear to me
Social presence	Sociability Warmth Personal focus	• [I] I had fewer small talks with the instructor compared to a typical face-to-face tutoring session • [I] I felt a lack of presence of the instructor • [I] I experienced great difficulty in trying to focus on the instructor
Media richness	Multiple cues Interactivity	• [I] I had difficulty following explanations because some cues were restricted • [F,V] The student repeatedly acknowledged receipt of messages • [I] There were plenty of delays in communication • [F,V] The student frequently sought clarification from the instructor • [I] Simultaneous work could not be carried out under such circumstances

complex ideas include having "some methods to decompose a complex idea into several simpler ideas before communication" as suggested by Instructor A and "asking her to transmit complete information rather than type like she talks with information gaps in between" as suggested by Student Y. On the whole, subjects felt this mode of education had "increased my interest in mathematics" because it was "interesting", "amazing" and "fun". The results presented in Tables 2 to 6 offer some suggestions on how to promote one-to-one tutoring sessions via desktop video-conferencing facilities. Some important benefits that can be

Table 5: Experience and Opinions of Student Y

Factor	Key aspects	Major issues
Background	Gender Age Education Experience	• Male • 18 • Final year science student in high school • Received mathematics tutoring for 1 year
System characteristics	Hardware Software Bandwidth	• [F] System was slow (15-20 minutes) to establish connection due to technical difficulties • [F] System was disrupted 1-2 times during each session but did not hang up • [F] White board for chat could not display messages typed in by the instructor • [F,V] Visual signals were unclear 80% of the time • [F,V] Voice signals were inaudible 20% of the time
Mode characteristics	Usefulness Challenge Attractiveness Clarity	• [I] There was a limit to how useful this system could be for mathematics tutoring • [F] Less material was covered in each session compared to an average face-to-face tuition session • [F] The student had some difficulty in understanding mathematical concepts • [I] The system increased my interest in mathematics • [I] The working spaces on the white board was inadequate • [I] The system was not quite enjoyable to use but could be improved in the future • [I] Information conveyed by the instructor was not clear enough • [F,V] The student had to repeatedly clarify with the instructor
Social presence	Sociability Warmth Personal focus	• [I] Because we had to communicate via the system, I had less discussion with the instructor • [I] I could not sense the continual presence of the instructor • [I] It was very difficult to focus on the instructor
Media richness	Multiple cues Interactivity	• [I] It was troublesome to communicate because some cues could not be used • [F,V] The student repeatedly acknowledged receipt of messages • [I] The delays in communication were a real pain • [F,V] The student repeatedly provide feedback to the instructor to demonstrate understanding

emphasized to prospective instructors and students include "savings on transportation costs and time", "flexibility in scheduling of tutoring sessions", and the ability to "electronically transmit questions and answers". The first benefit can be particularly important in big countries or congested cities where travelling is not convenient. It is a key motivator behind distributed work arrangements (Sia et al., 1998) and other uses of technologies to breach the distance gap. The second benefit implies that if the instructor and student are to engage regularly in tutoring sessions from the convenience of their homes or workplaces, the addition or

Table 6: Experience and Opinions of Student Z

Factor	Key aspects	Major issues
Background	Gender Age Education Experience	• Female • 18 • Final year science student in high school • Received mathematics tutoring for 1 year
System characteristics	Hardware Software Bandwidth	• [F] There were no hardware problems • [F] There were no software problems • [F,V] Visual signals were unclear 20% of the time • [F,V] Voice signals were inaudible 10% of the time
Mode characteristics	Usefulness Challenge Attractiveness Clarity	• [I] The system helped me to complete my mathematics assignments faster • [I] This way of attending tutoring helped me to save on transportation costs and time • [I] I had flexibility in scheduling of tutoring sessions • [I] I could understand complex concepts without difficulty • [F] The student managed to complete complex mathematics questions without difficulty • [I] The system raised my interest in mathematics • [F] The student often drew smiley faces to indicate satisfaction • [I] I had more privacy because the instructor could not see me • [I] I was unable to refer to materials covered earlier by the instructor • [I] I thought the information conveyed was clear
Social presence	Sociability Warmth Personal focus	• [I] I could easily start small talks with my instructor • [I] I could feel a real presence of my instructor although we were physically separated • [F] The student exchanged many personal messages with the instructor
Media richness	Multiple cues Interactivity	• [I] I had no difficulty working with restricted cues • [I] I could communicate rapidly with my instructor • [F,V] The student interacted very actively with the instructor

cancellation of such sessions at short notices may not cause much inconveniences. The third benefit suggests that instructors and students can quickly exchange large volumes of materials, at low costs. When instructors and students (e.g., Instructor A and Student Z) can see and exploit the benefits of this mode of education, they may enjoy it despite its current drawbacks of having to "cover less materials in each session".

Results on social presence and media richness suggest that subjects tend to form better perceptions of their tutoring sessions if they could feel the psychological presence of the other party, if they could send personal messages to the other party, or if they could get replies without waiting too long. Nevertheless, Instructor B felt that the "psychological distances should disappear if we have enough practice," and Student X thought that the lack of social presence and media richness might not be a problem "if we regularly acknowledge receipt of messages or reply to messages". The reduction in social presence and media richness, reported in Tables 2 to 6, has also been noted by researchers in other situations where face-to-face communication was replaced by computer-mediated communication (Dennis and Kinney, 1998; Rice, 1992; Rice, 1993). People who are less familiar with each other and with the new technologies tend to be bothered by issues such as delays in communication, difficulty in focusing on the other party, and the restricted range of cues that could be used. But when people have developed shared understanding on how to work with each other through the new technology, they tend to be less affected by changes in social presence and media richness (Lee, 1994; Walther, 1995). Therefore, instructors and students are likely to be able to free themselves from the restrictions of one-to-one distance education if "we have enough experience with such tutoring sessions". After all, Student Z noted that "there are solutions for each restriction and we just need to get used to applying these solutions".

FUTURE TRENDS

While the use of desktop video-conferencing facilities for one-to-one tutoring sessions has its limitations, this notion has a promising future too. The subjects have some suggestions on how to improve the quality of such tutoring sessions in the future (see Table 7). These suggestions can be broadly classified as technical or procedural improvements. While the technical improvements are answers to some issues on system characteristics presented in Tables 2 to 6, the procedural improvements are solutions to some issues classified under the other three factors in these tables. People developing one-to-one distance learning technologies or contemplating use of one-to-one tutoring sessions may want to incorporate these suggestions.

Some obvious research efforts in the near future are to implement or fine-tune software tools and to put in place procedural routines to improve one-to-one distance education via desktop video-conferencing capabilities. Other research efforts that can be carried out are to replicate this study with different topics of instruction (e.g., languages or sciences) and different levels of instruction (e.g., middle school or college), and to examine interaction between each pair of instructor and student as a single case. But beyond the immediate horizon, several long-term research directions may be worth pursuing.

First, the technological capabilities examined in this study focus on helping the student to access the instructor and other sources of information.

Table 7: Suggestions for Improvement

Category	Suggestion from subjects
Technical	• It is better and easier to use pen-based interface to draw pictures and write formulae • We should replace the white board with shared document to have more shared space • The system should somehow capture all the information transmitted for subsequent reference • We can consider using ICQ instead of NetMeeting to speed up connection time • We should bypass the Internet if other dedicated networks can be made available for the tutoring sessions
Procedural	• Instructors and students can speak slower with regular intervals to enhance quality of audio signals • We can consider doing away with video signals to improve transmission quality • We may be able to use multiple means to make explanation of complex concepts clearer • It is a good practice to solicit feedback from the other party at regular intervals • It is a good practice to respond quickly to suggestions or queries from the other party • Try to engage in more small talk or share jokes with the other party more frequently • Perhaps we should meet face-to-face for some discussion before using the technology • We should publicize this mode of tutoring by making a list of ideas on how to exploit benefits of the technology

By concentrating on the needs of the student, such capabilities are an operationalization what scholars termed 'the vision to informate down' (Leidner and Jarvenpaa, 1995). In an ideal learning environment, the technological capabilities have to meet the needs of both the instructor and the student. Thus, software tools and procedural routines that can help the instructor to play a more effective role are needed. Examples are tools and routines to systematically assess the understanding of the student and to adjust the pace of a session according to the progress of the student. Such capabilities can be considered an operationalization of what scholars termed 'the vision to informate up' (Leidner and Jarvenpaa, 1995).

Second, while this study examined each subject over five sessions, future research efforts can certainly study the behavior of instructors or students over a longer period of time (e.g., one year or even longer). Research has demonstrated that people tend to adapt their behavior over time in expected and unexpected ways when using technologies (DeSanctis and Poole, 1994). For example, some people who used electronic mails over time have been able to overcome limitations due to restricted social presence and media richness (Walther, 1995). It would also be interesting to see the types of procedural routines that may emerge over time to help instructors or students cope with technological limitations.

Third, this study has focused solely on instructors and students from Singapore but future research efforts can examine the same phenomenon in a multi-cultural context. Research has shown that culture does moderate the impact of technologies on human behavior (Tan et al., 1998). For example, while an objective of distance learning technologies is to provide students with more opportunities to challenge their instructors, this practice may be more acceptable in some cultures than others (Hofstede, 1991; SpencerOatey, 1997). Given that distance learning via desktop video-conferencing capabilities can potentially match instructors and students over vast geographically distances and cultural variations, it is interesting to investigate whether and how technological capabilities or procedural routines can be employed to breach the cultural divide between instructors and students.

CONCLUSION

This chapter demonstrates the promise of desktop video-conferencing technologies as a means for conducting one-to-one distance education. Given the widespread availability of low-cost Pentium personal computers and the widespread use of the Internet in the future, it is plausible that this mode of distance education may partially replace face-to-face tutoring sessions. More importantly, the benefits of the technological capabilities examined in this chapter can potentially extend beyond one-to-one tutoring sessions to larger-scale distance education efforts.

Information and communication technologies have permeated many aspects of education (Alavi et al., 1995; Leidner and Jarvenpaa, 1993; Leidner and Jarvenpaa, 1993). These technologies will continue to impact education in the future. An example of how such technologies may alter the future of education is a course on Global Project Coordination, jointly conducted by National University of Singapore, Stanford University, and the Swedish Royal Institute of Technology. In this course, students from the three universities enrol in the same global class. Faculties from the three universities take turns to give weekly lectures to the entire global class via a three-way video-conferencing facility, based on real-time multicast technologies. Students also form global teams to work on large-scale projects sponsored by the industry. As part of this course, faculties and students employ a wide range of technologies to communicate with and learn from each other. The desktop video-conferencing capabilities investigated in this chapter can certainly facilitate such learning efforts by helping to breach geographical barriers among faculties and students of such a global class.

   Although this chapter focuses on desktop video-conferencing technologies as a means for distance education, other existing and emerging technologies based on the Internet must not be neglected. In the 21st century, when information and communication technologies are likely to play a critical role in enabling effective education, knowledge accumulated on existing and emerging technologies can guide us in terms of what technologies are appropriate under what circumstances. Rather than seeing each technology as a solution to an existing problem, it is more fruitful to examine how the collection of information and communication technologies may complement each other to open up new and exciting possibilities for educating people.

REFERENCES

Alavi, M. (1994). Computer-Mediated Collaborative Learning: An Empirical Evaluation. *MIS Quarterly*, 18(2), 159-174.

Alavi, M., Wheeler, B.C., & Valacich, J.S. (1995). Using IT to Reengineer Business Education: An Exploratory Investigation of Collaborative Telelearning. *MIS Quarterly*, 19(3), 293-312.

Benbasat, I., Goldstein, D.K., & Mead, M. (1987). The Case Research Strategy in Studies of Information Systems. *MIS Quarterly*, 11(3), 369-386.

Borsook, T.K., & Higginbotham, W. (1991). Interactivity: What is it and What can it do for Computer-Based Instruction. *Educational Technology*, 21(10), 11-17.

Champness, B., & DeAlberdi, M. (1981). Measuring Subjective Reactions to Teletext Page Design. NSF Grant DAR-7924489-A02. New York, NY: Alternate Media Centre, New York University.

Chi, M.T.H. (1996). Constructing Self-Explanations and Scaffolded Explanations in Tutoring. *Applied Cognitive Psychology*, 10(Special Issue), S33-S49.

Cook, M., & Lallijee, M. (1972). Verbal Substitutes for Visual Signals in Interaction. *Semiotica*, 6(2), 212-221.

Cyrs, T.E. (1994). *Essential Skills for College Teaching*. Las Cruces, NM: New Mexico State University.

Czeck, R. (1995). Videoconferencing: Benefits and Disadvantages to Communication. (http://ils.unc.edu/~czecr/papers/cscwpaper.html).

Daft R.L., & Lengel, R.H. (1986). Organizational Information Requirements, Media Richness and Structural Design. *Management Science*, 32(5), 554-571.

Daft, R.L., Lengel, R.H., & Trevino, L.K. (1987). Message Equivocality, Media Selection, and Manager Performance: Implications for Information Systems. *MIS Quarterly*, 11(3), 355-366.

Dennis, A.R., & Kinney, S.T. (1998). Testing Media Richness Theory in the New Media: The Effects of Cues, Feedback, and Task Equivocality. *Information Systems Research*, 9(3), 256-274.

DeSanctis, G., & Poole, M.S. (1994). Capturing the Complexity in Advanced Technology Use: Adaptive Structuration Theory. *Organization Science*, 5(2), 121-147.

Eisenhardt, K.M. (1989). Building Theories from Case Study Research. *Academy of Management Review*, 14(4) 532-550.

Fowler, F.J. (1988). *Survey Research Methods*. Newbury Park, CA: Sage.

Gale, S. (1994). Desktop Video Conferencing: Technical Advances and Evaluation Issues. In *Computer-Supported Cooperative Work: The Multimedia and Networking Paradigm*. Aldershot, England: Avebury Technical.

Garrison, D.R. (1990). An Analysis and Evaluation of Audio Teleconferencing to Facilitate Education at a Distance. *American Journal of Distance Education*, 4(3), 16-23.

Graesser, A.C., & Person, N.K. (1994). Question Asking During Tutoring. *American Educational Research Journal*, 31(1), 104-137.

Graesser, A.C., Person, N.K., & Magliano, J.P. (1995). Collaborative Dialogue Patterns in Naturalistic One-to-One Tutoring. *Applied Cognitive Psychology*, 9(6), 495-522.

Halhed, B.R. (1996). Desktop Video: Not a Pots Solution Yet. *Business Communications Review*, 26(6), 55-58.

Hofstede, G. *Cultures and Organizations: Software of the Mind*. London, England: McGraw Hill.

Hume, G., Michael, J., Rovick, A., & Evens, M. (1996). Hinting as a Tactic in One-to-One Tutoring. *Journal of the Learning Sciences*, 5(1), 23-47.

Ishii, H., Minoru, K., & Jonathan, G. (1992). Integration of Inter-Personal Space and Shared Workspace: Clearboard Design and Experiments. *Proceedings of Conference on Computer Computer-Supported Cooperative Work*.

Jacobs, G., & Rodgers, C. (1997). Remote Teaching with Digital Video: A Trans-National Experience. *British Journal of Educational Technology*, 28(4), 292-304.

Kydd, C.T., & Ferry, D.L. (1994). Case Study: Managerial Use of Video Conferencing. *Information and Management*, 27(4), 369-375.

Lee, A.S. (1991). Integrating Positive and Interpretive Approaches to Organizational Research, *Organization Science*, 2(4), 342-365.

Lee, A.S. (1994). Electronic Mail as a Medium for Rich Communication: An Empirical Investigation using Hermeneutic Interpretation. *MIS Quarterly*, 18(2), 143-157.

Leidner, D.E., & Jarvenpaa, S.L. (1993). The Information Age Confronts Education: Case Studies on Electronic Classrooms. *Information Systems Research*, 4(1), 24-54.

Leidner, D.E., & Jarvenpaa, S.L. (1995). The Use of Information Technology to Enhance Management School Education: A theoretical View. *MIS Quarterly*, 19(3), 265-291.

Markus, M.L. (1994). Electronic Mail as the Medium of Managerial Choice. *Organization Science*, 5(4), 502-527.

Miles, M.B., & Huberman, A.M. (1994). *Qualitative Data Analysis: An Expanded Sourcebook*. Newbury Park, CA: Sage.

Milhem, W.D. (1996). Interactivity and Computer-Based Interaction. *Journal of Education Technology Systems*, 23(3).

Millbank, G. (1994). Writing Multimedia Training with Integrated Simulation. Paper Presented at Writers' Retreat on Interactive Technology and Equipment. Vancouver, BC: University of British Columbia.

Nunamaker, J.F., Dennis, A.R., Valacich, D.R., Vogel, D.R., & George, J.F. (1991). Electronic Meeting Systems to Support Group Work. *Communications of the ACM*, 34(7), 41-60.

Panko, R.R., & Kinney, S.T. (1992). Dyadic Organizational Communication: Is the Dyad Different? *Proceedings of the Twenty-Fifth Annual Hawaii International Conference on System Sciences*, 4, 244-252.

Poole, M.S., & Billingsley, J. (1989). The Structuring of Dyadic Decisions. In *Dyadic Decision Making*. New York, NY: Springer Verlag, 216-250.

Porter, L.R. (1997). *Creating the Virtual Classroom: Distance Learning with the Internet*. New York, NY: John Wiley.

Rice, R.E. (1984). *The New Media: Communication, Research, and Technology*. Beverly Hills, CA: Sage.

Rice, R.E. (1992). Task Analyzability, Use of New Media, and Effectiveness: A Multi-Site Exploration of Media Richness. *Organization Science*, 3(4), 475-500.

Rice, R.E. (1993). Media Appropriateness: Using Social Presence theory to Compare Traditional and New Organizational Media. *Human Communication Research*, 19(4), 451-484.

Rice, R.E., Grant, A.E., Schmitz, J., & Torobin, J. (1990). Individual and Network Influences on the Adoption and Perceived Outcomes of Electronic Messaging. *Social Networks*, 12(1), 27-55.

Rosen, E. (1996). *Personal Videoconferencing*. Ashland, OH: BookMasters.

Rutter, D.R., & Stephenson, G.M. (1979). The Role of Visual Communications in Social Interactions. *Current Anthropology*, 20(1), 124-125.

Sankar C.S., Ford, F.N., & Terase, N. (1997). Impact of Videoconferencing in Teaching an Introductory MIS Course. *Journal of Educational Technology Systems*, 26(1), 67-85.

Sankar, C.S., Kramer, S.W., & Hingorani, K. (1995). Teaching Real-World Issues: Comparison of Written versus Annotated Still Image Case Study. *Journal of Educational Technology Systems*, 24(1), 31-53.

Schloss, P., Wisniewski, L., & Cartwright, G.P. (1988). The Differential Effect of Learner Control and Feedback in College Students' Performance on CAI Modules. *Journal of Educational Computing Research*, 4(2), 141-150.

Short, J., Williams, E., & Christie, B. (1976). *The Social Psychology of Telecommunications*. New York, NY: John Wiley.

Sia, C.L., Teo, H.H., Tan, B.C.Y., & Wei, K.K. (1998). Examining Environmental Influences on Organizational Perceptions and Predisposition toward Distributed Work Arrangements: A Path Model. *Proceedings of the Nineteenth Annual International Conference on Information Systems*, 88-102.

SpencerOatey, H. (1997). Unequal Relationships in High and Low Power Distance Societies: A Comparative Study of Tutor-Student Role Relations in Britain and China. *Journal of Cross-Cultural Psychology*, 28(3), 284-302.

Tackett, R. (1995). Pain Worth the Gain? *Network World*, 42(12).

Tan, B.C.Y., Wei, K.K., Watson, R.T., Clapper, D.L., & McLean, E.R. (1998). Computer-Mediated Communication and Majority Influence: Assessing the Impact in an Individualistic and a Collectivistic Culture. *Management Science*, 44(9), 1263-1278.

Tan W.P., & Chan, H.C. (1998). A TAM-Based Assessment of Videoconferencing for Remote Tutoring. *Proceedings of the Fourth Annual Association for Information Systems Americas Conference*, 1094-1096.

Trevino, L.K., Lengel, R.H., & Daft, R.L. (1987). Media Symbolism, Media Richness, and Media Choices: A Symbolic Interactionist Perspective. *Communication Research*, 14(5), 533-575.

Walther, J.B. (1995). Relational Aspects of Computer-Mediated Communication: Experimental Observations over Time. *Organization Science*, 6(2), 186-203.

Webster, J. (1998). Desktop Videoconferencing: Experiences of Complete Users, Wary Users, and Non-Users. *MIS Quarterly*, 22(3), 257-286.

Webster, J., & Hackley, P. (1997). Teaching Effectiveness in Technology-Mediated Distance Learning. *Academy of Management Journal*, 40(5), 1282-1309.

Webster, J., & Trevino, L.K. (1995). Rational and Social Theories as Complementary Explanations of Communication Media Choices. *Academy of Management Journal*, 38(6), 1544-1572.

Wheeler, B.C., Valacich, J.S., Alavi, M., & Vogel, D.R. (1995). A Framework for Technology-Mediated Inter-Institutional Telelearning Relationships. *Journal of Computer-Mediated Communication*, 1(1).

Wilbur, S., Ing, S., & Wilbur, S.R. (1994). Early Experiences in Desktop Multimedia Conferencing. In *Computer-Supported Cooperative Work: The Multimedia and Networking Paradigm*. Aldershot, England: Avebury Technical.

Wright, N., & Cordeaux, C. (1996). Rethinking Video-Conferencing: Lessons Learn from Initial Teacher Education. *Innovations in Education and Training*, 33(4), 194-202.

Yin, R.K. (1994). *Case Study Research: Design and Methods*. Newbury Park, CA: Sage.

About the Editor

Mehdi Khosrow-Pour, BBA, MBA, MS, DBA, CSP
Executive Director, Information Resources Management Association (IRMA)

Dr. Khosrow-Pour received his Bachelor of Business Administration (BBA) and Master of Science (MS) in Computer Information Systems from the University of Miami (Fla.), a Master of Business Administration (MBA) from the Florida Institute of Technology, and a Doctorate in Business Administration (DBA) from the Nova Southeastern University. He is also a Certified Systems Professional (CSP). Dr. Khosrow-Pour has taught undergraduate and graduate information system courses at the Pennsylvania State University for 20 years where he was the chair of the information Systems Department for 14 years. He has also lectured at the Florida International University, American University, University of Lyon (France), University of West Indies (Jamaica), Kuwait University, University Carlos III - De Madrid, and Tehran University (Iran). He is currently the Executive Director of the Information Resources Management Association (IRMA) and Senior Editor for Idea Group, Inc.

He is also the Editor-In-Charge of the *Information Resources Management Journal (IRMJ)*, the *Annals of Cases on Information Technology (ACIT)*, the *Information Management (IM)*, and consulting editor of the *Information Technology Newsletter (ITN)*. He also serves on the editorial review board of seven other international academic information systems journals. He is the former Editor-In-Charge of the *Journal of End User Computing* and the *Journal of Database Management*.

During the past 20 years, Dr. Khosrow-Pour has served as a consultant to many organizations such as: United Nations, Mutual of New York, Pennsylvania Department of Commerce, and Foodynamics Inc. He is the founder and currently Executive Director of the Information Resources Management Association (IRMA), a professional association with over thousand members throughout the U.S., Canada, and 52 other countries. He has served as the Program Chair and Proceedings Editor of IRMA International Conferences for the past 14 years.

Dr. Khosrow-Pour is the author/editor of more than 20+ books on various topics of information technology utilization and management in organizations, and more than 50+ articles published in various conference proceedings and journals such as *Journal of Information Systems Management*, *Journal of Applied Business Research*, *Journal of Systems Management*, *Journal of Education Technology Systems*, *Computing Review*, and *Review of Accounting Information Systems*. He is a frequent speaker at many international meetings and organizations such as: the Association of Federal IRM, Contract Management Association, Financial Women Association, National Association of States IRM Executives, IBM, and the Pennsylvania Auditor General Department.

Index

U

ulaw encoding 197
unistructural outcome 254
unity/wholeness 238

V

Venn Diagrams 6
vertical disintegration 113
video compression 199
video conferencing 190
video streaming 190
virtual classrooms 135
virtual education 132
virtual educational organizations 60
virtual office hours 177
Virtual Reality Modeling Language 264
Visual Basic (VB) 228
visual beauty 236
visual complexity 99

W

wayfinding 102
Web enabler 204
Web page design 90
Web site design factors 90
Web teaching models 64
Web-based courses 180
Web-based education 1, 59, 60, 73
Web-based environment 68
Web-based instruction 90, 93, 94
Web-based teaching 66, 72, 78, 80, 87
Webwatcher 222
Wide Area Networks (WANs) 168
windowing environments 98
windows 98
word-processing software 84
WWW 252

NEW from Idea Group Publishing